HERE I WALK

Das lampartisch mer
Das venedisch mer
Das pomerisch mer
Denmarck

HERE I WALK

A THOUSAND MILES on FOOT TO ROME WITH MARTIN LUTHER

ANDREW L. WILSON

BrazosPress
a division of Baker Publishing Group
Grand Rapids, Michigan

Published by Brazos Press
a division of Baker Publishing Group
P.O. Box 6287, Grand Rapids, MI 49516-6287
www.brazospress.com

Printed in the United States of America

Library of Congress Cataloging-in-Publication Data
Names: Wilson, Andrew L., 1975– author.
Title: Here I walk : a thousand miles on foot to Rome with Martin Luther / Andrew L. Wilson.
Description: Grand Rapids : Brazos Press, 2016. | Includes bibliographical references.
Identifiers: LCCN 2016026014 | ISBN 9781587433054 (pbk.)
Subjects: LCSH: Luther, Martin, 1483–1546. | Reformation. | Christian pilgrims and pilgrimages—Europe. | Europe—Description and travel. | Wilson, Andrew L., 1975—Travel. | Wilson, Sarah Hinlicky—Travel. | Luther, Martin, 1483–1546—Travel.
Classification: LCC BR326.4 .W55 2016 | DDC 263/.04245632—dc23
LC record available at https://lccn.loc.gov/2016026014

Frontispiece: Erhard Etzlaub map (colored woodcut) / Wikimedia Commons. This south-up road map was made for pilgrimages to Rome for the Holy Year 1500.

16 17 18 19 20 21 22 7 6 5 4 3 2 1

To my parents,
who have always encouraged
my adventures

One
Two
Three
Four
Five
Six
Seven
Eight
Nine
Ten

Contents

Preamble 1

One 7

The wrong city—Etzlaub's map—Strasbourg station—Luther's metaphysically ambiguous cell—Arnstadt—the longest day—rusting Iron Curtain—mighty fortresses

Two 37

Fourteen Holy Helpers—thunderstorm on Staffelberg—a cross and a skull—some thoughts on saints—Bamberg—water for wanderers—Nuremberg and its clock

Three 61

Earthly vocations—Neuendettelsau—the limits of the Roman Empire—Oettingen with beer, Bach, and Brotzeit—crossing a crater—Nördlingen—Neresheim Abbey

Four 77

Ulm and the spire Luther didn't see—a jar of interconfessional honey—Memmingen—wars of religion—Genhoffen's mysterious chapel—into Austria with inadequate footgear

Five 97

Bregenz—little Liechtenstein—fortress Switzerland—some thoughts on translation—rescued—church and charnel house—Bivio's religious rivalries—snow

Six 115

Into Italy—at home in Chiavenna—chestnut groves beneath the Alps—Como, lake and city—sidewalks end—unfashionable in Milan

Seven 135

Augustine's mortal remains—the priest of Santa Cristina—the mayor of Orio Litta—ferry across the Po—Piacenza—over the Apennines—scatological issues—marble

Eight 157

Lucca—new wine in old Tuscany—Florence through Luther's eyes—souvenirs of San Gimignano—Siena's architecture of salvation—up with Dante, down with Luther

Nine 177

A soupçon of volcanic ash—fellow pilgrims—fortunati!—the Papal States—Lake Bolsena—a real Roman road—Etruscan caves—the good life with Mary Jane

Ten 195

Many Romes—St. Peter's—one thousand miles—St. Paul's Outside-the-Walls—celebratory supper—necropolis—Reformation Day—Scala Sancta—Luther and Rome, then and now

Epilogue: Wittenberg 215

From the Other Pair of Feet 219

Sarah Hinlicky Wilson

Gear 223

A Recipe from the Road: Pilgrims' Vegetable Stew 225

Notes 227

Preamble

It must have been while teaching Church History 101 and reading for the umpteenth time that Luther made a pilgrimage to Rome that I said absent-mindedly to Sarah, "You know, we should do this someday—walk to Rome in Luther's steps." I suppose it was 2005, and we were both siloed away at Princeton Theological Seminary working on our PhDs, she in theology, I in Reformation history.

"We should really do it in 2010," I added, since that year would be his trek's five hundredth anniversary.

"Sure," she said, looking up from her preparations. "Sounds nice. We've got a few years to figure out how." Then we both went back to our books.

It was really just a lark at first, a desultory distraction from work. I remember the moment quite clearly. I was sitting at my desk—the shining sun at my back (always at my back)—and thinking as I often did and still do that I would rather be outside. I grew up hiking in the mountains, and when I wasn't I was dreaming of it. My childhood was full of ramblings all over the Cascade Range of the Pacific Northwest. I spent my college summers in the mountains of Colorado, guiding youth on backpacking trips, among other adventures. In 1998, I'd managed with my friend Paul to hike most of the Pacific Crest Trail through Oregon and Washington. And then I went to grad school and sat.

And dreamed.

With all this sitting, all this reading, all this soaking up of text—and all this dreaming—I'd somehow missed that Martin Luther was a hiker, too. His inner life I felt I knew quite well. For the sincere young man that I was,

Luther was an antidote to my fruitless introspection and obsession with God's will. His *Freedom of a Christian*, with its vision of God's descent to free us from our sin so that we may serve the world, was visceral relief for a soul too troubled by minutiae, too waffling to act. That little book was also my initiation into theology. I went on to complete a Master of Divinity, becoming ever more familiar with Luther's writings along the way. Yet my inner resonance with Luther remained abstract, somehow utterly divorced from my other, less cerebral avocations.

But there it was before me in the textbook: in 1510 the monk Martin Luther made a pilgrimage to Rome. As I read the story this time, it finally struck me that I could make this pilgrimage too, and read instead of a book the buildings, instead of an abstracted history the landscape upon which it was written. Surely this would turn up something more than could an arid text; surely walking would divulge data hidden from the bookish, isolated scholar. Luther was a man, after all, with flesh and feelings, who occupied space, who felt and saw many things he never mentioned in writing.

Luther's pilgrimage to Rome, despite how little was known about its practicalities or purpose, attracted powerful and misleading metaphors. All the evidence we now have was filtered through the trials yet to come. As the supposed capital of the antichrist, Rome came to symbolize for Protestants all that was both highly immoral and materially seductive in papist religion. The fact that Luther went *himself*, that he both witnessed and partook of Rome's iniquity, lent credence to his strident whistle-blowing. For generations of faithful Catholics, on the other hand, Luther's unhinged slander of the martyrs' city, of Peter's See, of the holy orders and their mountains of charity, was ample reason to dismiss the so-called reformer—the arch-heretic—from any further consideration whatsoever, to banish the merest hint of Lutheran taint. Luther's pilgrimage provides the consummate set piece for centuries of confessional polemic.

For secular historians, too, Luther's pilgrimage provided a convenient cusp upon which to turn the soon-coming schism, a step in the march toward modernity. Renowned French social historian Lucien Febvre makes this point about as brazenly as anyone; his thoughts tie up in a single, concise, and shining piece of rhetoric the confessional stereotypes that have accrued around both Rome and Luther for almost five hundred years:

> At the end of 1510, for order business, brother Martin Luther went to Rome. A great hope carried him. He went a pious pilgrim to the city of true pilgrims,

> the Rome of martyrs, living center of Christendom, common homeland of the faithful, august seat of the vicar of Christ. And what did he find? The Rome of the Borgias become, only just, the Rome of Pope Julius II.
>
> When, distraught and fleeing cursed Babylon—its courtesans, "good-men," ruffians, its simoniac clergy, cardinals with neither faith nor morals—Luther returned to his native German lands, he took with him in his heart an inexpugnable hatred of the Great Whore. The abuses that would wither all Christendom he had seen embodied, alive and blooming insolently under the pleasant Roman sky. He knew its source and origin. In the convent, from 1505 to 1510, he could measure the decadence of Christian teaching. He had tested, to the depths of his sensitive soul, the desiccating poverty of the doctrine of works. In the Rome of 1510 it was the hideous moral depravity of the Church that appeared to him in its nakedness. The Reformation was effectively complete. The cloister and Rome handed over, from 1511, a *Lutheran* Luther.[1]

But is it really true? Was his experience of Rome the last straw? Was Luther so upset, so "desiccated" by his church's empty doctrines, that he struck out in righteous rage against the broken promises of youth? Stark contrasts are compelling, as Febvre the lecturer clearly knew. As is the case with many convenient interpretations of the past, what makes perfect sense is also very often wrong. Squeaky-clean plotlines are simply too convenient to be true.

I remember looking briefly into the subject not long after the idea for the pilgrimage first popped into my head. While rummaging through the recesses of Luce Library, I managed to find an article here, a book there. These treatments, most of them a century old or more, placed Luther's journey within the context of an arcane dispute among the Observant Augustinians, a party of which Luther was a member and perhaps even a leader. Everyone agreed that Luther went primarily on order business—to lobby the vicar general *against* a merger of Luther's stricter Augustinians with their less strict brethren—and that the pilgrim angle was a happy parallel.[2]

This seems less certain now than it did one hundred years ago. The first and chief witness for this interpretation turns out to be Luther's vehement opponent Johannes Cochlaeus (1479–1552), whose slanderous biography of Luther eagerly recounts how the young monk was well conditioned by his extremist brothers to resist authority. What could be expected from such a renegade within such a mutinous milieu? We—and many generations of historians—ought to have been more circumspect of such a source.

The gathered wisdom of the library agreed that Luther left from Erfurt in 1510. In Rome he would have done the usual pilgrim things—saying mass and praying at holy sites, visiting various churches and their relics. In brief, he accumulated not a small amount of merit for himself and for his family. The literature had little to say about the actual trip, mostly due to lack of evidence, though one of the books laid out a brief though entirely speculative itinerary.[3]

This particular lacuna sent my scholar's—and hiker's—mind a-whirling, and soon I was even more smitten with the notion of a historical re-creation of Luther's most famous—and unexpectedly mysterious—journey. As those who study Luther professionally lament, there's precious little new to say about a man who wrote more—and about whom more has been written—than almost anyone before or since. Add to this his role as font and touchstone for nearly every aspect of later European history, and it's difficult to find anything new to say at all. Yet in briefly scanning through all this chatter I couldn't find much about Luther's walk itself, only comments on the destination. Since so little was forthcoming from the written evidence, I reasoned that the road might tell us something new or as yet undiscovered. Here, I thought, was something I could do. Andrew the scholar *and* the hiker might find something yet unsaid to say.

For several years the dream remained just that—a dream, a lark. Soon after I had that initial vision, Sarah and I adopted a baby boy, our Zeke, and with that we were occupied as all new parents are. But in the fall of 2008 Sarah got a job at the Institute for Ecumenical Research in Strasbourg, France. We now were at least geographically closer to our starting point. And with our move to the Institute, a new angle came to us: we could make our re-creation ecumenical, a pilgrimage bookended by Luther's familiar Germany and distant Rome. It could be an exploration of distance—not only between two places but also between our time and Luther's and between two great theological traditions that diverged because of this one man. By the act of walking we could show as well how close these two supposed termini really are, and with our slow steps illustrate the reconciliation that has happened in recent years between Protestants and Catholics.

Such were our thoughts when we presented the idea of the walk to the Institute. To our great delight, Sarah's colleagues and the board approved the project as legitimate ecumenical work. And so commenced several months of preparation. We had to find a route, make travel plans, and book places to stay. I worked up a blog and assembled the gear to document the trip. As

Facebook at the time was beginning to dominate social media, and Twitter was taking flight as well, we'd be on both. Our trek would not be for us alone but for the public—a proxy journey for the world of Luther's friends.

Zeke by then was not quite five years old. Would he come with? Stay home? If the latter, then with whom? The perennial facilitators of my adventures, my parents Roger and Virginia, solved that dilemma by agreeing to accompany us for several months. While we trekked through nearby Germany, they would look after Zeke (who adores his Farmor and Farfar) during the week and visit us on weekends. Once we had gone beyond the Alps they would tag along in a small camper van. It all came together swiftly and remarkably well, as things tend to do when deadlines loom. And so by the end of August 2010—five years after we were sitting there studying in the Princeton sun, dreaming of distant adventures—Sarah and I finally set off to see what we could learn not just from Luther's words but by walking in his footsteps.

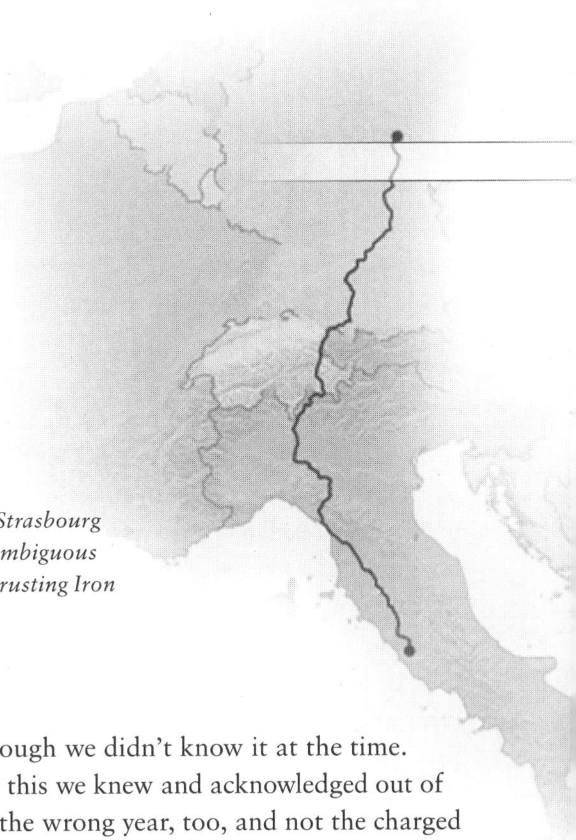

One

The wrong city—Etzlaub's map—Strasbourg station—Luther's metaphysically ambiguous cell—Arnstadt—the longest day—rusting Iron Curtain—mighty fortresses

We left from the wrong city—though we didn't know it at the time. It was also the wrong month, but this we knew and acknowledged out of necessity. It was in all likelihood the wrong year, too, and not the charged five hundredth anniversary we were hoping to commemorate. So much for our heady pretense to re-create, half a millennium later, the storied journey of the young monk and soon-to-be-infamous friar of the Augustinian order, Martin Luther. It was probably in 1511 and not in 1510 that Luther took up his pilgrim's staff and walked to Rome.

Looking back, our catalogue of errors should not have come as a surprise. Swept up in the prospect of the event, full sails to the winds of time, we mistook a consensus for a truth and forgot just how murky a thing the past is—even such a simple matter as establishing a date or a place. Our story, our meandering trajectory itself, was wound up from its outset with the very errors we sought to unravel. It was as complicit insiders that we would have to confront, over the next thousand miles, our own inadequacies and ignorance.

We had been warned. A mere week before our departure, we got a consternated email from a Thuringian pastor. She'd just heard of our ambitions from a colleague and took vigorous umbrage at our itinerary. "You must by no means go through Paulinzella!" The right path, the authentic sixteenth-century road, she insisted, went through her own parish, as everybody there knows. And so we abruptly changed our plans in deference to this vociferous local tradition. We weren't about to throw away a precious morsel of on-the-ground evidence.

For it's surprisingly difficult to follow in someone's footsteps. We know much less about where people walked than where they stood. And we often don't know much about that either. The oldest record of what we now think of as a Christian pilgrimage, the *Itinerarium Burdigalense* recorded in AD 333, isn't a travel account at all but a staccato of waypoints and horse-changing stations between Bordeaux and the Holy Land. Some of these we still know, for they remain great cities: Milan, Belgrade, Constantinople, Beirut. But on the identity of many others we can only speculate; they are little nothings buried beneath centuries of forgetfulness and dust. And about life between the milestones the chronicler tells us nothing whatsoever, nary a peep about the beauty of the countryside or the terror of the mountains. The modern pilgrim may holler, "The journey is the destination!" but this is not a sentiment we could glean from the *Itinerarium*. It reads more like a financial report than a travelogue, with Jerusalem as the wealthy pilgrim's bottom line. In the radiant afterglow of Christ's worldly presence, the surrounding world faded to nothing.

Luther lived more than a millennium after the *Itinerarium* was recorded, yet we know still less about his route. Even someone with his historical weight walked rather lightly on the land, leaving little but the odd impression. We were diligent in our research, but when it came to Luther's pilgrimage to Rome, the world of scholars seemed less interested in his location than in his state of mind. Luther's writings don't offer us much either. And what he does note comes filtered through the blustery events and years to come, an aging man's reminiscences taken down by dinner guests during the last years of his life—what we now call his *Table Talk*, the least trustworthy source of Luther's words.

Despite all his later conflagrations with the Roman Church, Luther seems to have appreciated the journey; it was by far his longest trip and certainly the most exotic. We can sense a particular kind of wonder in the tidbits that have come down to us in his sermons and *Table Talk*.[1] He mentions the marvelous clock above Nuremberg's market square and Ulm's cavernous (but at the time still towerless) cathedral. Luther the practical mendicant approved of Florence's well-run orphanage, but we hear nothing of its flowering Renaissance. The Alpine peoples impressed him by eking out a life from barren rock and ice. He clearly noticed the natural world, too, which seems to have been charged with allegory. The always green, ever-fruiting lemon trees prompted spiritual lessons for Luther the northerner. But beyond these scattered impressions: nothing. The details of Luther's multimonth trip are left to speculation.

Scholars much more able than Sarah and I have tried their hand at the task. We based our initial itinerary on the 1914 work of Heinrich Böhmer, *Luthers Romfahrt*, which seemed to be the definitive work. After sifting through the meager evidence, Böhmer fixed 1510–11 as the only possible window for the trip and suggested a westerly route from Erfurt southward through Ulm and over Graubünden's Septimer Pass. For the return trip in 1511, Böhmer supposed Luther took the lower Brenner Pass to Augsburg. Lacking anything better, we considered these waypoints enough to get us started.

After we spent some weeks flexing our hard-earned academic and linguistic muscles trying to get a bit more specific, Sarah's colleague Theodor Dieter emailed us an obscure East German article about a certain map printed in 1500. Its title promised very helpful guidance: *Römerpilgerkarte*, "Rome-Pilgrim's Map." Just what we were looking for! Its drafter was one Erhardt Etzlaub, cartographer and pocket-sundial maker who taught mathematics in Erfurt; young Luther may have even known him. The map's printer was based in Nuremberg, right in Luther's neighborhood; perhaps Luther collected some pointers before his trip. After picking up my jaw and counting our good fortune, I noticed a link in Theo's email: it turns out we could have found it on Wikipedia all along. So much for our hard-won scholarly skills.

As comforting as our newfound guide was for us, the detail given by the map would hardly have been necessary for Luther. Dirty and dangerous as travel may have been in the late Middle Ages, it was a simple matter to arrange. His world was, in its basic infrastructure, a much simpler one than ours. The fastest mode of transport was a horse, and even royalty shared the road with everybody else. If your destination was Bamberg, there was certainly no need for a map (let alone a GPS): you just joined up with all the other carts and horses and pedestrians headed southward on the *Bambergerstrasse*. The same went for traveling amenities. Just as your feet began to complain, you would likely come across an inn, or the next town would appear around the bend. Luther's world was built for a human pace. Going to Rome was no more complicated than going to the next town, again and again and again. All Luther really needed was a list of cities, with Rome as his guiding star. It's not as if he could have called ahead for reservations.

We were grateful for Etzlaub's guidance nonetheless, for he freed us from the mounting pressure to conjure sure knowledge of Luther's route out of historical thin air. There, right in the middle the map, just below the hatched swath of green indicating the Thuringian Forest, lay "Erffurt," our starting point. Whence, linked together in black and white like so many pearls on a string, our walk rolled out before us: *Erffurt, Arnstet, Ulimeno, Eysfelt, Koburg, Pamberk, Forchem, Erlang, Nurenberg* (Erfurt, Arnstadt, Ilmenau, Eisfeld, Coburg, Bamberg, Forscheim, Erlangen, Nuremberg). No more archival spelunking needed. Just follow the dotted line.

We are five people leaving Strasbourg, our home of nearly two years. After helping with last-minute preparations, my parents will accompany us to Erfurt. The adventure is a whole family effort, and we're happy not to be leaving home alone.

The first stop on our way is Strasbourg's renovated *Gare Centrale*, a great glass bubble of a building—like a terrestrial burp through soapy soil. By day the outside is a panoramic reflection. Clouds race across the sky above, celestial voyagers coming and going. At eye level the shining glass mirrors the hotels across the plaza, shrinking them fun-house style, taunting lodgers with the smallness of their rooms and the greatness of the travels about to begin. But at night, that time of dreams, another world glows within the now transparent dome: the former station shimmers into view. Ornately appointed with the wealth of the Gilded Age, it bursts with Teutonic confidence, having been built when Alsace was part of the German Empire. The neo-Renaissance façade draws us still further back in time; its sturdy arches and frivolous scrolls recall yet another, erstwhile age of Classical Rome and Greek philosophy.

Crossing the motion-actuated threshold into the great glass bubble, we enter the liminal world that will be our home for months to come, a no man's land where past and present are strangely confused. The airy atrium seems a fitting waiting room, a timeless lobby between an unyielding, stone-built past and a hopeful but indeterminate future. The architects put the old *gare* under glass to inaugurate the arrival of the high-speed train in 2007. Their work awakens hope in us that we can have our historical cake and eat it too.

But they deceive us. For our eyes can only see what nature and human love have condescended to preserve. A frozen past is an anomaly, a trick sustained by our present selves. As our high-tech train rushes us away, the protective dome disappears, and the naked countryside opens up before us. Here among the fields the past is gone, swallowed quickly by the dirt.

Our trip is quick, just a few hours to cross a former empire. But it is made to feel much longer by our lack of a place to sit. Among the thousand preparatory details, we forgot to make seat reservations, and the train is very crowded. Jumbled on the floor among chatting youth and their teetering piles of luggage, we race past fields and forests, factories and mines. Stations with vaguely familiar names scroll by, places where something important happened sometime: Fulda, Hanau, Gotha. Somewhere not too far from Eisenach we spot a mountain of tailings so unbelievably huge it seems a hallucination: a perfect, twin-peaked, lopped-off cone, like a displaced Kilimanjaro. Luther's family owned copper mines nearby, we recall. His ambitious father sent him here to Eisenach as a teenager to learn the trivium. We spot the Wartburg castle too, perched above the town. There Luther later lived, protected and clandestine, after he was condemned for heresy at Worms in 1521.

At last we come Erfurt. The station here looks somehow just the same as Strasbourg's old one: the same smooth, rosy sandstone blocks, the same classical arches, the same Gilded Age garnishing. We've plunged deeper into the same Germanic world. A quick ride on the tram delivers us near the Augustinian cloister.

The Luther that the world knows and remembers got his start in Erfurt. He was at first a student in the faculty of law, but then—seemingly abruptly—he gave up his goods and ambitions to join the Order of St. Augustine, one of several religious orders of the day that drew upon the broad spirit and teachings of the esteemed fourth-century bishop of Hippo.

The standard account of this apparently rash conversion is both familiar and obscure. Walking home from visiting his family in Mansfeld, we're told, Luther found himself quite suddenly in the middle of a frightening storm. Overcome with fear he swore an oath: "Help me, St. Anne, and I will become a monk!" And being a young man of exceptional scruples and apparent sincerity, he made good on his vow and after coming through the storm unscathed entered the life of the cloister.

Why he chose to join the Augustinians in particular is not as clear, for he certainly had other options. Erfurt—with its population of 20,000—was a large and wealthy city for the time, and chock-full of religious orders and their attendant foundations and facilities. The abundance of its chapels and churches earned Erfurt the moniker "city of spires." Luther could have just as easily become a Franciscan or a Dominican. He would not even have had to become a monk at all but could have approximated this vow by joining one of the popular and more loosely organized lay movements such as the Brothers of the Common Life, whose members had educated him in Magdeburg.

Whatever his reasoning, when Luther entered the Augustinian Cloister he walked into a new and different world from what we today tend to think of as monasticism. He would not have spent his days in *ora et labora* (prayer and work), as did monks under the Benedictine rule, who lived cloistered lives in sprawling, often wealthy, rural estates. A warming climate and new farming techniques had helped Europe's population to balloon after 1050, sending many country people into city life. The resulting urbanization was accompanied by growing pains more associated with the nineteenth than the twelfth century. The swelling cities saw a heartrending concentration of squalor and a disturbing dissolution of traditional morals as the uprooted masses foundered in their new environment. Monks shut up on distant farms could offer but their prayers. A new kind of religious order arose to address the trials of city life.

These were called mendicant or "begging" orders, for they owned no property from which to feed their members, as did conventional monasteries. The first so-called friars are still the most renowned. Franciscans, inspired by St. Francis, did works of charity among the new urban poor. The vocation of the Dominicans can be surmised from its members' Latin suffix OP, *ordo praedicatorum* (the Order of Preachers). Parish priests of the day performed the mass and the other sacraments, but neither sermons nor the study required to compose them were common; Dominicans filled that gap. Mendicants also catechized the disturbingly ignorant masses and soon filled the teaching ranks of Europe's burgeoning universities. Because of their flexible apostolate, the friars (as they were called) did not remain behind closed doors like rural monks. They left their quarters daily to work in the city alongside the people.

We are tempted, and with good reason, to imagine Luther's Augustinians descending in unbroken succession from their famous patron. But they did not. The Order of St. Augustine (or more historically precise, the Hermits of St. Augustine) dates only from 1244, when some reform-minded religious repurposed and updated the bare-bones rules written up by St. Augustine for his community at Hippo. Luther's Augustinians were all that you'd expect of medieval mendicants. They begged for food and served the city mostly with their ministry of teaching at the University of Erfurt. Maybe Luther knew a professor or two before he joined the order, maybe not. But when he entered the Erfurt Priory, it was not to set the world aside completely—as he might have done in other times or places. He joined to serve a bustling urban setting from within a community of already reform-minded friars.

Luther's *Augustinerkloster* has long since been *evangelisch* (the German word typically translated not as "evangelical" but as "Protestant"). More startling still, until recently the cloister was run by a cadre of celibate Lutheran deaconesses. Despite the early zeal of the sixteenth-century reformers against the religious life and a resulting mass exodus from it, in certain places it was reborn with "evangelical" overtones.

Walking through the low-slung modern gates and wandering about, we try to see the space as Luther might have seen it when he entered. The large but unpretentious church is dimly lit by tall and slender Gothic windows, not quite as abundant as one would like. The adjacent cloister is both quiet and lovely, as it should be—a grassy emptiness surrounded by an airy, covered walk. Beyond the nave the sisters have planted a walled-in garden full of medicinal herbs, a reminder that the friars healed bodies as well as souls.

Cloister of the Augustinian priory in Erfurt

But it is difficult to ignore all the subsequent alterations. The stained glass is almost all gone, victim to some or another generation's hatred or neglect; a few of the panes are out for restoration. All the friar's cells (except for Luther's) are gone too, long ago transformed into classrooms, then dormitories, then yet again as conference halls and guest rooms. When at last we find our own quarters, in an authentically old-looking edifice, they smell distinctly of wet plaster and recent paint. Adaptation and upkeep are constant, and we too confidently assume that this recent facelift comes, long expected, after Communist neglect.

But we are wrong. The entire cloister complex was ripped apart by blockbuster bombs in the last and shameful days of World War II. At one point nearly three hundred innocents perished below the old library. They had taken refuge beneath an insufficiently protective shield of valuable rare books. Their cellar-turned-tomb is on display as a memorial, weather-washed as a Roman ruin. To perpetually honor the innocent, the wreckage has been put behind glass.

What at first seems old and timeless has in fact been almost entirely reconstructed. The steep roofs are newly framed and tiled; entire walls are puzzled together from piles of rubble. The wooden guesthouse where we stay is completely new, rebuilt after the bomb-induced conflagration. Neither did the seemingly ancient cloister escape the explosion unscathed: its contemplative colonnades caved beneath the blast. What stand as sturdy watchmen of a hushed and former age are, upon closer examination, carefully restored impostors. Crisply cut new stone mingles with pitted, reassembled pieces.

Luther's cell alone endures, zealously maintained. It is bare save a writing desk; we're meant to imagine his immense mind wrestling with ideas, a scholar fighting with his pen. It's a convincing period piece: exposed half-timbering and plaster, a flagstone floor. But the bombing partially destroyed that building too, letting in the weather for many years. To stave off a certain end in decay and collapse, the whole surrounding structure was dismantled, its punky wood treated against rot, then reassembled inside a more protective enclosure.

Perhaps Luther did work here. But it strains one's metaphysics. How many times can you take apart and move and reassemble a room and have it still be Luther's? How many times can you rebuild a cloister and call it the same cloister? Does it matter that the stuff is the same when the hands that assembled it span a thousand years? Does it matter that the form remains, when the stuff that makes it spans several centuries? It's a question we can ask of any tenaciously maintained antiquity: what is it that we see? The past? Or the long chain of cradling hands that brought it forward for us to contemplate? Luther's Erfurt is just like Strasbourg's station: a preferred past safely guarded by its own iteration of glass bubble—protected quite literally from the winds of change.

On the morning of our departure I wake early in anticipation. Sarah still sleeps, peaceful and warm, soaking up her last moments snuggled closely with our son. While they rest, I take another trip around the grounds. The skies are clear in the crisp fashion of a northern summer, darkish blue and free of haze. The red tiles of the roof are redder; the angles of the buildings sharply defined in the crisp morning air. The cloister walk seems more silent and more manicured than yesterday. Circumnavigating at a contemplative pace, I meditate on Luther's steps, for here I can be sure that I am right on top of them. It was along this very walk that Luther exercised his soul for nearly six years. Within these (reconstructed) walls, he studied the Bible for the first time, learned the science of theology, and recited the entire Psalter weekly as he, together with his brothers, prayed the canonical hours seven times a day. It was here that he exhausted his superiors with his ceaseless and disturbed confessions.

We know more about Luther than we do of nearly anyone else of his era. He wrote incessantly and soon was followed by stenographers eager to record—and possibly to profit by printing—his every word. The critical edition of Luther's writings runs well beyond one hundred volumes and is still growing. But all of this comes later—in many cases much, much later. Of his time in Erfurt in 1510, we have nothing save some reminiscences of an elderly Luther with a gift for storytelling—notes taken down by students of their conversations with a beloved professor. These are hardly sufficient evidence for our skeptical age.

A whole crop of historical psychoanalysis has grown from the fertile field of Luther's silent youth. Was Luther paranoid? Manic? Depressed? Did Luther's fervor arise from a troubled relationship with his father? These lacunae play particularly well in movies, which cannot really capture the religious terror that seems to have dogged the young monk—and many people of his epoch. The latest *Luther* film (2003) sums up half a century's worth of guesswork in an imaginary scene, memorable for its simplicity. I think of it as I pace over the very spot where it is supposed to have occurred. In the movie we see the overwrought and hungry look of actor Joseph Fiennes, on his knees and scrubbing his assigned patch of this very cloister's floor with an unhealthy obsession. His strip of stone is already bone white, and yet he labors unabated, convinced against all reasonableness of his indelible imperfection.

There is no such bone-white strip in Erfurt's cloister. But neither is there any overwhelming evidence to distinguish this young zealot, who certainly took his obligations with exceptional seriousness, from a thousand other novices negotiating the spiritual ropes here and elsewhere. To the contrary, Luther himself reports quite confidently late in life that his early days in Erfurt were among his happiest. The rigors of the religious life do not appear to have been particularly difficult for him; Luther's self-control seems to have been as native as his genius. His mind proved a more fickle servant.

That he was exceptionally talented is sure. He was quickly marked for scholarship and given much to study and to read: the Bible and Gabriel Biel, and soon Aristotle and the Sentences of Peter Lombard. All this was in addition to serving as priest and confessor. His earliest extant letters show a peculiarly intimate concern for fellow friars he otherwise hardly knew.[2]

It's likely that for the same recognition of ability he was chosen to go to Rome. His superiors were well trained in the care of souls, and they certainly would not have sent a wide-eyed lunatic or lascivious libertine (as later polemicists would proclaim) on such a weighty and independent journey. They sent Luther because of his promise as a rising star, since Rome was the ultimate destination for ecclesiastical networkers. There he would meet the people he needed to know to make it in the scrabbling religious politics of his day.

I circle the inner cloister again. Over the years, over these flagstones, Luther walked more than the thousand miles before us. Could we not learn more about him by walking here in Erfurt for seventy days on end? We'd surely see more of what he actually saw. We could dedicate ourselves to read and pray the words he read and prayed; of those, at least, we have a pretty good idea.

Of his thoughts on the eve of his departure to Rome we know not a thing. We know only that it was in the years leading up to the pilgrimage that he reports having suffered his infamous *Anfechtungen* (spiritual attacks). In these he was overcome by theological convulsions that he describes as

> so great and so much like hell that no tongue could adequately express them, no pen could describe them, and one who had not himself experienced them could not believe them. And so great were they that, if they had been sustained or had lasted for half an hour, even for one tenth of an hour, he would have perished completely and all of his bones would have been reduced to ashes. At such a time God seems terribly angry, and with him the whole creation. At such a time there is no flight, no comfort, within or without, but all things accuse. At such a time as that the Psalmist [32:22] mourns, "I am cut off from thy sight."[3]

Luther's superior Johann Staupitz was certainly privy to his young protégé's turbulent inner life. Perhaps it was upon hearing of these *Anfechtungen* that Staupitz assigned a vigorous cure for the overwrought Luther. Confession and absolution can only go so far to ease the mind. Sometimes you just have to get outside and take a long, long walk.

It's Sunday morning, so we head to the cloister church. We're joined now by two friends who will hike with us for a few days. Hans is a longtime friend, a Lutheran pastor, and church history professor. He's tall, wiry-haired, and goateed, with a huge smile inside a bright face. Anne-Sylvie I'd met the year before in Geneva, where we both pursued a postdoctoral fellowship in interreligious dialogue. She's quiet and attentive, with thick black hair and round French cheeks. She's Catholic, a complement to Lutheran Hans, so our pilgrimage is ecumenical from the start.

At the conclusion of the morning's worship, the head Lutheran deaconess offers a special ceremony of blessing for us pilgrims. Sister Katerina raises her hands to speak over us: "The Lord has placed a path before you and taken your journey upon His heart. May He watch your steps with compassion. May He himself uphold your feet, that they dash not upon a rock. May He hold your head high, that you see clearly and far. May the eternal God, Who ever waits upon the way, Who led his people through desert and darkness to the Promised Land, be with you." To Sarah she presents a small bronze angel, cast from old church bells; to me she gives an unadorned cross of olive wood from Jerusalem hung from a simple leather lace.

Sarah and I, my parents and our son Zeke, Hans and Anne-Sylvie walk away together from the *Augustinerkloster*. We wend our way through Erfurt's numerous steeples and spires toward the city's cathedral square. There we linger, double-checking our backpacks and chatting nervously, reluctant to leave. We press the bronze angel into Zeke's hands, a token of our presence and a reminder that God is watching over us all. After a tearful good-bye with the family, we strike out across the broad plaza dragging out the farewell with repeated looks and furtive waves. It will be less than a week till we see them again in Bamberg, but it also will be our longest time ever apart from Zeke.

At the far end of the plaza we climb a small rise to the looming *Marienkirche*, which rules the city both in setting and in opulence—far outshining the plastered box of the *Augustinerkloster*. It was between these Gothic heavenward-soaring columns and full flying buttresses that Luther was ordained a priest and said his distraught first mass. And it is at its doors that we become pilgrims in a recognizable sense. For here we pick up the trail, blazed with the yellow shells of the *Jakobusweg*—better known to English speakers by its Spanish name, the *Camino de Santiago*—that will lead us to Alps. Here we join the august ranks of those marching toward the bones of the saints.

Trail markings for the Camino de Santiago and other paths

The mere mention of the Camino conjures images of ancient, well-worn paths and earnest, humble hikers. Since long before the discovery of the disciple James's bones in the Middle Ages, pilgrims of one kind or another have walked toward Spain's far northwestern tip to contemplate Europe's terminus before the crashing sea, the end of the known world. Some sections of the path and many of its sites are very old indeed: way stations and chapels, hostels used by centuries and generations of wayfarers.

But old roads can be hard to find and even harder to identify. For the most part it's not the path that's old but only the destination. Most of the Camino as we know it now is disappointingly recent, created and promoted in Iberia by the Spanish board of tourism beginning in the 1980s. Some famous books and travelers launched a new wave of interest, and with the crowds came accidents. The route was only occasionally marked, and often walkers found themselves on highway shoulders facing streams of hurtling traffic. At least initially as a public safety measure, the government moved pedestrians off the major roads and onto less traveled trails.

Though far from Spain, even Erfurt feels the ripples of the resurrected Camino. There's no official path to Santiago de Compostela. Spiritually speaking, any way you go to get there is a Camino. But the success and reputation of Spain's trails have sparked a kind of renaissance in pilgrim paths. All across the continent today, clubs maintain, mark, and promote thousands of miles of pathways headed Spainward. All this is quite convenient for us, as there's a made-to-order trail for us to walk nearly all the way to Rome. Until Bregenz, Austria, we'll follow bits of the Jakobusweg; once we are past Milan in Italy, we'll walk its newer sister, the *Via Francigena*, a path that commemorates a separate medieval route to Rome. Though each of these itineraries is longer and more circuitous than Luther's route, we'll hit all his major stops. And equally important, these routes will keep us (mostly) off the roads that now lie atop the premodern tread.

On the backside of the cathedral, we descend the modest height that we had gained approaching it, then walk out of town through the parks and suburbs along the Gera River. The skies are clear and the sun is warm—as if in supernatural benediction. Very soon we leave the city and thread among the fields of recently harvested wheat. Combines and trucks tend the oats and barley. Their rumble warns us of the weather soon to come; when Germans work on their tenaciously guarded Sundays, it can only mean that rain must be threatening. *Ohne Sonntag gibt's nur noch Werktage* ("Without Sundays there are only workdays") goes the slogan. Others profit from the sunshine in a different way, and we walk among those out for their weekend promenade.

After several miles under placid skies, the farmers' omens bear out and the heavens threaten. Beneath the mounting, darkening clouds a gray past shows itself too. So far we've noticed nothing of the former East Germany. But now, well beyond bright and tidy Erfurt, signs of this dismal period become more obvious. Among the many crumbling monuments is an abandoned *Kinder- und Jugendzentrum* (Children and Youth Center). Its glazed façade cracks away pane by rock-shattered pane, windows destroyed by its intended tenants. Communism failed not for a lack of vision but for its shocking naïveté. Here children of the proletariat not only played games and learned their slogans in unison; they also began a life of jockeying for competitive positions within the party structure. There's no solution to human ambition, and Communists merely exchanged one way of sorting people for another. It's not too hard to conjure up the anger of those children, now grown, who were so carefully catechized in this doublespeak. Did one of them toss the first stone? Unlike Strasbourg's station, this unloved era has no glass dome to shield it.

Thunderheads pile up black to mountain heights, preparing to release their flood. Just as the rain begins to pelt us with fat drops, we hurry inside a protective spinney to don our rain gear and deploy umbrellas. We scurry onward through a blurring downpour past more miles of forgettable, unloved architecture.

Just at the outskirts of Arnstadt, the buildings suddenly brighten. Homes new and old are cheerfully painted; the streets are freshly paved. The rain patters upon sidewalks muddy with evidence of recent landscaping: rows of freshly planted saplings promise to shade the streets in due time. In the old town proper a glittering playground—all yellow and blue and stainless steel—shows they city's loving care for today's capitalist children. The historic district is completely refurbished, positively bursting with civic pride. The contrast with the dilapidated *Jugendzentrum* couldn't be more extreme. The whole of Arnstadt is an updated, bustling seventeenth-century village. Here is a history deemed worthy of protection.

Old East Germany is full of such juxtapositions, as if the whole populace cried out to bury the gray and joy-draining Communist past. It makes me think of Ypres, Belgium, which was rebuilt in perfect copy after being obliterated by the shells of World War I. Its burghers had fled with their city plans and family photos and later reconstructed the whole thing, brick by painstakingly accurate brick. Today's visitor sees nothing of the war, only the height of Walloon prosperity. On the one hand, rebuilding these old towns gives them honor and demonstrates a defiant hope; on the other, the reconstructions function as a massive mental dam, erected to hold back the terror of what might have been the last word.

Dripping wet, we knock at the home of Angelika and Detlef, a local pastor couple. Angelika is tall and thin beneath slacks and sweater; her smiling face is framed by a slightly wavy, shoulder-length bob. Taciturn and calm, she fits the part of the conflict-soothing superintendent of the local Lutheran diocese. Detlef is her opposite: round in every way, jolly, balding, bearded, voluble. He's a social activist and coordinates the church's *diakonia* in the form of international service projects and exchanges. They wave us warmly into their cozy home, offer us hot showers, dry out our sopping things, and share with us a light supper, for which we're joined by their two teenage daughters.

Over our bread, beer, cheese, and cucumbers, Sarah and I speak haltingly, struggling to awake our dormant German tongues. The assembled family enthusiastically approves our ecumenical aim of linking Luther and Rome with our feet; but as well-catechized Lutherans they are much more tepid about pilgrimages. They proudly show us the morning's newspaper, where our departure from Erfurt has been announced. The church's press service has mistakenly identified us as French and exaggerated our numbers; neither does the notice mention our blog as we had hoped. We're happy for the publicity nonetheless.

"Arnstadt looks really nice," we observe ingenuously. "There's obviously been a lot of work done recently." Detlef and Angelika remind us that Arnstadt was the first post of Johann Sebastian Bach and is quite famous as a result. At the age of just eighteen, the young organist and composer inaugurated one of the first modern, multi-rank organs in the now eponymous *Johann-Sebastian-Bach-Kirche*. Thousands of visitors come each year to make a musical "pilgrimage" on his account. These visitors want to see the church, hear a concert, take a stroll in the forest nearby, and see the town just as it was in Bach's time. Another city under glass!

It all looks historic, but the buildings we see restored bury a still deeper past. The record of human settlement in this location runs into prehistory. Arnstadt was one of only a few permanent settlements north of the old Roman borders. The medieval city was twice decimated by the plague, then finally leveled by fire at the close of the Thirty Years' War. We see only its latest incarnation, which dates from the late seventeenth century. Luther's steps lie well beneath all visible trace.

But signs of Luther are everywhere. Bach was as Lutheran as they come, and Bach is certainly Arnstadt's patron and still the source of its prosperity. Visitors who come to see his church can't help being assaulted by Lutheran piety. The Johann-Sebastian-Bach-Kirche is self-consciously modest from the outside—a simple box of rough stone. Inside too it is neither grand nor fancy. Its wooden vault is intimately proportioned and surrounded by two wraparound galleries. It feels as much like an opera house as a church—just without the fancy decoration. The association is far from chance, for the whole space is conceived to channel sound—that privileged, sacramental medium of Lutheran worship. It is a perfect size for music, for singing, for listening attentively to a well-articulated sermon. We have no idea where Luther may have slept in Arnstadt, but reminders of him are everywhere, echoing like fugal counterpoint through a city rebuilt in his faith and spirit.

In the pastors' study, we inaugurate what will become our nightly ritual: Sarah blogs about the day's events, while I edit and caption some photos to put online. We plug in our electronic paraphernalia, then we sleep.

Only one day's walk behind us and we're already unsure of how to proceed. Our original plan of following the Camino has been upset by the aforementioned protests of a local Thuringian pastor against our planned stop in Paulinzella, and we have yet to find an "accurate" alternative. We ask Detlef to help us find an appropriate route. Myriad maps descend from dusty shelves, and he plots us a course: continue up the Gera River, head over to Stützerbach, take the well-known Rennsteig trail to Masserberg, then descend from the Thuringian Forest down into Eisfeld.

It seems like quite a lot, and he's a bit fuzzy about the distances. "We have to be in Coburg in three days," we worry aloud, "so Hans can catch his train." He has family and classes waiting for him in Minnesota. But it isn't just Hans and his train that concerns us. In precisely six days—next Saturday—we must rendezvous with our son and my parents in Bamberg. Our itinerary is already fixed. We have appointments and reservations in almost every city southward. We've already booked our nonrefundable flight from Rome! There's but the slightest room for error, and we don't want to throw everything off already on day two.

Detlef assures us that his route is possible, and we accept his three pages of typed notes. Perhaps we ought to have heeded his transparent enough caveat emptor: *Ich wandere nicht gern* ("I'm not so keen on hiking"). But swept up in his helpful enthusiasm for the proposed route and determined to take the most historically accurate option—not to mention lacking any convincing alternative—we gladly accept his painstaking plans.

The previous night's rain has calmed to a drizzle as the four of us leave Arnstadt, ducking through the old south gate. The guardhouse issues a topsy-turvy threat: *Kein Sturm, kein Ungewitter, kein Feind, kein Trug und List kann dieses Haus erschüttern wenn Gott der Schützer ist* ("Neither storm nor tempest, nor enemy, nor deception, nor trick can shake this house if God is the protector"). But we pass through that gate and walk beyond its protection. Outside those walls God's vigilance seems more tenuous.

One might think a pilgrim to be a jolly sort or at least lusty: to trade the workaday for a distant and exotic destination, to exercise the body's native yearning to move, to wander, to respire the wholesome rural air, to suspend pretensions of autonomy and accept the stranger's embrace. But this morning finds us feeling dour and irritated by the weather. The pilgrim marches openly toward his own death, I ruminate, trying on a medieval imagination. Were we to walk in Luther's day, we would have left a will behind on the realistic assumption that we might die. Such was fitting for pilgrims of that age, who sought not to contemplate pastoral countryside but to visit distant bones of saints. These relics were terrestrial harbors of eternity, remains whose demise and decay had brought not oblivion but a new awakening—a final judgment of resurrection and new life.

Using Detlef's notes, we follow the Gera upstream toward Plauë. Idle pastures glow shamrock green under glowering skies. Uneaten thistles stand tall, like pink torches on the grassy sea. Cheery blue chicory lines the roadsides. Having worked through a dry Sunday to take in the harvest, the farmers rest, satisfied. All is hushed and wet. Each time our legs dry off, we plunge through more brush, painting our legs again with dew.

Damp and withdrawn beneath our umbrellas, we trudge past an unassuming park and are drawn in by a weathered brick memorial, which is half obscured by soggy, drooping foliage. It exudes some mysterious, heavy gravity. *Todesmarsche* ("Deathmarch") reads a bold header, chastening me and my dour mood. It's April 1945. Their guilt awoken to terror by approaching Russian drumbeats, the rushed SS emptied their death camps, marching the living evidence of their crimes away from the front. Past this very point stumbled a doomed and necrotic column fleeing Buchenwald: thirteen thousand victims, claims the rusty panel, going nowhere but away from one death toward another.

Here and everywhere, herding soldiers struck a curfew in the town, ordering shutters closed and blinds drawn as they prodded their charges toward an unknown fate. There were already too many witnesses to their crimes of obedience. What strange humanity, what peculiar devotion to procedure saved the doomed from being mown down into an open pit, as happened elsewhere. And what childish admission of culpability by the soldiers, who so frantically desired to destroy the evidence.

Ihr Vermächtnis lebt in unseren Taten fort ("Their legacy lives on in our deeds") reads the inscription, which I take as our own generation's anguished cry: Let them have died for something! Let us not remember only Bach and bustling city centers but graveyards and guilt. Memory is only half glory. The other half is well-deserved shame. Those prisoners—Jews, gypsies, Communists, homosexuals, the mentally ill—they yearned for the future described by Zechariah: "Stronger than the sword is my Spirit" (4:6), a poetic but apt translation I recall from the lintel of Strasbourg's synagogue.

We soon enter a small valley, both absolutely lovely and completely conventional. Luminous pastures merge into forested slopes that rise to modest heights. A stream runs through it. All that's needed is a thin ribbon of smoke drifting up from a gingerbread house and we would be transported into a sentimental dreamscape of Thomas Kinkade. But then the sun breaks through, illuminating a towering viaduct—white concrete set against black clouds beyond. Cars and trucks rip across the wet highway, oblivious to our slow footsteps—and Luther's—beneath.

My thoughts are likewise formulaic as I draw the obvious contrasts between walking and driving, slow and fast, the old and the new way of getting about. But I'm unsatisfied. The old pilgrim left the rhythmic life of fields and harvests to head toward the eternal harbor of the saints. The modern pilgrim does the opposite. She leaves the fast track to join the rhythmic life of the road. The two eras, the two exchanges seem too incommensurate, too fake to make our re-creation of Luther's walk feasible. At least we're somewhere near his track, I comfort myself—though I will later learn that even this is a false comfort.

We pass through Angelroden, then Elgersburg. Their buildings are sided with slate, as is the style throughout the Thuringian Forest. The flakes of stone are not merely utilitarian but are expertly worked into delightful, scalloped patterns. Trompe-l'oeil pillars, ornamental flowers, butterflies—all of them pointillated with little slates of different colors. Here there is no distinction between technical prowess and artistry.

From Elgersburg we climb from the Gera valley into the misty Thuringian Forest. Along our winding forest track, well-managed firs reach straight and high from the mossy litter. All is gentle and hushed in their airy shadow, even the calm drip of the rain. Old stumps nourish spongy new growth. Springs, one after another, bubble up beside the needle-softened road. A family grinds slowly past in a rusty Fiat. (Or is it a Trabant?) We pass them up at a concrete catchment. The hatchback is now stacked high, its body sunk low, with crate upon crate of fresh spring water.

The beginning of a long walk is the hardest. After a few weeks each step becomes routine: one million two hundred thirty-nine thousand nine hundred forty-eight, forty-nine, fifty. But at the outset, the feet fail to comprehend their new and unrelenting routine. And they protest, understandably. They demand a hearing.

On first reflection, modern life may seem disconcertingly portable. Our massive and recent urbanization has left many pining for the family farm and the rhythm of the seasons. It's easy to lament our own unease and then assume that stability, rootedness, a "sense of place," are how things ought to be. But our pilgrim feet tell another tale. For civilization itself is founded on the rift between the settled and the unsettled, and it is no longer possible for us to say which is more natural. The rift cuts straight through the Bible too, starting with geographically fixed farmer Cain slaying migratory herdsman Abel.

Scripture's God seems to prefer mobility. Great Abraham himself, the father of nations, was first of all a man who left his home: a "wandering Aramean" (Deut. 26:5). And no sooner had his descendants settled in Canaan than famine drove them to Egypt. For all the talk of a promised land, God seems forever to be sending the chosen people packing off to some far-off place. Even the Lord's home was at first a tent, struck and raised at each move. It probably should have stayed that way too, for the costly temple lasted no longer, nor did it protect the holy of holies more thoroughly than the tabernacle's insubstantial fabric. Moreover, the tabernacle was a good reminder to the Israelites that their divinity lived neither in a tree, spring, rock, or high place, nor in any mighty monument of man, but in the midst of their unsettled assembly. The one God is not fixed, but mobile.

Our aching feet beg us to forget this foundational fact. Recall how Rachel stole her father's household gods when fleeing with Jacob, how the Israelites longed for the savory stews of their Egyptian slavery, and how quickly they forged their plundered gold into an idol-reminder of their settled, suffering existence. Modern people also have their household gods: protective spells woven of salaries and calendars and insurance. In an immoveable abode, bound in their native niche, our little paper gods do their work, shielding hearth and health from unforeseen intrusions.

But who is to protect that wandering Aramean, the wandering Hebrews, the pilgrim, us? The wanderer's home is no place—his gods rebel. Unsettled from their stable niche, squirreled away in the baggage, the nomad's gods can no longer provide protection; they demand to go home. When the Hebrews longed for their fleshpots, when they lamented their aching feet, they confessed allegiance to their frightened, uprooted idols. Away from home, we hide our household gods from the prying eyes of that great idolocide Moses, who teaches that God's home is not a place, but among his people. The pilgrim's aching feet let us feel the ancient angry protestations of dying household gods, who tolerate no bread from heaven but are fueled by toil and worry. Once unchained, the gods renounce the wanderer's liberty as blasphemous and demand the comforts of their imprisonment. Adam and Eve lived blissfully in a garden, only to be exiled to toil. But we cannot undo the fall by re-creating paradise, for God lives not in a garden, nor in a solid temple, but in a tent.

Past the springs and farther into the dripping forest, we happen upon a public spa, a U-shaped pool of mortared stone set in the middle of the wilderness. The sign says *Barfußpfad* (barefoot path) and invites us to cool our screaming feet with a slow soak in its simple labyrinth. We roll up our pants and descend the steps, like those of an ancient Roman baptistery, and shuffle slowly through the frigid, cleansing ablution.

After the pool we continue toward the crest and join a trail blazed "Bach to Goethe." Further signs call the world-weary to fugal reveries and bright epiphanies in the foggy mist. It was here that the harried Goethe took his cures, retreating from Weimar and ingesting fully the book of nature. His choice vistas over sprite-filled hollows are now built up for the Romantic pilgrim: wooden platforms and poetry-laden panels aid our contemplation of his mystical woods.

Here as well once summered the favored among East Germany's Communist elite. We descend to their old resort near Stützerbach, where we will spend the night. It has seen better days. What's left of proletariat splendor is now a vast field of repurposed campers and mobile homes. Ours is pungent with old vinyl and barely tamed mildew. Not precisely the cleansing air that party officials might have hoped for. Several scratching mice take good advantage of our trailer's tubular ventilation. Hans, Anne-Sylvie, Sarah, and I cook up a simple spaghetti dinner in our trailer kitchen. Our tongues loosened by the addition of wine from the campground's kiosk, we talk long and volubly of hiking, Germany, Luther and theology, the unknown distance of tomorrow. The rain pounds down hard upon the thin roof as we go to sleep.

Awakening late but well-refreshed, we hike from our trailer home down into Stützerbach. This vacation town is exceptionally well-manicured and bustles with walkers and holiday makers, who are out like us to buy their morning bread. Its narrow streets are lined with cheery gardens bursting with color—all the brighter for the ubiquitous backdrop of Thuringian slate. The designs worked into the siding are even more intricate than those we saw the day before: roosters crow, multicolored flowers bloom, whole murals grow out of meticulously worked rock.

We're still on Detlef's detour, but we grow suspicious as we climb up the valley wall and gain the crest. The old road surely lies below toward Sühl. But our recent change of plans means we have no map to plot a surer course, so we plow on with our written directions. Even as we doubt our route's authenticity, we're quite sure of its wisdom. For the car-filled road below winds for miles through narrow canyons—with neither sidewalk nor shoulder. In contrast we cut high above on the Rennsteig, a former border road that is now a popular hiking trail. The chances that Luther went this way are—we later learn—well-nigh null. But we're happy enough to leave the traffic behind and stroll through forests scented by the gentle aroma of recently felled pine.

This is an old, old trail, and its milestones are weathered enough to prove it. We pass the time imagining aloud what Luther's thoughts would be as he braved such forests. It was much wilder then than now, we speculate. Bears and wolves ranged freely in Luther's day—to say nothing of brigands. Sprites and devils hid in hollows and behind the trees. Here was ample spawning ground for tales of talking swans and magical bears such as were gathered by the Brothers Grimm. Modern people—confined to cities and desks and protected from the wilderness by rifles, machines, and tight regulations—are more apt to pine for the wilds than did the people of the Middle Ages, who feared their dark recesses. What devils did Luther hear beneath owl hoot and creaking tree? Was he calm and sober as he walked along chanting his Psalms? Or did he jump at every snapped twig?

Dampness follows us along the Rennsteig and fuels now and again a powerful fungal odor. Next to the hiker's lean-to where we stop for lunch, we discover cached a basket full of mushrooms. Its absent owner must be out to gather more. The mushroom harvest will follow us southward. All along the way to Rome we're accompanied by this insistent evidence of decay. In nature, a single season is enough to consume the evidence of the previous one. What is five hundred years to this? Only protected things do not rot. And what is civilization itself but one giant shield against nature's inevitable entropy? The peripatetics and even Moses in his way knew the curse of our species well: that all our toil is but a constant battle against oblivion.

We press on, now through thickets as silent as death, now beside open pasture. The skies are suddenly cleared by brisk wind; the light shines so hard, as if it and the local slate were hewn from the same flinty quarry. A trailside chapel ringed with split-log benches—just like those I remember from the summer camps of my youth—invites us to settle for our evening prayers. We sing beneath the trees, the light, and a simple hewn cross. Luther might have done this on his pilgrimage too as he measured out his days with the liturgy of the hours.

Approaching dinnertime, we wander into our penultimate town of the day, Masserberg. We've already walked more than thirteen miles, and all hope to find our beds soon. Instead a road sign whips us to attention; "Eisfeld 18km," eleven more miles. Detlef! *Ich wandere nicht gern* indeed! Sarah suffers her first crash as we contemplate the strenuous evening still ahead. She's never walked so far in a single day before. I had planned longer distances but only for much later in our trip, after we had hardened ourselves to the routine. Yet we must arrive in Eisfeld tonight. We have our reservations and plans. Hans has his train to catch; a few days later Anne-Sylvie has hers. Then there are other meetings and schedules to keep.

A weary pall settles over us all as we stumble into the only open restaurant. The gruff owner agrees to stay open and serve us, but with obvious unwillingness. He unwraps frozen pizzas in plain view, as if to show us how little he cares, and puts them into a cold oven. When we eat them not too many minutes later, they taste exactly as you'd expect: like stale, starchy cardboard. Exhausted as she is, Sarah can't even stomach hers. Hans and Anne Sylvie manage, as do I, to eat something—but only just enough to rekindle our flagging energies.

Slightly sick to the stomach, we steel ourselves for the remaining miles and make the most of a pleasant enough hike down from our crest. The trail is springy with moss. Rays of golden evening light stream through the coniferous canopy. We exit the dusky forest just before nightfall, only to be greeted by the bright orange of a full harvest moon. We are glad for its brilliance, as we still have several miles to march—along a highway. But hurtling cars negate any solace the moon might have given. Inside a car one forgets the noise. But on the outside we can hear the screeching juggernauts approaching from miles away. The lights are a blinding glare. We curse the darkness and gnash our teeth as we stumble along with ears perked to sense the next approaching threat. We're forced to leap across the drainage ditch each time we fear a distracted driver. During one such evasive maneuver, I plunge my foot into an invisible concrete drain and scrape my shin nearly to the bone on a rough corner. Sarah hastily cleans and bandages the wound. I console myself with the thought that it's better than the broken knee it easily could have been.

St. Augustine in his *City of God* supposed all Christians to be pilgrims, suspended in expectation by baptism and foretasting in that sign a future resurrection of the dead. Marked with the cross of Christ, the Christian's life cannot be settled, but is a constant pilgrimage. What for humans now is the visible and recurring spectacle of work, of the harvest, of sordid politics would soon be sloughed off in the resurrection as so much terrestrial baggage. We are all foreigners, he opined, whose citizenship lies uncomfortably far away in an exotic yet familiar paradise: the celestial abode of the saints.

What for Augustine was an allegory of the soul is for us a reality in the flesh. There's nothing like walking against traffic on a highway in the dark to feel the point quite viscerally. Over the last centuries humans have incrementally succeeded in creating a world in which our own bodies are unwelcome. A late night for Luther on his pilgrimage meant following a cart and its lantern. Under a full moon it meant nothing but taming familiar, primordial fears. For us it means walking on the only right of way, which happens to be ruled by two-ton hunks of steel speeding along at a mile a minute. Wincing from my scrape, I pine for Luther's woods, looming black behind us. They may be full of phantoms, but our plains have equally menacing monsters.

We finally limp up to our hostel in Eisfeld at ten o'clock, worn thin after twelve hours of ups and downs. It turned out to be the longest day of our whole trip: we covered almost twenty-four miles. Our best estimates put Luther's pace at around a marathon a day. We almost equaled Luther. Once. Then again, he got up early and didn't have to blog or make hotel reservations. We're impressed with ourselves nonetheless.

As we collapse into our beds, we voice ill-tempered thoughts about pushy Thuringian pastors and their local pride. But it was we who took the bait of authenticity all too easily. So smitten were we by the prospect of retracing Luther's steps through space that we forgot how much has changed through time. Enough has happened between then and now to make any re-creation at best an approximation. That night on the highway into Eisfeld wore through the first of myriad illusions.

We make another late and aching start. Our few hours of sleep are just enough to take the edge off of yesterday's fatigue. Three-quarters of us are feeling rather unwell after last night's partially unfrozen pizza. But after a light breakfast of rolls, ham, cheese, and ample coffee, our spirits lift and we set off under clement skies. The protests of our legs quiet quickly as we start to walk, and our moods warm with the gentle rays of the sun.

After two days of blurry navigation through the forest, we're relieved to be on Luther's tracks again—or at least somewhat nearer them than before. Even if Luther didn't come this way on his pilgrimage to Rome, the next station on Etzlaub's map, Coburg, is a certified Luther destination. In 1530, he was holed up above the city in the *Veste Coburg*—its mighty fortress.

Ein feste Burg ist unser Gott ("A mighty fortress is our God"). With these opening words of his most beloved hymn, Luther presents God as an unassailable refuge, a medieval castle's keep, safe from the endless assaults of sin, death, and the devil. Against this trinity of evil—Luther often mentions them together—Christ rises insurmountable and builds up a sturdy bulwark of faith around each beleaguered believer.

Luther's theological fortress was an appropriate martial metaphor for a warring and warrior age. Fortress-as-refuge was a reality he knew well. Twice his own life was spared by the protection of nonmetaphorical mighty fortresses. His first retreat came after the infamous deposition before Emperor Charles V at Worms in 1521, where Luther was officially condemned as a heretic. This label earned him the imperial ban, a fancy way of saying that anyone who killed him would go unpunished. Luther's prince and patron, Frederick the Wise of Saxony, promptly kidnapped Luther for his own protection and secreted his young celebrity to the Wartburg castle. Luther's second fortress was the Veste Coburg. Here the more mature reformer of 1530 was compelled to remain while his colleagues, led by Philip Melanchthon, presented their confession of faith once again before Charles V at yet another imperial diet—this time convened further south in Augsburg. Coburg was as far as Frederick's power reached, and beyond it Luther, who was still under the ban, seriously risked his life.

At both fortresses Luther turned toward Scripture. Removed from the exhausting demands placed upon him as professor, pastor, and busy spokesman for the reforming movement, he read and translated. It makes sense that ensconced between thick protective walls he would work to create a spiritual defense. For the Reformation, taking so many of its cues from the Renaissance, also sought the uncontestable source of things. In studying the Bible *ad fontes*, back to the sources, Luther sought the stable rock from which all could be built upward and insurmountable. In the Wartburg castle he drafted a translation of the New Testament into German. There had already been other German Bibles before this, but Luther's was the first to work not from the official text of the Western Church, the Latin Vulgate, but from the original Greek, a critical text of which had recently been published by Erasmus. Just as important and revolutionary as its source was Luther's intended audience: the common people. When Luther took refuge in the Veste Coburg in 1530, he was still working on his translation of the Bible, though by then he had moved on to the Old Testament.

With fortresses on our minds, we turn a corner and suddenly find ourselves face to face with the Iron Curtain. It would be easy to miss, actually. A modest watchtower empty above a gas station and some sprawling highway margins is all that's left standing. We snack at a lonely picnic table beneath the bygone vigilance of the vacant tower. Beside the table a sheltered sign diagrams the old checkpoint. On each side of the official border was a fence, but on the side of the German Democratic Republic (GDR) was a further no man's land one hundred yards wide. Beyond that was a minefield enclosed by yet more fences topped with razor wire. Patrol roads and more watchtowers complete the scene.

The deserted setting—all spindly wire—is the opposite of a fortress. But it's much more menacing for that. A castle's purpose is quite simply to keep the nobleman and his wealth as safe as possible. Its hilltop bulk sends an unmistakable message: do what you will, but I am unassailable. This border sought not to protect a single person but to control every last one of them. The informational panel evokes with a few statistics the extent of the pressure held back by that slender metal gate: "On 10 November 1989, when the crossing was opened at 4 a.m., 800 people passed in the first minute. A thousand cars per hour were crossing by the beginning of December."

A separate panel tells a more hopeful story. At up to three miles wide, the old border was a fairly substantial strip. Forty years of military protection unintentionally left behind a ribbon of undeveloped wilderness. When Communism fell, some perspicacious activists seized the rare opportunity to create a nature preserve straight through the middle of the world's most built-up continent. From the Baltic to the Adriatic now stretches the European Green Belt. What once warned certain death now sprouts unfettered life. Bunkers are dens for foxes, badgers, and endangered wolves. Humans made themselves unwelcome and have thus welcomed the rest of life. The meandering trail is part of an even longer Iron Curtain Cycling Route that begins at the Norwegian-Russian border on the Arctic Ocean. With the slightest shift, a menace has become a source of life and health.

Heads spinning with contradictions, we leave our no man's land and walk out of the old GDR. Another sign reminds the quickly passing cars of the significance of their humdrum passage: "Up until 10 November 1989, here Europe and Germany were separated." Half a century of fear and hegemony ended at the stroke of a clock. From the safe distance of twenty years, it now reads as an inevitable fall. But an entire generation was raised on the utter certainty of a final, devastating conflagration. Even my recent youth in the 1980s was saturated with cloak-and-dagger spy tales, hunts for Red October, and Olympic boycotts. All such intrigue has been very quickly abandoned. That old watchtower now guards not the border but the past itself, hoping for its remembrance.

At first one side of the border looks much like the other. Geese honk, awaiting Christmas slaughter in their barnyards. Ripened maize dries out in the sun. Oat stalks are bent double under their own fullness. Granaries and barns stand ready to accept their portion. Then we perceive a bright cheerfulness about Bavarian farms that was lacking in the East, but perhaps that's just the years of propaganda we heard as children.

Emerging from under a murky Autobahn underpass we finally glimpse the still distant Veste Coburg standing guard over the old city. It takes a while to get there. Like most modern cities, Coburg is surrounded by a belt of light industry and commerce, the ubiquitous and forgettable office buildings and warehouses that make the backdrop of our civilization. They're impossible to avoid on foot. We pass a large distribution center with numbered loading docks. Then as we briefly join the ring road, we're confronted by a very new monolith of gleaming glass—home to an auto insurance company—surrounded by an expansive and utterly pointless garden. We're surprised to come across a baseball field. A hand-painted banner invites passersby to support the local team, the Coburg Cubs. And as if to confirm the city's international pedigree, a further sign announces sister cities in Canada, the United States, and other European countries.

The global connections are not new. Local royalty, the Saxe-Coburgs, ruled half of Europe during its industrial age. Uncles, cousins, and brothers reigned from Edinburgh to Athens. Today's Coburg longs to tap this historical well for tourist cash. At the city limit, a sign reminds us upon whose august steps we tread. Our Luther, we happily note, tops an impressive list that includes Queen Victoria and Prince Albert as well as Johann Strauss. Coburg sells them all, just like it sells insurance.

Once we climb up to it the Veste Coburg proves, as did Erfurt's *Augustinerkloster*, that age is deceptive. Even amid the obviously old, the past lies hidden beneath remodels, additions, structural reinforcements. And maintenance. Constant, unceasing maintenance. That's what keeps old structures up and decay at bay. A tall tower dominates the castle's height. It is stamped with the rippling crowned lions of the Saxe-Coburg heraldry. Surely this is the hoary cornerstone, we assume. "This tower erected in 1911," a panel tells us when we approach. So much for ancient history.

Our ambition to experience the past is already muted as we tunnel together into the renovated interior. Manicured grass and tidy half-timbering tell us that we're in a museum. An exhibition poster confirms it. The castle's nobility were great patrons—and continue to be. Their commissions and collections still attract crowds. We set aside these later wonders, though, and head instead to the greatest treasure of them all: the jewel in Coburg's tourist crown is the *Lutherkammer*, the Luther Rooms, the very site of his 1530 sojourn.

Hans, Anne-Sylvie, Sarah, and I all pay at the kiosk and head up some dark and creaky stairs to Luther's chambers. The wooden entryway is carved with an advertisement for the room's significance: "As the Confession was presented in Augsburg, Luther stayed and worked here." It is a dim and severe place, spare of decoration, demanding of the intellect rather than the senses. A grotesquely scourged Christ painted by Albrecht Dürer overlooks the study, putting us in the proper mood: Jesus holds the cat-o'-nine-tails that will become the instrument of his own flogging. Beside this agonized Christ hangs an immediately recognizable portrait of the older Luther by Cranach.

I've never seen the two together, but they make much more sense this way. Side-by-side they complete a *fröhliche Wechsel* or joyful exchange, one of Luther's favorite gospel metaphors. A well-fed, academically robed Luther sits in placid comfort. Any sign of his youthful terror is long gone, transferred fully and miraculously onto Christ in the painting opposite. Whereas Jesus holds the cords of his own pain, Luther holds the Bible, which also works God's will upon those who study its mysteries—but to comfort and heal, not to whip and destroy.

Luther's rose is painted on the wall, as is his Latin motto from Psalm 117: *Non moriam sed vivam et narrato opera domini* ("I shall not die but live and declare the works of the Lord"). A sketch of Luther's death mask completes what might incorrectly be perceived as a grave scene. As in the painting, Luther's plaster face is calm, comforted, lifelike; the vitality that was Christ's is now his. The Psalm is fulfilled, for while Luther's body is absent, his words live on, declaring the works of the Lord.

But there's more to Luther's presence than an intellectual heritage. The building itself stands because of him. It is a shrine, I realize with Protestant shock, if ever there was one. But a shrine uncomfortably transformed from the original purpose of that genre. There are no bones, fingernails, garments, or any material remains of Luther's person, but rather entire rooms, halls,

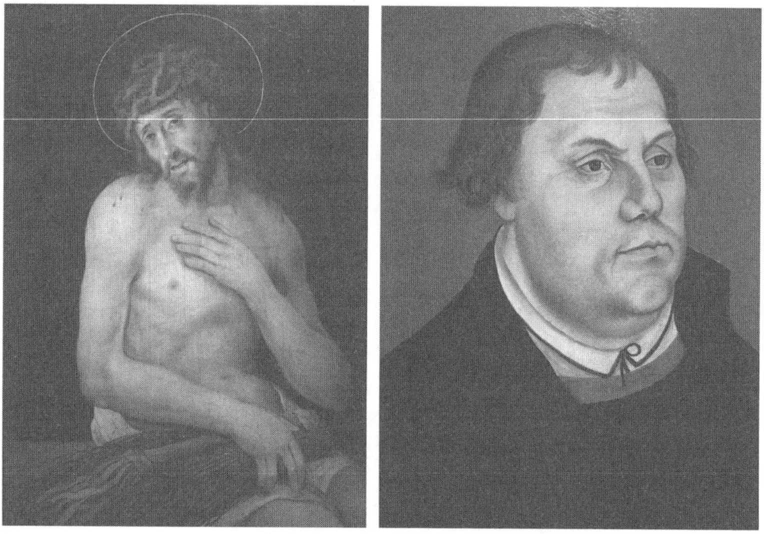

Paintings of Christ and Luther by Lucas Cranach,
now hanging in Luther's quarters at the Veste Coburg

and chapels are maintained because once upon a time, five hundred years ago, Luther was here.

In the next room hangs a painting that illustrates the practices of Reformation churches. A child begowned in white is baptized. Pastors, open books in hand, teach Bible lessons to children. Priests share the communion cup with the laity, a practice nearly unheard of in the Middle Ages. Women and men sit in pews—a Protestant invention—attentive to a preacher high in his pulpit. In a discrete corner, a pastor offers absolution to a troubled soul. The anonymous artist has made his message loud and clear: all that the Roman church has—from baptism until death—we have too, only purified. It is a useful reminder to us that, even as they struggled for their freedom, Lutherans didn't see themselves as revolutionaries at all. Here the Reformation is portrayed not as a negation of what was before but rather as a perfection of all that was good.

The same artist has also rendered the diplomatic events that happened as Luther worked on his translations in these rooms: the presentation of the Confession at Augsburg. It is a proud, peaceful scene. Charles V presides. A papal legate sits on his right, a prince of the Augsburg League on his left. All the Protestant magistrates are standing in a line with their hands raised to take an oath. In Luther's era there was little distance between prince and bishop: both worked to ensure the proper worship of God. It's easy to forget what a deadly serious matter the Reformation was—hardly a mere theological dispute among religious fanatics, as many moderns have been tempted to think. Thousands had already died by 1530, heretics had been burned and drowned, peasants slaughtered. Global politics played a role as well. The Turks besieged Vienna in 1529, and the fate of Christendom itself seemed at stake. The painting makes quite clear that the famed Diet of Augsburg was every bit as much the sealing of a military and administrative alliance as it was a theological agreement. In 1530, one couldn't happen without the other.

We take leave of these polemics. Outside the study a sunny reading nook is preserved, and beyond it the Luther Chapel. Here prayed Luther. On one wall, glowing in the stained glass, stand Saints Peter and Paul. Catholic and Protestant may as well be a preference for one over the other. But here in Luther's house of worship the two saints stand side by side.

On the way out a gift shop sells *Luthersocken*, cute socks sporting our own motto's inspiration: *Hier stehe ich, ich kann nicht anders* ("Here I stand, I cannot do otherwise"). That is what Luther purportedly said at Worms when he was asked to recant his new evangelical teaching. We chuckle at the play on words and walk on. We ourselves can stand there no longer. We must walk out of the museum and its archived greatness into the open, where moth and rust destroy.

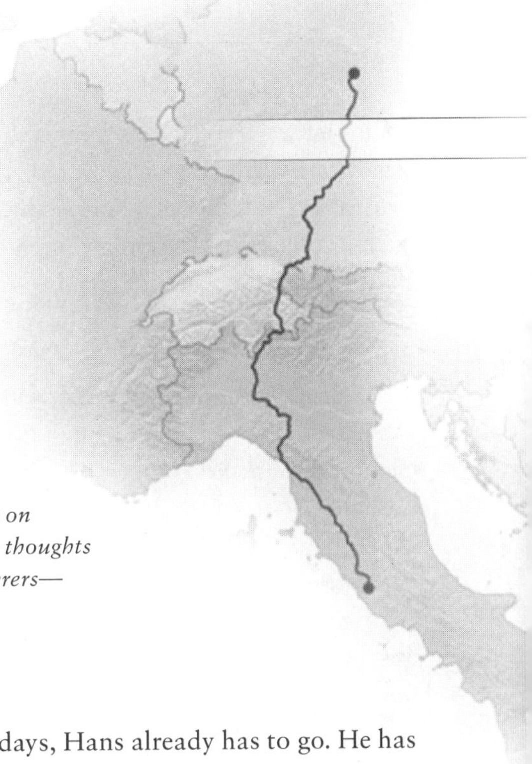

Two

Fourteen Holy Helpers—thunderstorm on Staffelberg—a cross and a skull—some thoughts on saints—Bamberg—water for wanderers—Nuremberg and its clock

Though he's been with us only four days, Hans already has to go. He has family to visit in Holland before heading home to the States. Anne-Sylvie, Sarah, and I walk him down to the station where we say our good-byes. It's late, and by the time we locate our hostel just outside of town all the staff is gone and the building locked up. But the friendly bustling crowd of youth let us in and even clear out a room for us to sleep in. Their welcome is a boon, and not the last time perfect strangers will get us out of a bind.

Over breakfast the next morning we chat with another hiker, Robert, who sits beside his ponderous backpack. He's a photographer laden with gear, walking the length of Germany to take pictures of the people he meets along the way. He finds our idea of following Luther's steps both curious and inspiring. As we don our packs and take up our hiking sticks, he adds our portrait to his collection. We thus become part of recorded German history!

Once on the road, Anne-Sylvie, Sarah, and I breathe the outside air with renewed vigor. The sun shines, the air is clean and cool, our legs are ready to stride: a welcome change from yesterday's heavy atmosphere and plodding pace inside the Veste Coburg. We follow the yellow shells of the Jakobusweg out of town—at first along a busy road lined with parking lots and commerce, then past unassuming homes surrounded by extravagant gardens bursting with color.

Beyond, waves of wheat break across the hillside, driven before a passing squall. Barley and oats give way ever so slowly to maize. Hops grapple up trellised walls. A picketed horse makes his way around an overgrown soccer pitch—some farmer's son having moved on to more adult pastimes. At a construction site, scaffolds clamber and cranes sway, as if to the same wind, and as if the bridge, animated by some parallel vital force, were being summoned upward from the earth itself as giant trunks of concrete.

A village church fronts the road with a hammered bronze door, upon which a radiant lamb proclaims, "I am the host for all who enter." Roadside shrines, memorial crucifixes, murals of saints confront us from all sides. We're in Catholic country. Or so decreed the Peace of Augsburg in 1555, whose edict *cuius regio eius religio* ("whose the region, his the religion") parceled up the faith like so many congressional districts. After 455 years, countless wars, and an ongoing and massive secularization, the landscape itself still proclaims this division of the faith—much more loudly than the silent populace. Even the stones cry out.

On a main street, looming over a particularly blessed parking meter, stands a gaudy profession of faith. A huge diorama of Golgotha in the mannerist style of a late Michelangelo hangs sheltered under an imposing classical pediment. Backed by baby blue sky and puffy clouds, larger-than-life statues of two robbers twist energetically as they plead with a muscular Christ, who hangs limp and serene. Perhaps it is an original. Perhaps it came from the prestige section of a nineteenth-century church statuary catalogue. The proportions are so grand, the setting so mundane, that we spend some time afterward wondering who paid for it—especially its evidently recent restoration. Was it a local landowner, thanking God for an excellent harvest? Did a rich merchant—or his son—outlive a mortal sickness and give this in return as an ex-voto? Was it a vision? And now, what can it possibly mean to the thousands of passing drivers and those who pay to park at its base?

We plod for a while along a freeway, our heavy steps mute beside the swooshing traffic. Suddenly, beyond the Autobahn rise two gaudy towers of pinkish stone, green-topped, like giant sequoias stretching toward heaven or two tall mushrooms sprouting with statuary and ornament, such as to make of mere stone a glowing beacon of spiritual light: the Basilica of Vierzehnheiligen.

We ascend toward the blooming basilica through fields of verdure. From cropped pastures burst clutches of gentians glowing electric indigo in the bluish northern light. The place seems hallowed—set apart for life, abundance, blessing. Even our pilgrim's hostel, plagued by the indelible modernity of, say, 1973, cannot suppress nature's opulence. Its impeccable long-grained woods and sumptuous woolen upholstery ooze with warmth and hidden wealth. All is pristine, as if here we are suspended from the natural tendency toward wear and decay.

The aging Franciscan sisters are solicitous in their welcome and seem happy enough for the interruption we offer their clockwork lives. On the way to our rooms I'm shown a cabinet fully stocked with the abbey's own brew, *Nothelfer*, loosely translated "help in time of need." It's named for the fourteen saints, the Vierzehnheiligen, who appeared on this hillside and gave the basilica its name. Our rooms are arranged with grandmotherly care. A framed computer printout chirps a *Herzliche Wilkommen* to *Herr and Frau Wilson*. Upon a staged tea towel sit a prim vase of silk flowers and a bottle opener. (Don't forget the *Nothelfer*!) Without a hint of luxury, it is the very distillation of elegance.

Luther's path must have lain along the Main River below. But it is fitting that we should ascend to this holy place. For it captures, in a way obscured for us by polemics of the Reformation itself, the strangely democratic spirit of medieval religion. The Standard Narrative would have us believe the late medieval church a fascist dictatorship in form and a spiritual conspiracy in substance, maliciously concocted to rob the widow of her mite. Nothing could be further from the truth.

We arrive too late to visit the church, so instead we read the story of Hermann Leicht, the shepherd boy who founded this mighty basilica. According to our abbey guidebook, it was in early fall of 1445 that young Hermann, standing watch over his flock on the hill above, heard the cries of a child. When finally he found the source and reached down to comfort the distraught infant, it disappeared before his very eyes. One can well imagine his conundrum: whether to confess such a pious apparition or guard his supernatural secret closely. But two days later, in the very same place, the child again appeared, this time silent, accompanied by two floating lights. His first experience having been confirmed, Hermann confessed immediately to the abbot of the nearby Cistercian monastery, who urged the boy to keep watch and also to keep quiet.

This he did until the next summer, when again, in the very same place, the child returned. A red cross now shone from the babe's tunic—symbol of the

Templars, widely recognized as the sign of healing for the invalid—and he was surrounded by a host of others. These were the Fourteen Holy Helpers—the *Vierzehnheiligen*, the *Nothelfer*—as the child told Hermann. Should he build a chapel here for the helpers, they would help others in return. The same two bright lights again descended upon the place, and the vision vanished. Then began the miraculous healings. A chapel soon grew from the spot, and the field of the Vierzehnheiligen began to draw pilgrims from all over Franconia, seeking cures and help of all kinds.

The Fourteen Holy Helpers were certainly known and venerated in nearby Nuremberg. And if Hermann's catechism was typical for his time, then he had been stuffed with wild tales of martyrs and miracles, which in the form of the *Legenda Aurea* ("Golden Legend") made up the most popular literature of the age. And so Hermann, making good use of his well-fed imagination, saw no reason to exile these resurrected souls to another dimension entirely.

The tale has the stamp of fantastical truth about it, yet its outlines are tired to our sterile rationality. After Juan Diego at Guadalupe, the Giraud children at Salette, Bernadette Soubirous at Lourdes, and the children at Fatima, among many others, shepherd boys and girls with visions are cliché, little nobodies upstaging bishops with fanciful tales of supernatural favor. Then comes the popular support. Then comes the church to trim back the weeds of this unruly indigenous piety.

It was the particular genius of the medieval church to manage such outbursts of devotion. Later Catholic officials, just as much as their Protestant nemeses, wouldn't have brooked such chaos. Vierzehnheiligen itself was proscribed for several decades at the height of the Counter-Reformation. But Hermann's vision had the fortune to fall on fertile ground. While the Cistercians cleared the land and turned the soil, making Europe burst with agricultural productivity, they also prepared all of Franconia to receive Hermann's revelation. But it was neither Hermann nor the Cistercians—and certainly not the bishop off in Bamberg—who turned Vierzehnheiligen into a holy place. It was the feet of the masses, churning up that rich soil, dressing it with their hopes, wetting it with their tears, turning it over generation after generation. Thus frothed by popular acclaim, it became a soothing balm for the grinding Gilead of peasant life.

Except for the power of the papacy, there was no other aspect of medieval religion that so maddened the Reformers as the cult of the saints. Their complaints were manifold: the people looked to saints for all manner of help in distress and illness, praying to them instead of to God; rather than caring for their neighbors, people preferred to build shrines, go on costly pilgrimages, or visit relics. Side altars dedicated to saints were often better attended than the mass. In short, it seemed that little had changed since the dark and pagan era when the people appeased the local spirits with suffering and sacrifice, holding the gods at arm's length with a web of spirit magic. Europe's faithful certainly feared God, but by any visible measure they loved and trusted the saints a fair bit more.

It was not merely a matter of ecclesiastical corruption. As Luther distills in his explanation to the First Commandment in his *Large Catechism*:

> To have a God properly means to have something in which the heart trusts completely. Again, consider what we used to do in our blindness under the papacy. If anyone had a toothache, he fasted to the honor of St. Apollonia; if he feared fire, he sought St. Lawrence as his patron; if he feared the plague, he made a vow to St. Sebastian or Roch. There were countless other such abominations, and every person selected his own saint and worshiped and invoked him in time of need. In this class belong those who go so far as to make a pact with the devil in order that he may give them plenty of money, help them in love affairs, protect their cattle, recover lost possessions, etc., as magicians and sorcerers do. All these fix their heart and trust elsewhere than in the true God. They neither expect nor seek anything from him.[1]

This theological perversion, according to the reformers, was propped up by a religious system that assigned to such acts of devotion the weighty label of "good works." Nowhere can we see this clash of pieties more clearly than in the controversy over indulgences, which reveals less the emptiness of popular piety than the utter poverty of the doctrine of merit that had come to dominate the discourse of salvation history. It fits very well within the columns of a bookkeeper's ledger: humans are born tainted with the sin of Adam; baptism into Christ's body atones for this original sin, but actual sin continues to accrue a carefully accounted debt; post-baptismal sin must be repaid by corresponding good works, a lifetime of which would rarely suffice; purgatory provides an in-between place for baptized sinners to repay their remaining balance with requisite suffering; after being properly purified, those dying in the faith would finally end up in heaven. Saints, on the other hand, were so good in life as to die with more merit than debt; this surplus was deposited upon their death into a kind of common chest, a "treasury of merit" managed by the church; this excess was accessible through various pious acts, such as visiting saintly relics or purchasing letters of indulgence. In this tidy schematic, the saints' holiness powers the whole ecclesiastical machine. Priests become cashiers, bishops mid-level managers, and theologians accountants, making the pope a distant CEO of a giant, multinational monopoly on the saints. No wonder there was a Reformation!

The indulgence that was propagated by the archbishop of Mainz and made its rounds through Saxony in 1516 and 1517, against which Luther so (in)famously and successfully preached, was a clear exercise in spiritual capitalism. Becoming archbishop had cost Albert a lot of money, most of it raised as loans from Germany's rich banking families. They were only too happy to finance the debt, for he had at his disposal a most remarkable fund-raising tool: letters of indulgence, granted by the pope himself. In return for the privilege of dispensing these affidavits of reduction in purgatorial debt, Albert was required to turn over a portion of the revenues to Rome, where they helped finance the construction of the new St. Peter's. For officials within the system, it was simply bureaucratic business as usual; for those outside, it became the stuff of revolutions.

But as shockingly egregious as this affair may seem to our era and its economic scruples—Catholic and Protestant alike—the church was always exceedingly careful never to sell *salvation* itself. Indulgences relied, rather, upon the secondary market in saintly merit, which hedged against a muted, distant, and all-judging Christ with the softer doctrine of purgatory. In fact, one didn't even receive an "indulgence" proper but rather a "letter of indulgence," which confirmed the proper outlay of cash and good works. And this was a doctrine that was at its base profoundly popular and eminently democratic. For it was founded not upon the speculations of some scholastics but upon the longing of the people to help and receive help from the dead. That this came to take the form of commercial transaction was only natural, too, especially among the highly urbanized populations of the Holy Roman Empire and the Low Countries, where barter and trade had succeeded the exchange of gifts as the principal pattern for social commerce. If Albert erred in his calculations, it was not in mixing economics and religion. For as long as there are buildings and staff, how can they be separated? His error was rather in trying to bait a newly market-savvy populace with the logic of the gift when they knew enough about finance to cry foul—especially when they began to suspect that the product itself was dubious.

Storms brood beyond our dormitory windows as we stuff our packs the next morning. On our way out we meet Anne-Sylvie coming back from morning mass in the basilica. She seems dazed, not by the service, which offered nothing unexpected, but by the edifice itself. "It's all . . . clouds and . . . gold and . . . fat cherubs!" she blurts in a cry of aesthetic alienation. "Where is my God in all of that?" What a transformation from a windswept shepherd's field! We're immediately curious to see the mighty thing that had once raised so many spirits and now had cast another so low. After a hasty, *herzliche* farewell to the solicitous sisters, we all step outside to face the blustery morning.

The basilica looks more and more alive as Anne-Sylvie guides us toward its pink and green façade. Clouds whip by beyond its spires, which seem to sway like living masts rigged with leafy sails, or like great fir trees bowing in the gale. The main entry, guarded by cool episcopal likenesses, stands calm below the squall. Its grand ceremonial portal is closed, so we take a deep breath and dive inside through the side door.

Just as Anne-Sylvie had warned, the scene takes our breath away. The organic vitality we sensed without is redoubled within; suddenly we are swimming in a sea of life, caught at the very moment of being overwhelmed by a seething, supernatural tide; we are divers in a coral reef, washed by a foaming sea above, surrounded by darting schools

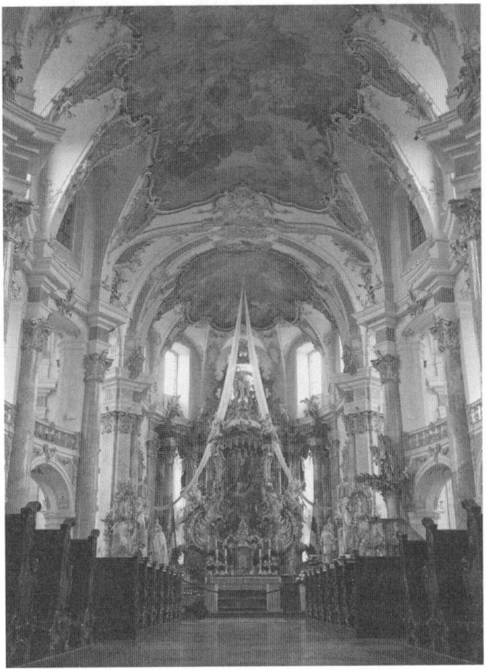

The Basilica of the Fourteen Holy Helpers

of cherubs. The precisely conceived geometries of the space are shrouded by plaster foam and churning frescoes. Soaring above in radiant lightness, golden arcs and twisted scrolls lead beyond the tumult toward an immense and heavenly canopy. Sarah can hardly tame her squeamishness at the cloying scene. "It's like the work of an evil cake decorator," she utters with a kind of architectural nausea.

At the center of it all, thrusting upward with geological force, rises a vast assemblage of marble, lifting statues of all fourteen saints heavenward. The whole churning pile is crowned by the Christ child, who bears the red Templar's cross of Hermann's vision. He is flanked by two fluttering streamers, slowly dancing textile flames dangling from above. Out of my childhood psyche pops a less than pious association: it's somehow like that great floating bust of the Wizard of Oz. Who is that man behind the curtain?

Luther never saw this Basilica of Vierzehnheiligen, which was not built until the eighteenth century. But we can't help wondering as we float among the clouds what friar Luther might have thought. Like Ulm's cavernous Minster, it's certainly no good for preaching. I judge it with austere and modern eyes: overwrought, expensive, too sweet by far for me. Is not all this decoration billowing up before my eyes one vast veil to hide God's majesty? And if this magnificence is but a veil, is there another beneath it? Is it not veils all the way down, each accumulated layer hiding not God's radiance but a primeval fear of being utterly alone in the universe—that there will be in the end, and was in the beginning, nothing? I shake myself from these rehearsed Protestant polemics and try to appreciate the clutter of beautiful things, to contemplate the accumulated labor that cast them into plaster, to imagine generations of pilgrims streaming up the hill laden with their gifts. Such an offering cannot remain mere art—nor mere history.

But then I find the Oz-like curtain and see that the fiercely ornamented nave is but a magnificent antechamber. The basilica's beating heart lies hidden in a tiny chapel to the side, a *Votivkammer*, or votive chamber. Less than fifteen feet square and almost as tall, the room is stuffed from floor to ceiling with guileless tokens of thanksgiving: plaster impressions of healed limbs, abandoned crutches, disembodied eyes, crude drawings notarized by barely literate scribes, cases lined with treasured dolls, infant effigies swaddled upon miniature cradle-boards—all signs of some straightforward healing or deliverance. This little room is the key. The whole building is not an emblem of earthly wealth or power but a colossal material offering to the saints. Before the pricelessness of salvation and the immeasurable benefit of miraculous healing, all the architectural opulence is but a tiny token of gratitude.

The whole ensemble gives me a strange feeling, a rising wave of seasickness. I've felt it before in my aunt's apartment, before her shelves chock-full of Hummel figurines. Despite the immoderate frippery—or better, because of it!—Vierzehnheiligen professed a stoutly populist piety. Common people have offered here their best and brightest. I recall my visits to humble churches in the mountains of Honduras—how they coruscated with plastic streamers, blinked with strings of Christmas lights. The Rococo interior of the basilica shares with those country churches an unmitigated love of ornament and festivity, sweetness and light. Protestants usually imagine that their form of Christianity is the more democratic one, but that is clearly not the case here.

I could appreciate Vierzehnheiligen more as a mirror of popular sentiment, for it expresses with a child's delight the preference for frosting over cake: a voluptuousness that can only spring from the most profound awareness of life's common preciousness and fragility and so seizes what is sweetest and devours it immediately. When—if ever—will it come again? Here is a peasant's heaven, a world of light, a cloud city full of familiar vegetal life that is fully organic yet reborn, purified, unsoiled, magnified. Those whose life is always brown and gray don't want to contemplate yet more rustic simplicity but rather to look upward toward a true place of worship, to gaze upon a world of abundance—purified. And who would want to take from the peasant this vision of a better, brighter place?

But what we witness upon our exit soon taxes this brief eruption of magnanimity. While we were awash in the heavenly tide within, a long row of booths opened their shutters across the street. There they hawk not only walking staffs and umbrellas but also a vast pageant of kitschy wares: candles, cards, bookmarks, holy memorabilia. What had seemed so innocent, heartfelt, and honest inside the basilica now came across as cheap and exploitative. Too much sweetness. Too much light. Too much finance. I cannot shake my Protestant austerity after all. Money changers in the temple, I judge, and I urge our little pilgrim band to hurry away from the crashing spiritual shoals.

Behind the basilica we pick up the trail and tack a blustery path up toward the next point of interest, the Staffelberg. Our recent and unshriven surliness is soon repaid as the threatened storm arrives. Sprays of windblown wetness now beat the undulating swells of Franconia. The already rain-softened stalks of grain buckle under the strain, too weak to support their carefully-bred-to-be-heavy heads. Whole sections lie flattened upon the waterlogged soil, black-specked with mildew, victims of their own abundance. Fallow fields shine with riotous bursts of wildflowers, which fare much better. Pressing on, hunkered behind our flogging umbrellas—born shield-like to fend off the horizontal rain—we pass by bench after bench, each judiciously placed to aid that particular Germanic love of contemplating nature. The view must be superb in fine weather; today we notice little but the clouds, the sheets of driving rain, and our growing cold.

We reach the summit of the *berg* in a full tempest. Lightning strikes. Thunder booms. There's an open chapel on the hilltop, thankfully, and we duck in. "St. Adelgundis," says the lintel, and just inside stands a painted statue of the Merovingian abbess, carved to the not-quite-correct proportions of a skilled amateur, and holding what appears to be a lobster. Adelgundis, we read, is the patroness of cancer victims; her giant red crustacean must be the yeoman artist's idea of a crab—only in landlocked Franconia it came out as a giant crayfish.

Safe from the punishing weather and away from the aggressive piety of the basilica, we breathe a breath of spiritual fresh air. Flat wooden benches line the floor, fading frescoes decorate the walls, elsewhere all is simple stone. This is more our style. No veiling, no haughty symbolism of light, no sky-distant eternity. Just a refuge of cold, hard rock—a tomb from which to rise. The altar alone is overwrought. Its hand-tatted mantle is identical to the one found in the basilica below and reveals the grassroots faith that was sown in both locations. In the place of a full and gaudy realization of dreams, here all that remains is hope. Human love itself fills the spacious void left by the modest decoration. We use the respite to say our morning prayers, then wait for a break in the weather.

We leave too soon. Just beyond the point where we could easily retreat, a new wave of lightning crackles shockingly close. Bounding down an unsheltered slope to the beat of thunderbolts, we feel momentarily assaulted by Luther's biography. One of us jokingly shouts, "Saint Anne, help me! I will become a monk!"

Once we're safely on the valley floor, we warm up in a *Bierstub*, a little village pub. It's so cozy and *gemütlich* as to be a caricature of itself—as are its round, white-haired patrons. Over steaming plates of sausages piled high atop mounds of sauerkraut, we reflect upon the day's striking contradictions. Between St. Adelgundis and Vierzehnheiligen, we get a very different picture of medieval Christianity than the usual. Outwardly hierarchical Catholicism turns out to be quite bottom-up. Instead of uprooting the spiritual seeds that fall willy-nilly into its soil, Catholicism cultivates them, tends them, and trains them to the true trellis. Contrary to what a Protestant—haunted by visions of papal bulls and inquisitions—might expect, the Catholic Church doesn't wrench up local pieties as errant weeds, at least not without much reflection.

There's something kind and generous—not conspiratorial at all—in all the veiling of God, too, all those layers to protect the laity. For if God is in fact creator of the universe, its glorious redeemer and final judge, perhaps we should rather shroud him in clouds and drapery, surrounding him with a more accessible heavenly host. Moses wore a veil, after all. The faith of Protestants, which insists upon direct contact with the living God, seems by contrast rather terrifying.

Architecture tells more about us and our piety than we'd prefer. Sitting there after lunch, still sipping my beer, I mentally recollect the churches of my youth. First Presbyterian in Yakima, Washington, was grand in the style of middle-class dreams with its stolid Florentine nave topped by an Italianate tower. Inside it looked a bit more Presbyterian: dark wood, red carpet, colonnades, a trumpeting organ, a grand wooden pulpit under spotlights whence theological orators held biblical court.

Next was a Vineyard Fellowship: an office building, pure and simple. Just recently rid of its cubicles, it was complete with neutral gray carpet and a hung ceiling buzzing with fluorescent lights. So successful was its original intent to dampen noise that large speakers and bright lights were needed to make the musicians and preachers seen and heard. But the building's design could not be altogether exorcised. At the height of the charismatic service, the people didn't come together for a common rite, but each withdrew into a personal theophany—a spiritual cubicle.

And then there was my first brush with Lutheranism in the lofty attic above Eastvold Auditorium at Pacific Lutheran University. We gathered beneath the giant and night-blackened rose window, illumined by simple tapers. The music washed over us simply and harmoniously, so that we felt at once to be resolutely among humankind—for this was not the heavenly music of the spheres—but still clearly, uprightly, and eternally among the angels. The next week the same service continued as if no time had passed: the same elvish music played by the same elvish pianist. Yet rather than being boring to repeat, it was a comfort.

Each building and each style of worship presents convictions about people, about the nature of the church, about God, about salvation. They tell the social story of their age: of lords and kings and peasants, of professionals and laborers and middle managers. Christianity has had its sway upon these spaces and these liturgies, but each also grew from different ground and from still unfolding histories. Staffelberg is an ancient holy place. It served the Celts as both temple and fortress. Hermann's vision of the Fourteen Holy Helpers was nourished by popular acclamation, built up to foamy greatness by the devoted gifts of the lowly. The primitive reverence for that mountain has been transmuted to Christian ends. In Vierzehnheiligen and in St. Adelgundis's chapel we behold the fundamental genius of Catholic thought according to Thomas Aquinas: that God's grace does not destroy but rather perfects nature. These buildings and the pieties they represent are but the summits of a vast and subterranean spirituality; the church takes and forms correctly their raw and unruly roots.

My evangelical Protestant catechesis seems to have had a preference for blank slates: a revelation, a *creatio ex nihilo*. But it is cruel to be cynical about the Catholic way. For didn't Christ cast out demons in order to sanctify liberated bodies? Did not the holy places of Canaan cede their gods to the Lord? And did not God's revelation over several centuries turn that high place, high above all others—Jerusalem—into the cultic center of the entire universe? To say God's grace perfects nature is neither foolish nor uninformed but is writ into a story of God's inhabitation of the material world.

Protestantism hums a different tune, one also fully Christian but rooted less in the promised land than in the exile, the diaspora. And this is not without its own kind of sense. For it was within the dispersed Hellenic world of displaced Judaism that Christianity spread and took root. We're back to the dialectic between wanderer and settled, which is written into our very consciousness as humans, who alone among earth's creatures have the capacity to be alien to ourselves. And if religion is a natural faculty, it conforms to this divided nature. In our estranged consciousness, by the quest that seeks to find a home, we are made and remade into pilgrims and visitors, ever sojourners. Like the Son of Man into whom we are baptized, we have no roof, no home, no place to call our own. As Christians, our home is nowhere, which means that it is everywhere.

From our dry and cozy Gasthaus, we climb a muddy rut up to another holy hill. This one is dedicated to St. Vitus, another of the Fourteen Holy Helpers. All around now we can sense the fertility of the farmland, the bursting granaries, the agricultural wealth that fills the well-stocked cellars of prosperous hamlets. Places none of us have heard of line our path: Dittersbrunn, Prachting, Oberluterbach, Renthlos. Despite their obscurity, they are as full of life and beauty as anywhere on earth. The countryside is so lovely and clean, the air so crisp, the fields so perfectly mown and harvested, the houses so well-kept. One can well imagine it having been this way forever.

And then, in the most precious and prosperous of all the villages, we meet the subtle negation of all we have seen. Beside a crucifix hung with wilting flowers we see a waxed black hatchback, souped up to engineered perfection and guarded by a fist-sized silver skull dangling from the rearview mirror. Here is the sterile product of an imagination that had ceased to be exercised by life and light: speed, skulls, black. Life itself is nothing more than a carnival dance with death, not in worship but defiance. Keep the enemy near and visible.

This conceit rings hollow and adolescent among the surrounding fields and their cornucopia. I imagine the owner's mother: she has adorned the nearby crucifix with all that is natural and beautiful. She is eager to share and show the wealth of God's land and to plow underfoot all that is decay and death. She is justifiably confused that her care of life could be so mocked, that the pearl she had protected from every danger through a long childhood had chosen in the end not to love life but rather to flout death. Perhaps she had never taught this son about God? Or perhaps what she had passed on to him was all flowers and no crucifix? The cross is more revolting than that skull, for sure. It points to a gruesome execution at the hands of merciless authorities. Yet it is infinitely more nourishing than flowers and sunshine, because it speaks not of inevitability but of overcoming the inevitable—that even the supreme horror of death will not have the last word.

After a night in a musty room above a bar in Zapfendorf—what a comedown from our rooms among the friendly sisters!—the three of us strike out onto the floodplain of the Main River. We pass a seething sluice, white with the flood. Flocks of doves and geese glean among the plowed fields, reaping the excess fruit made possible by relentless engineering.

Channeling nature's energies is clearly the local passion. Even the preferred saints are farmers. A village house is stuccoed with a homespun fresco of St. Leonard brooding over his flock with staff in hand, his mantle spread like a mother hen's. An accompanying verse says:

> St. Leonard, in your loving hand
> we trust to you our fertile land.
> Spread wide your shielding pallium
> o'er beast and harvester and home.[2]

Another *Nothelfer*! St. Leonard of Noblac is normally depicted girdled with chains, as befits the patron of prisoners. But in Bavaria all things point to life: here he guards horses and other draught animals from sickness and injury. A horse's game leg, just as much as a deluge, could leave a harvest to rot. So pray to him the farmers did, to protect their ever-besieged livelihood. Leonard's feast, November 6, fell during Luther's passage through Bavaria. Would he have seen the horse-drawn, harvest-full carts in their festival parade?

This Leonard, of purported Merovingian pedigree, appears *ex nihilo* in the eleventh century. Peddled by enterprising locals who served the pilgrims heading to Compostella, his cult spread throughout a Europe littered with debtors' prisons and teeming with fickle judges. Today we tend to see it all through skeptical Protestant eyes. But we should hear the clanging of justice's hammer rather than the plinking of coins into some dubious saint's coffers.

Yet it is we who are impoverished by our parsimony. Safe behind our laws, our science, our insurance policies, we have at our disposal an arsenal fit to slay a thousand saints and their patrimony. And so we conveniently avoid the true work done by that old-time religion, which was not to hoard money for the church at all but to unite the incommensurate worlds of heaven and earth. With a Father stuck in heaven, a resurrected Son passing cool judgment from far above, and a Holy Spirit caged by the episcopacy: to whom could the people turn for the petty matters that daily worked their way between life and death? The saints! Who was God Almighty to concern himself with the small affairs of farmers? Better to keep God safe and distant. It is with good reason that people protected themselves from God's frightening power and otherness with a healthy padding of holy men and women: if it wasn't for the saint who kept watch over their crops, there was only God, who wrought the people's starvation.

Luther's Reformation may have coalesced around the eminently offensive gaffe of indulgences, but the true problem was far deeper than mere theological bookkeeping. The motor behind the people's devotion to the saints—and why they seemed so willing to pay for their affections—can be seen hovering in apses across Europe. There, floating high above the altar, an icy Christ, draped in finery and glowing with gold, directs the upright sheep into heaven and the reprobate goats into the insatiable maw of eternal punishment.

Luther's education with the Augustinians did not shy away from such disturbing possibilities. Quite the contrary. His was what we now call a mystical tradition: a disciplined drive to probe spiritual matters to their source and to contemplate the very being of God. It was an upsetting task. Against God's righteous flood, the church alone, with its righteous sacraments, could stand. The spiritual directors of Luther's Erfurt priory tried to direct their charge toward this theological softer side, to point young Luther toward God's generous means of grace—toward the certain ways by which sinners could achieve pardon, correct wrong, and enter eternal life. But this was cold comfort for Luther, who fixated—with a seldom matched obsession—on the chasm between God's glory and his own inner inadequacy. Saints, indulgences, all manner of churchly hedges melted to nothing before God's white-hot holiness. This new mystical piety had breached the fortifications of the rood screen only to be scorched by the terrifying vision of what that screen sought to hide.

The liveliness of people's devotion to the saints was due to a theological problem: the incarnation itself had been strangely forgotten. The Son sent by the Father to take on human nature had lost all solidarity with humanity; once risen and ascended, Christ now lived in eternal conflict with the elect. The saints were a democratic exception to a derailed doctrine. If Christ ruled from his judgment seat, floating off-limits in the apse of the church, then the people would get close to God through more accessible mediators.

The great triumph of Luther's Reformation was not a berserker demolition of a fetid ecclesiastical edifice. It was a rediscovery, a reorientation of *where* to look for God—and for our salvation. Much of the medieval church—like so many of our churches today!—played vicar for an absent or at least a very distant Christ. What God's people needed, Luther insisted, was not one more mediation but an encounter with the one who had already bridged that insurmountable gap—to know the triumph of God's mercy over his judgment.

To dismiss the whole Catholic tradition on this account is woefully unfair. Luther himself drew on a strain of piety that, while perhaps not dominant, was ever-present in medieval Catholicism and today finds expression in the most beloved modern saint, Thérèse of Lisieux (1873–97). Our Catholic companion Anne-Sylvie shares all of our concerns about the valence of the piety we have just witnessed; she's as put off by the pomp and grandeur as we are—perhaps even more. We spend much of that afternoon discussing Thérèse, who after strenuous spiritual efforts toward achieving holiness concluded that it is God and not our human efforts that draws us up: "I mean to try and find an elevator by which I may be raised unto God, for I am too tiny to climb the steep stairway of perfection."[3] She called this elevator her "little way," and it had nothing to do with great earthly edifices or temporal power. This "Little Flower of Jesus," as Thérèse is now affectionately called, drew instead upon the contemplative tradition of self-negation: becoming lesser that God may become greater. Her growing comprehension of her own insignificance sounds conspicuously like Luther's own dying motto: "We are beggars; this is true." It's not wholly insignificant that both Luther and Thérèse—together with diverse other sixteenth-century lights like Calvin, Erasmus, and Ignatius of Loyola—knew and drew upon that other aspect of medieval Christianity, the contemplative inner piety espoused by Thomas à Kempis: the *devotio moderna*.

This discussion of the beloved Little Flower opens us to a much less dubious regard toward the saints, one we can find throughout Luther's writings. It was not for special intercessory powers that Luther drew attention to the saints, but for their witness, their faith, their example of the Christian life. The very first hymn he wrote, "A New Song We Raise," was dedicated to the faith of his fellow Augustinians John and Henry, who were burned at the stake in Antwerp as the first martyrs of the Reformation. Luther published various martyrologies lifting up the lives of Henry Zütphen, Matthias Waibel, Caspar Tauber, Georg Buchführer, Leonard Kaiser—the last of which he even subtitled "A Saint's Life." To encourage the formal education of girls, he invoked the example of Saints Agnes, Agatha, and Lucy. He even goes as far as to place the lives of saints above all other pious reading:

> Next to the Holy Scripture, there is indeed no book more helpful for Christendom than the legends of the dear saints, especially those which are pure and authentic. For example, in them we find such sweet descriptions of how the saints believed God's Word from their hearts, confessed it with their mouths,

> praised it with their deeds, and honored and confirmed it with their suffering and death. All of these things give immeasurable comfort and strength to the weak in faith, and they make those who are already strong even more courageous and bold. If we teach the Scriptures alone without the examples and stories of the saints, though the Spirit does work abundantly within, nevertheless it is a very powerful help if we also hear or see the examples of others externally.[4]

Saints were hardly banished or forgotten in Luther's Reformation but repurposed as examples, as witnesses, as living sermons through which the Word of God had overflowed abundantly.

The growing noise and traffic close to Bamberg mute our high-minded conversation—as does the visual confusion of our age, mash-ups that make the kinship between Luther and Thérèse seem perfectly obvious. We trudge along the noisy road, lined left and right by global commerce. A garden shop peddles a clamor of religious confusion: bathing Venuses, Mayan calendars, impish gnomes, all jumbled haphazardly under a single roof. They're dishearteningly generic, but they must vent some suppressed memory of an earlier and not inferior age when the alchemy of fertility below dwelled on the same plane as the stars above. Opposite the nursery is a cabaret, shuttered in advance of the evening review. A niche above the entry houses a half-sized Mary, queen of heaven. She cradles the Christ child, who mirrors her sign of benediction. The gesture is so tiny, so subtle above the flashing neon sign. Is she still queen of that house?

Once in town we gleefully unite with our son and my parents at the Hotel Lieb. They've just arrived by train from Strasbourg. Zeke regales us with tales of kindergarten intrigue. My parents coo how good he's been for them. It's so nice to see that they're managing so well together.

The temporal and geographical confusion of outer Bamberg continues through the evening as we head downstairs for dinner. The Café Bug next door offers a "Deutsche & Thai" fusion: *Frisches aus dem Wok*, "fresh from the wok." Heavy beams and herds of trophies from the hunt press in from all sides. One particularly massive rack of elk serves as a plinth for an oriental crucifix; its horns are draped with a rustic rosary—like an atavistic Jägermeister logo. So as not to be trapped in a cliché German dream, the café also boasts a fat golden Buddha, smiling and utterly unfazed by the Bavarian ambience.

He seems perfectly content with a reincarnate gemütlichkeit. Our taste buds happily awake to Thai spices after a weeklong somnolence of sausages. And we wash down our Asian fusion with the local beer, St. George, Europe's dragon-slayer in an Asian bar.

We say farewell to Anne-Sylvie at the station in the morning, thanking her profusely for her company. Her week's break is up and she can remain a pilgrim with us no longer. We'll miss her quiet, steady company. For the first time on our trip it will be just Sarah and me afoot.

Today's our first day off from walking. After Sunday service at the local Lutheran church, my parents, Zeke, Sarah, and I step back into Bamberg's preferred past. We were prepared to be skeptical by yesterday's miracle miles and our fusion hotel, yet we gawk nonetheless. A crisply cut stone hotel, seemingly unaltered by its six hundred years, boasts in conspicuously blocky capitals: "Since 1437." Luther might have seen it! The Bambergers of today reach far back, and we can feel the high-octane pride. Here they build things to last—Roman-quality stuff. With its thirteen museums and twelve hundred protected buildings, Bamberg boasts a venerable, hand-crafted ambiance.

Bamberg is the last navigable stop on the Main River, the commercial gateway between the watershed of the Rhine and that of the Danube. As if to evoke the distant destinations of its waters, the city hall perches like a pilot house on a galleon-sized shoal in the middle of the river. Its prow cuts the foaming torrent; its wake eddies downstream. The timbers are even scrubbed down like a good ship's deck. It's as if the city wasn't built but rather grew from a felicitous confluence of roads and rivers. And in a sense it did, for trade financed it all.

Bamberg's old city hall on the River Main

What we can sense among Bamberg's streets is not mere decoration laid upon mass-produced elements but buildings and entire city blocks built to the dimensions of human bodies. Our present world is measured in panels of 8′ × 4′, sized to fit oceangoing containers 8′ × 8′ × 20′, things designed not for our delight but for the convenience of our machines. A handcrafted city such as Bamberg becomes art by its very existence and perdurance.

But its age of bourgeois splendor faded away. Stuttgart, Ulm, Nuremberg, and many others blossomed with industrial success while Bamberg was left behind, the same half-timbered vestige of a former age. This recent unimportance, though, saved the town from the Allied bombing that razed its neighbors' historic city centers. And in a postwar Germany where intact old towns are rare, Bamberg is now a jewel preserved. It retains the charm exacted from its more significant siblings.

The morning arrives with frigid rain. I swear I see snow outside our hotel window. Sleet at least. What a climate in which to say good-bye to the comforts of family! We shiver under our umbrellas as we bid farewell to them in the half-shelter of the station. Then we scurry quickly on, heads down and shoulders shrugged, shivering with the wet and cold.

After a few minutes racing through the deluge trying to stoke the internal fires, we finally huddle in a passageway and put on every last scrap of clothing. Sarah even dons a rain-skirt fashioned from a garbage sack to keep her legs dry. We ought to have gotten used to cold and rain already, but today's onslaught has a polar vigor. It's still August, for goodness' sake! I check the forecast on my phone: more of the same all day long. Then I check the map: the Jakobusweg meanders a dozen miles through an isolated forest south of town. It's a scenic detour, no doubt fit for the balmy summer's day it should be. Instead we take a shortcut straight to Forscheim along the flat path of the Main-Danube Canal.

In less than an hour the weather breaks, and a furtive sun warms us ever so slightly. Sheets of rain luff down on all sides but not on us. We are protected in a tiny pocket of calm. The hills above, where our Jakobusweg meanders, look very wet indeed. Despite the morning's forecast, we arrive at our destination dry.

Forscheim is a stop on Etzlaub's map, so we poke around the old half-timbered center briefly, looking for details that Luther might have seen. At first it looks promising: more half-timbering, more stone churches. But here, as almost everywhere else along our way, we can't find anything to speak of.

I'd hoped before we started that we'd have time to explore, to investigate potential Luther locations a bit more thoroughly. One might think that our human pace would slow down the landscape sufficiently. But not enough. Even as we crawl along at a few miles per hour, the centuries speed beneath our feet. The fleeting shadows of past souls summoned by our insistent contemplations scurry about busily, erecting the buildings, then painting and repainting the plaster a hundred times. We can't take it all in. As we walk slowly by, the past races around us like a sped-up film.

The next morning we set off cross country from Forscheim in hopes of avoiding the roaming Jakobusweg. Just outside of town we meet a stagnant slough some thirty feet wide. Our map tells us there's a bridge, but in fact it's just a bunch of used train rails set up side by side. They wobble rather comically—and disconcertingly—as we shuffle over the muddy stream one at a time.

We pass more fields of corn and see more half-timbering with romantic nostalgia inscribed in the local patois across a timbered gable: *Ober Fragn is mein sheens heimadland . . . do seem mir dahamm* ("Oberfranken is my native land . . . here I am at home"). It's a cozy place afloat a sea of agricultural richness. The sweet sentiment links the land itself with all that is good in life: a protecting shelter, abundant food, clement weather, a goodly number of children. It's as close as a Christian gets to worshiping the earth itself.

Then, finally, for the first time on our August trip, we feel a touch of heat! And for the first time, predictably, our water runs dry. The trouble with careful planning is that we've not had to rely upon anyone but ourselves so far. So as we enter the little town of Effeltrich, we start searching for a pious-looking door. Surely there's a retired lady who will fill our water bottles. We see a stuccoed house with a crucifix high in the gable. We knock twice before the door opens to reveal a puzzled octogenarian in a housedress. We introduce ourselves as pilgrims headed to Rome, and she immediately relaxes and lets us into the entryway. Out of a reflexive hospitality she offers us a whole trayful of cold drinks, but we take only the icy water. Seeing us drink and fill our bottles and noticing our packs and hiking sticks, she lets her gaze wander off toward an imaginary horizon. Coming to, she looks questioningly at our meager footgear. We ask if she's ever been to Rome, and she giggles as the elderly often do when thinking of their youth. She digs deep into her memory and tells us very briefly that once, while she was still in Catholic school, her entire class went to Rome to visit St. Peter's.

I somehow imagine we were to her as those angels were to Abraham and Sarah, announcing something almost as incredible: walking to Rome! She had learned her own catechism well enough not to laugh outright. For why should God—who could bring forth such abundance from the fields around, and who could, at the end of all things, bring the entire universe through the final barrier of death itself into a new creation—not empower a couple to cross the infinitesimally small distance between here and Rome?

Our journey seemed to animate a hidden, flickering excitement in her mind, a vague hope that this isolated valley in which she had confined her existence would soon through us spill over—that the great distance to the tombs of the apostles, to the age of Christ himself, could by our vicarious action be brought to nothing. With our drinks finished and our bottles filled, we make to leave when she stops us in the threshold and asks us to pray for her when we get to Rome. We agree with open hearts.

In Effeltrich we find more gardens, more half-timbering. Then out of town, we pass still more fields of corn. Soon we rest and take refreshment at the foot of yet another crucifix. This time it is a memorial addressed directly to us wayfarers: "*Wanderer!* Remember our dear child Michael, son of tradesman Konrad Schmittlein von Effeltrich, who on February 24, 1891, at the age of three years, died here in an accident. 'In the evening it is different from in the early morning.'"

Seeing and contemplating that crucifix, we feel part of that liminal world of saints. And as we continue on our way, we notice a new lightness on our feet that comes from a palpable sensation that our ridiculous desire to walk through history has found us wading through seas of souls—as if we ourselves have somehow joined their company and now pull behind us a long train of the departed toward that distant and unreachable horizon. At this cross we grab Michael's soul too, add it to our luggage, and pull it along with us. The skies now clear completely. As the late summer sun settles slowly in the west, the whole country glows in its benevolent, golden embrace.

For the first time in a week, the morning is hazy with the kind of damp that promises later sunshine. The path out of Kalkreuth (where we slept in rooms above the butcher) is a fairy tale of Old World charm. Branches heavy with pears and apples sag over our walled path, almost but never quite blocking our way. As we brush by they sprinkle us with their friendly dew.

At the outer limit of Nuremberg we walk into a forest. Its groves—or rather bogs, as there is so much standing water—are full of pine trees that reach high above, straight and tall. We scurry along before clouds of aggressive mosquitos. At the darkest, quietest corner of this hundred-acre wood, we spy a wooden arch painted red, some dry rock fountains, pagodaed pillars, a handful of well-cropped bonsais, a bridge to nowhere. It declares itself a *Japanischer Zen-Garten*. Just beyond, and rather suddenly, we walk into a vast field, blooming all around with acre after acre of goldenrod. It's the airport! A few planes come and go, their screaming turbines jetting busy people here and there. We blink, and they are gone.

Luther saw this very clock in Nuremberg just a year (or two) after its installation in 1509.

We greet the city from the castle up above; its banners are up and fluttering cheerfully in the breeze. We descend the bulwarks into the town and into the far past. At last we reach a place that Luther actually mentions in the sparse record of his pilgrimage. He notes briefly in his *Table Talk* that he saw the wondrous mechanical clock above Nuremberg's market square.[5] It dates from 1509, just a year or maybe two before his arrival, and would have been the town's touristic centerpiece. We await the hour to see the clock's king salute, to witness his mechanical heralds lift their golden trumpets in welcome, then valediction. It's a rare case of seeing something that Luther actually notes and unequivocally saw—something much less frequent than we imagined at the outset.

Luther certainly would have found fellowship in Nuremberg. The Augustinians here, along with those in Erfurt, were partisans in the same small network of strictly observant priories. Apparently it was here among his brethren that Luther gained his travel companion for the months to come. Some suggest that this person was Anton Kreuz, an Augustinian brother experienced in the ways of the Roman Curia;[6] others Johan Mecheln.[7] This colleague would have served Luther as both guide and living letter of recommendation among the well-rubbed shoulders of Rome. In any case, friars—for justifiable reasons of moral accountability—were not permitted to travel alone.

Despite what is for us a significant tidbit of historical evidence, Nuremberg's past is otherwise hard to detect, little more than a clink from that old clock. The imperial city of Luther's day is nearly gone. As a center of Teutonic mythology, it was conscripted as the rallying point for Nazism, and for this reason American and British bombs flattened 90 percent of the old city—a gratuitous bombing at the tail end of the war designed to break an already broken German morale. As a cry against this ensemble of shame, a grand colonnade has been erected in one part of the rebuilt city with one pillar for each article of the United Nation's Universal Declaration of Human Rights—monumental amends for a sordid past.

We're almost desperate to take it all in, for everything seems so important. We should see the Dürer house, at least. I take picture after picture and grab tourist pamphlets like a rat for his bedding, but I'm quickly exhausted by the strain of it. I'm tired by famous saints, tired from unseasonal cold, tired from the rain, tired from mosquitoes. We are not tourists. We are not tourists! We are *not* tourists! In our frenzy to gulp down the past, we choked. We are pilgrims, whose walking pace is still too fast to take in a historic city. We sit for a while on a bench, watching mutely as thousands of lives mosey down the carless cobblestones.

We are treated to dinner by Larry and Nordis, Americans who just happen to be visiting their son nearby. They've been leaders in the Lutheran charismatic movement. Since this is one of Sarah's ecumenical specialties, we are curious to meet and talk. We get a full testimony, as one might expect, but also tales of slander, embargo, and knee-jerk pigeonholing by churchly bureaucrats who see such things only through the sixteenth-century vocabulary of *Schwärmerei*—a term of derision used by Luther for those who "swallowed the Holy Spirit, feathers and all." Peacekeeping and conversation are needed not only with historical adversaries but with all the shifting faces of an unfolding global Christianity.

After this happy hour of fellowship, we stroll together for a while about the well-lit city. Sarah and I then find our hotel and sleep, fully in the present.

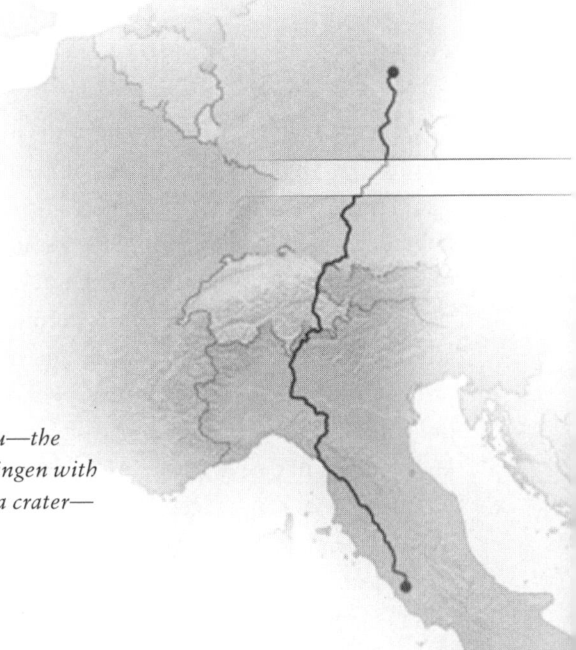

Three

Earthly vocations—Neuendettelsau—the limits of the Roman Empire—Oettingen with beer, Bach, and Brotzeit—crossing a crater—Nördlingen—Neresheim Abbey

A murky fog blankets all of Nuremberg when we awake. We shiver out of town wrapped in its chilly embrace. The brume turns our vistas into ghosts and mere suggestions. A great onion dome hovers spectral above us. Is it a steeple? Some futuristic temple? No. It is an antenna, a bulbous tower of Babel built not to breach the heavens above but to penetrate each head on earth below with radio waves. It's somehow fitting that a Protestant town would be dominated by something so visually inescapable but whose looming amplitude only hints at its even greater purpose: to broadcast sound.

Below the tower's pulsing emissions buses putt and trucks grind; the mechanical city sputters to life. We wade against the waves of traffic breaking into town. Beside the babbling flow of commerce a bulky silo of an apartment building juts into the sky—all square, all gray, unfinished concrete stained by streaks of damp. People do their best to humanize the haggard world of cement and asphalt: inside each window hangs a delicate veil of decorative lace and sits the obligatory vase of fake flowers, as if a breath of tatting and a soupçon of faded silk could transport the mind to country fields and meadows full of cheerful flowers.

The first bright colors of the morning are—fittingly—artificial. They stream in technicolor brilliance from a dull brick factory lined along the Rednitz River: the Faber-Castel company. Rainbow ranks of colored pencils gleam through the haze, billboard signs of glowing greens and lemon yellows outshining the dimmer trees and duller flowers of the garden with their mineral blaze. The real world fades before the shimmering luminosity of imagined possibilities.

Once we reach the countryside, all the leaking piety, the crosses, shrines, and frescos, the festive garnishes of Catholic Bavaria are gone. This is Protestant territory, dotted by hygienic barns, crossed by high-tension wires, its interstices filled in with geometrical stands of pine, acre after unending acre of quadrilateral abundance—but not a single Jesus, Mary, or Joseph is in sight. Even the houses seem bare, painted recently and brightly, but without adornment. The aesthetic is utilitarian: roofs bedecked with solar panels, walls bristling with wires and sprouting satellite dishes. Here the wealth of field and imagination is not placed on extravagant display, nor found in decoration, but manifest in elegant utility.

Faith has its many faces, only some of which are outwardly apparent. This was the insight of Max Weber, whose *The Protestant Ethic and the Spirit of Capitalism* has cast a long shadow over the interpretation of the Reformation and its social consequences. Weber's work interprets the diverging economic fortunes of Europe's prospering North and struggling South as extensions of their religion, roughly speaking. Protestants from Luther onward abolished the significance of "religious" work and created in its place a notion of holy secularization. Your daily life, your "vocation" or *Beruf*, as Luther called it, was not aggrandized in the eyes of God by additional obligations of prayer and fasting, penance or pilgrimage. Rather, your vocation *in itself*, well done and carried out, was the locus of your Christian life.

Luther spared no rebuke for those who shunned lowly callings in the world in favor of avowedly higher spiritual vocations. His 1520 treatise *The Babylonian Captivity of the Church* warns that "the works of monks and priests, be they ever so holy and arduous, differ not a whit in the sight of God from the works of the farmer toiling in the field or the woman going about her household tasks, but all works are measured before Him by faith alone. . . . [Indeed] the menial housework of a maidservant or manservant is often more acceptable to God than all the fasting and other works of a monk or a priest, because the latter lacks faith!"[1] Work for Luther and later Protestants was hallowed not by a pilgrim's stamp or priest's surplice, bishop's mitre or monk's tonsure, but by Christ's presence in faith, which showed itself most powerfully not in outward pieties but in service to neighbors in need.

Over decades, then centuries, the resulting shift in resource allocation slowly but inexorably diverted vast sums of very real money that might otherwise have gone up in candle smoke, indulgences, extravagant funerary legacies, military campaigns, and architectural improvements. The accumulated wealth of the people instead found itself in banks or city coffers, stored in farmers' barns, invested in capital improvements. Once a burden and a punishment, work itself took on a sacral hue. In this vocational approach to life, your God-given lot was to labor hard and long. What was formerly just a job had become a holy calling, a fulfillment of religious duty. Weber's theory may have a thousand holes and just as many exceptions. But as we traverse this Protestant countryside, the change from other, Catholic parts of Bavaria is plainly visible—or rather absent, absorbed into the land itself.

Elsewhere certain Protestants vandalized Catholic churches, defaced their statuary, smashed up sacred implements and furniture. But all that furor was never truly necessary to rub out medieval religious practice. We see around us a different form of cultural erasure: the slow iconoclasm of neglect. Time and the unpremeditated prescription of forgetfulness were every bit as effective. For in making *now* the time of salvation, the Protestants prescribed under their *semper reformanda* regime a powerful visual and ritual amnesia.

Here the swarms of individual saints, so lovingly on display for us the week before, have lost all individuality, their particular substance evaporated one by sublimated one, only to condense into a great and indiscriminate cloud of witnesses above. This collective holiness rained down upon the land, whose soil itself somehow soaked up a sanctity it never had under the previous order of things, so that a farmer's hands tilled his newly sanctified vocation straight into the dirt. The builder's hammer and plane, too, glowed ethereal, for what he worked and ate was harvested from that sanctified dirt. God's elected people bore in their molecular being the structure of salvation itself—holiness from on high to bless all work, all growth, all the diking and channeling of nature's energies to build, upbuild, and reproduce.

Is this the heritage of Protestantism? A renewed and ancient paganism? What a strange outcome for a movement bent on sanctifying the vocation of all life through Christ alone, to drive all traces of that sanctity underground. It's a peculiar thing for the heritage of Luther to be most present in silence, in absence.

Overt religion hereabouts shows itself rather in hard work. The only church we note today in Regelsbach is Saint George's, a cubic fortress of a building. There is little sign of God to see. Only several clocks and a sundial mark it as something celestial. But above it we see something more fitting: the roof undergoing renovations. A yellow crane beside it hoists great pallets of red tiles to waiting workers. One roofer tosses them deftly to another, who chinks them three by three between the battens. A well-maintained and protected building—not the superiorly decorated—is the mark of Frankish Protestant piety.

By noon the ripples of urban commerce and industry have dissipated—fine for the eyes but a trial for our mouths and stomachs, which are eager for some lunch. In one small town the lone shop is closed, but the bank is open, strangely. Inside we ask a dapper, dazed young man to fill our water bottles, but he can offer us no food, he states apologetically. On our way out of the village, however, stands an open and unguarded cupboard on the roadside. Its shelves are stacked with eggs and piles of potatoes out for sale. *Selbstbedienung*! Self-service! How wonderful, after such a down-to-business morning, to meet a dim glimmer of something wholesome and human in this trusting exchange of goods.

We drop a few coins in for our provisions, walk a ways into the fields, and plop down on a recently mown patch. Embraced by the sweet fragrance of the hay, bathed in the soft autumn rays, we light our little stove and fry up some hash browns and scrambled eggs. Rather than eating beneath the blessing of a crucifix, we let the grass, the scent, the warmth of the sun itself pour upon us benediction.

That evening we arrive in Neuendettelsau, a tiny town known for its onetime preacher Wilhelm Löhe and the missionaries and deaconesses he sent around the world. Our beds are in the *Lutherrose*, the Mission society's headquarters. But it's getting late and after our field lunch we again are out of food. The town is small and its shops aren't open late, something that still astonishes us Americans. At six o'clock we start to jog, making quick work of the last six kilometers despite the painful pavement. But our last-ditch efforts are in vain. The shutters all along the main street are rolling down as we walk in. With aching feet, we follow the hints of traffic heading out of town, hoping to find an open eatery.

Eureka! A Greek restaurant huddles in the evening chill under its flashing red sign. Germany may be closed, but on its outskirts ethnic enclaves keep more indulgent hours. We are the lone diners. A sympathetic server leads us to a cozy corner and plunks down some complimentary ouzo. We quickly warm up, and soon we're scarfing savory lamb and grilled eggplant, washed down with tumblerfuls of wine. The seaside scenes painted on the walls transport us to the beach: we sit on virtual verandas caressed by affable Aegean zephyrs. But it's Boreas who meets us as we leave. In the chilly twilight, we scurry like autumn leaves toward the *Lutherrose*.

The next morning we're up early and ready to go, only to be delayed by the discovery of free WiFi, still a rare thing in 2010. We frantically work online for almost three hours, catching up with photos, blogs, and numerous other bits of business. Two weeks into our trip the initial excitement has worn off, and we realize that we're exhausted. Sarah answers emails while I procrastinate with Facebook, watching lives of friends and families go on as before, as if nothing in the world has changed. And it hasn't.

It's already afternoon before we even begin to walk the sixteen miles to Gunzenhausen. The steely autumnal edge of last evening has dulled. Fluffy clouds and fresh breezes push us quickly on and over the undulating countryside. Gigantic leathery leaves of ripe tobacco flap gently in the wind, white flowers tipped with glowing coral hue. Sweet perfume rises from cut hay, raked into windrows, drying in the mild sun—auguries from absent farmers that the clement weather should hold for a few days at least. The harvest hangs heavy on the orchard trees, though now, with so many people moved to town, what used to be the guarded fruit lot is largely abandoned. Rows of weedy, unpruned apple and plum trees drop their wormy produce uncollected to the ground; it rots and reeks with sour smells of fermentation.

In a forest we come across a meticulously stacked pile of wood, the first of many we will see. A nailed-on panel urges us to give thanks, not for the wonder of the trees but for their biospheric generosity: "The forest gives oxygen necessary for life. It stores up damaging carbon dioxide. It takes the edge off the winter and tempers the summer." For all of which—at this wooden altar, raised to a panentheistic god—we should "Nourish and cherish it; it's worth your while!"

Beneath the fertility and austerity of the Protestant landscape lurks a piety that did not so much eject holiness as spread it out toward ubiquity. Now there's not a field or forest or woodpile that isn't enchanted with the aura of God's providence. The workaday arcs of scythe and axe are transformed by Protestant transubstantiation into priestly gestures. Human work—all of it, everything dedicated to serve the neighbor—has gained not the mere patina of alms or indulgences but the corporeal substance of divinity itself. The enchantment of the woodpile, the priests of the cordwood altar, the order, the pattern, the beauty of the inner workings of things: Is this not the extension of a movement inward that, far from rationalizing the world, filled its furthest recesses with the mystery of God's presence?

After hours of quick walking and heavy thinking, we make it to our camp just outside Gunzenhausen. I finally have a chance to flaunt my outdoor acumen, pitch my high-tech tarp, test my home-made quilt, and manage our survival with a pocketful of gear. We've carried all this on our backs since Erfurt, just in case. It's been a disappointment for me, a trained and skilled outdoorsman, not to have used my kit. I had imagined at the outset a more adventurous wilderness walk: we would wander until twilight, pitch our camp in a sheltered hollow, wake with the sun, and press on. But we're more beholden than I'd thought to our electronic paraphernalia. Each night we must update our blog, process pictures, charge up all our devices. It's also basically illegal here in Germany to camp on public land.

To fixate on this lack, however, is to ignore the fact that thus far much of Europe seems far superior to America for walking, where one must drive for hours or days to find extensive scenic trails. Germany is by no means a wilderness, but neither is it cordoned off by endless runs of barbed wire and off-limits areas bristling with "no trespassing" signs. The whole country is open to the wanderer. For days we walk unannounced and unmolested across farmers' fields and private forests.

In our campground all my meticulous preparations—the tarp, the quilt, the sleeping pads, the tiny flashlight—work as planned. Everything, that is, except the ambiance, which is decidedly unnatural. Beyond the thin shrubs that surround our tiny plot a gaggle of French scouts keeps bursting into laughter. Finally we fall asleep, lulled by the droning of a dozen Dutch generators. This turned out to be the only time we camped out on the entire pilgrimage.

As we depart in the morning, we meet our first bona fide remains of the Roman Empire. Right next to "Martin Luther Platz," a sign announces the location of a second-century watchtower. Upon its place local amateur enthusiasts have built from lengths of timber a mock section of border wall to hold back imagined surges of the barbarian tide. It's Emperor Hadrian's *limes*, the furthest limit of Rome's official territory. We climb a hill above Gnotzheim, the Spielberg, and gaze north upon the *limes* spread out below. A panoramic panel marks the buried posts and encampments, a whole horizon bristling with imperial vigilance.

It's not just that. Bits and pieces from several warring epochs are piled upon each other—fortress walls dating back three thousand years, when Venefelder and Hallstatt warriors were raiding everybody and protecting their hard-won booty. Scrolling through my archaeological memory, I make the connection: defenses. Nothing is left but defenses. What stands long against the fire and sword of humans will likewise withstand the assaults of nature. The same goes for our religious confessions: it is the defenses and their evocation of imminent assault that stand best the assault of time. This bears further reflection, as in our faith we tend to fixate on the fortress borders while ignoring the treasure within.

This particular *limes* is also the limit of an event recorded still further back in history—so far back that it dwarfs all human time. Some fifteen million years ago a mile-wide meteor struck nearby and sent its seismic ripples to a radius of eight miles, leaving standing waves of earth around its crater rim—of which this is the outermost one. We spend the rest of the day walking gently up and down the frozen shockwaves toward the round and pancake-flat Nördlinger Ries.

The harvest hangs dusty in the air. Horizons of hay lie tumbledown in the sun, the air infused with its grassy sweetness. The still green corn scrapes and cracks as it dries more and more with the passing days. The touch-me-nots explode as we brush by. The bees suckle from pink foxglove blooms. A farmer sprays his field with foul pig silage. And slugs, the sign that the great decay of fall has begun, creep after each other, everywhere streaming a wake of slime so that our paths are crisscrossed with the shimmering tracery of mollusk love.

Our first human encounter of the day is with Gerhard, who hails us with a silent wave while we are walking through his hamlet of Höhentrüdigen. Medium height, medium build, sunburnt face flecked with grass from the haying, he's in his thirties, or maybe forties. With a warm but stoic gesture he offers us glasses of ice-cold lemonade, fetched quickly from somewhere within. He probes in roundabout farmer fashion where we came from and where we're going. When we tell him Erfurt and Rome respectively, he's neither shocked nor incredulous. Instead he simply stares toward the south, flying in his mind though the forests of Franconia, across the Rieskrater, piercing the Alps and Apennines and hills of Tuscany to arrive—feet tired and soul at rest—before the tombs of the apostles. I've rarely seen such a silent longing before. Or perhaps I'm mistaken and it's just polite bafflement.

After this pregnant pause, Gerhard tells us of Höhentrüdigen's peculiar Protestant church. An eighteenth-century surge in local population outstripped the capacity of the old nave. More space was clearly needed, but so beloved was their old building that the townspeople were loath to tear it down—a habit quite common in that era of Baroque "improvements." So rather than begin anew, they simply embraced the old edifice inside a larger copy, creating a church within a church—an ecclesiastical matryoshka doll.

This tale is ripe with peasant wisdom—full of a faith expressed not in stylish architectural decoration nor Renaissance dreams of equilibrium but in the manner of a farmer and his expanding barn. Once, poking around a dusty hayloft on an Alsatian farmstead, I came across a complete horse-drawn carriage, wheels and all, hung on the wall. I asked the farmer why, and he was adamant that it was not for nostalgia or display but "just in case." Do we raze and start anew? Or do we conserve and keep things well past their time? Here above Höhentrüdigen the peasants have given us both: adaptation and conservation under the same (well-maintained) roof.

Leaving Gerhard and his village behind, we meet another interrogator in a wood, a spry sixty-something who is splitting logs with an axe. When we admire his colossal stacks of firewood, he looks reproachfully at our shoes and prophesies: "It's going to be a long cold winter." Our minds turn from the warming sun above toward the still distant Alps. We hope the snow will wait until our late September crossing.

Oettingen is a town that all Germans seem to know of, though less for gemütlichkeit than for the cheapest beer around. For decades its brewery's cutthroat practices have flooded Germany with economical drink. We glimpse the town as we descend from the Rieskrater's rim at dusk. Liquid sunshine floods down upon it in golden streams; we flow down into its yeasty embrace.

In town we happily reunite with my parents and our son, who have again come for the weekend from Strasbourg. It's Zeke's fifth birthday, and we celebrate with a calorific Italian dinner and cake followed by a romp in a park. Zeke is captivated and ecstatic with his first chomps of chewing gum. We lounge about in each other's company over books and games, spread out in our hotel.

Pilgrims next to a statue of St. James at the Lutheran church in Oettingen-in-Bayern

It's an unfortunate fact that our lodgings cannot complement our domestic feelings. The Hotel Rose is suffused with an inexpugnable odor of cigarettes; even the blankets are greasy with the cumulative residue of smoke. When we wake up in the morning, we're not very disappointed to realize that we forgot to make a second night's reservation for ourselves. After numerous phone calls, though, we discover that there is not a single vacant room in all of Oettingen. A famous violinist is in town, and her concert is tonight.

So all of us head out to church on this Sunday morning determined not to leave without an offer of hospitality. Our hopes rise as we spy standing before the Lutheran church of St. James a full-sized statue of a pilgrim, complete with jaunty hat, walking staff, and drinking gourd—all cast in bronze in honor of its patron. We've come upon a church for pilgrims! The jangling bells above call us in to worship.

We settle in our dark wood pew. A Bach prelude comes floating down from the towering organ in back. Like many older churches here, the somber Gothic has been frosted with triumphant Baroque. The plaster ceiling writhes with scrolls and acanthus, while the central frame depicts the risen Christ, standard in hand, pennant fluttering, rising muscular and triumphant from the vanquished tomb. A wispy-haired pastor, robed in his black academic gown with twinned preaching tabs shining white beneath his collar, mounts the high, gaudy pulpit to proclaim. To better project and reiterate his frail words, he's backed by a large shield declaring the Reformation's motto VDMA, the Latin acronym of a verse from Isaiah 40: "The Word of the Lord remains forever." It serves as an appropriate backdrop for a sermon on John 1. The hymn of the day squishes from the organ, proving that schlock is primarily a confusion of content and medium, for there's only so much a great Baroque instrument—conceived to trumpet the might of God's majestic trinitarian interrelations—can do to ignite the heart with muddled strains of "It only takes a spark . . ." This unfortunate error in musical judgment is soon compensated, though without great gusto on the part of the aged assembly, with the Reformation classic *Nun Danket Alle Gott*, "Now Thank We All Our God."

During the service we are left conspicuously alone by the congregants, who seem not to know quite what to do with strangers. But after worship we insinuate ourselves upon the pastor and ask if he could help our search for lodgings. He's rather stunned at first, then apologetic that he can't help more, as he's only filling in while the local pastor is on vacation. But as we elaborate for him our quest to follow Luther's steps, he warms up quickly and trundles off to find the church's warden.

The pastor comes back with Hans, a sprightly dark-haired septuagenarian with sparkling, slightly gibbous eyes. He's head of the church council and claims to know a lady with a room to let. Leaving parents and child to pack up in the hotel, we follow him hurriedly up the street a ways and find said lady's house. The prospects don't look good when we arrive: a chatty foursome sips tea possessively on the porch. Her rooms are already taken, predictably, by violin concert-goers.

No trouble, we tell Hans. We have our tarp and a sleeping bag. A postage stamp of grass is all we pilgrims need. He waves off all our suggestions while ushering us to his own home and installs us in the sunny garden, leaving six choices of cool beverage on a table while he goes to consult with his wife. Some short minutes later he returns with his wife Regine, who is thin and quiet and some years his junior. "I've talked with my wife," he announces momentously, "and though we are not a hotel, and probably cannot offer you what you'd expect, we have a spare room, and you're welcome to it."

Were we ever! Soon we're up the tasteful wooden stairs in a light and airy room. Hazy memories of the Hotel Rose fade quickly. Herr and Frau have business to attend to at the soccer pitch: Oettingen's soccer club has a match, apparently. So they give us a key and the run of the place. We head back to our family for more fifth-birthday festivities, then say our sad farewells as they drive off. Returning to Hans and Regine's home, we fall into a deep sleep in the warm and sunny guest room.

We are groggy when our hosts return and call us down for *Brotzeit*. A foaming pint of local beer is set before each of us, along with mustard, cheese, and a selection of *Würste*. In the middle of the rich wood table sits a basket spilling over with many shades and weights of bread. Our hosts request that

Sarah say the blessing—because she's the theologian. Then we munch and smack and sip our way through this "light" Bavarian supper.

Over mouthfuls of bread and meat, we set out tomorrow's morning schedule with diligent precision. "Since you must leave so early, can I wake you with some Bach?" inquires Hans, beaming with contentment as we enthusiastically consent. Tomorrow's lunch is contemplated and planned for. We work out our itinerary to Nördlingen. Though there's a cycle path that's shorter, we agree the church at Maihingen deserves the detour. Regine works at a bookshop, so she'll give us a good map in the morning. The pair expresses concern for our poor family, driving back and forth on the Autobahn from Strasbourg to meet us. In Ulm, we assure them, they'll come by train. "That's so much better," Regine sighs in relief.

Then we turn to weightier matters. Hans tells us of his frightful wartime youth. In 1941, when he was only four and his brother seven, his Austrian father died on the Russian front. With their mother completely alone, he recounts, "We had to wander through the country, begging door to door for bread and eggs. They gave us nothing." Like so many other towns around, he notes, Oettingen was bombed at the end of World War II. Reflecting simply but with gravity, he mentions US troops in Afghanistan and says as he shakes his head, "War, it is a plague . . . but not from God—from humankind!"

Our meal dispatched, we retire to a salon lined with books, where sit a harpsichord and a grand piano. Hans was church organist for many years at St. James. He used to have an organ, too, a small one built by his long dead Salzburger father, but he's since given it to the church. The other instruments will go as well: "We're giving all we have away."

Hans sits and plays a few bright bars on his harpsichord, then turns to the piano and gives us a kind of layman's catechism on what he deems the greatest works of Bach, starting with the "Toccata in E Minor."[2] The theme begins afar, slowly, hesitantly, like a butterfly in a breeze that's just barely too strong. The music mounts unhurriedly both in confidence and harmony, each phrase threatening dissolution, then promising deliverance. At last the left hand, then the right resolve their dueling dissonance with an ultimate and spine-tingling reconciliation.

It's a dance that's not without its trials. "If I want to play a toccata in good form," Hans assures us, gravely, "I need half a year to prepare it."

"So difficult!" we say, astonished, for it sounded simple and straightforward.

"Yes, yes! But it's pleasant work. Listen." Then he flips some pages and demonstrates another. "You see here's the theme. . . . Very simple, nice. You can sing to it! But now comes the real genius of Bach. Listen closely." The theme repeats and reproduces, propagating contagiously, echoing now higher in the right and now lower with the left, with myriad tiny variations.

"That's as far as I've gotten!" he apologizes after a few bars, bursting with amazement at the uncanny, eerie artistry of Bach. "Everything fits within the whole, so when one listens carefully one has to ask what finally will come from all of this. . . . Then the fourth voice enters with the same theme still! It's hard to even imagine how music can be so beautiful. . . . Sometimes it's said that in such music one can feel God's presence. I think so."

It's but a tiny step from these fugal confrontations to the deeper narratives of life. "What's been given to us all on earth—nature, or the opportunity to walk to Rome—we ought not to take for granted. I see everything as a gift from God! These gifts are tasks for us as well—to share them with all humanity. Perhaps some people don't know God; perhaps they'll be inspired by such gifts, such beauty, to say: 'We have a great and good God, who's given us much. We can make something of his gifts.'" And turning to us with a brightening face, he exclaims, "You've made something of your lives!"

The fonts of faith unleashed, a flood of reminiscence arrives in their wake. "Three years ago," reports Hans, "I became so sick with an infection they were ready to amputate my leg. They gave me such a powerful antibiotic that it was judged that I would either recover or it would kill me. I came through—but with a coronary. I'm no theologian, but I've thought about theological time. One never knows in the morning when one leaves the bed what the day will hold, whether anything can happen, which joyful or painful things may occur."

It turns out our organist is a preacher, too. He takes up his lay priesthood with great skill and comprehension. "The dear Lord God has given me a bit more time. I must therefore make something proper of it—not to let his help go by the wayside. I'm thankful for each day I'm still on earth. I've been much preoccupied with death, which might meet us any morning, tomorrow morning, even today!"

His life bookended by near misses with mortality, Hans bears a solemn, joyful mien, not of the carpe diem kind so praised by youth—for this reckless pabulum assumes control it cannot have—but peaceful wisdom grown from close acquaintance with caprice and a resulting trust in God's great overarching providence. It's not a morbid vision, as many think, but a pilgrim's mind-set, full knowledge that today's trials are tempered by the presence of that life to which one soon may be called. And it's a presence that did not make him a tourist, a passerby, but one on his way to love, serve, lay down, and indeed enjoy life with these companions who may at any time become fellows for eternity.

"My wife and I already have our grave plots, our gravestones, too," he assures us as if it was the most natural progression of topics. "And on the gravestones our names—mine and my wife's—are already inscribed! We're well prepared there for the other side, for death; and as for this side, for life," he gestures to the kitchen, "the brewery still lets us savor it rather well! And so we live—"

"Between death and life!" Sarah interjects, quoting Luther. Hans nods. He seems to have imbibed all of Luther's funereal wisdom. In a 1519 sermon on preparing to die, Luther admonished Christians to "familiarize ourselves with death during our lifetime, inviting death into our presence when it is still at a distance and not on the move."[3] Hans's brush with death pushed him not into terror or paralysis but, in a paradoxical way, toward life.

"You've listened well," he rejoices as he beams at us and claps his hands, bringing what might have been a melancholy lesson to a joyful close.

Retiring to our clean, fresh-smelling rooms upstairs, we marvel at our host. He embodies a sober Lutheran zest for life, a jolly apocalypticism born of stalwart, simple faith. He embodies as well that Lutheran preference for the ear. For there's something oddly ephemeral and slippery about this faith, captured by the transient nature of sound that, once created, resonates a while, then disappears, only to be reborn in the resurrection.

The next morning at six o'clock we awake startled, as forewarned, to shuddering fugal strains of Bach, blaring from the hi-fi down below. Now that's a Lutheran way to rise—as if to choirs of heavenly host! Again at table we eat more bread, ham, and cheese and pack more of the same for lunch. On the way out of town we stop at Regine's bookshop; she presents us with the promised map of the Nördlinger Ries and sends us off with a tender smile.

There's one more lesson—this one ecumenical—that Oettingen has to teach us. It's as obvious as the meteor impact once you notice it. At the Peace of Augsburg, each princedom was required to decide whether it would be Catholic or Protestant. But here in Oettingen the difference is starker than almost anywhere, for the town itself was split in two. This shows clearly in its architecture: one side is half-timbered and Protestant, while the other is plastered in the giant scrolls of the Catholic Baroque. Even the Jews had their sides, for the ghetto lay atop the dividing line that created not just one but two conflicting Jewish camps, who even called each other Protestant Jews or Catholic Jews, depending on which side of town they lived in.

The rift reached still more subtle depths—beyond the theological. The bisection of the town rent the very weft of time itself, a feat unachieved even by meteors. Oettingen's Protestants resisted the corrections to the calendar promulgated by Pope Gregory in 1582. For decades, even centuries, crossing a street meant jumping from Sunday to the following Tuesday, from feast to fast, from the new year back into Advent.

A few minutes' walk and we're already out of town, striding down an arrow-straight Roman road under a pearly sun. We move quickly through the abbey-town of Maihingen, stopping only to gawk at yet another foamy Baroque basilica, kid brother to Vierzehnheiligen. All afternoon we fight against a stiff and desiccating wind, blowing undisturbed across the level fields of grain and sugar beets that quilt the crater's bottom. Rumbling tractors tumble the beets onto mountainous piles, sweetness ready for pressing and processing. Exhausted by the wind and sun, we come to Nördlingen, a proud Protestant island of a town. The intact circular city wall glitters with a million minuscule diamonds, their facets scintillating in the sun, geological relics of the meteor's prehistoric impact.

We're still atop Etzlaub's dotted line. Luther must have stopped or slept here somewhere, in some mendicant hollow beneath a meager pile of rough blankets. There are no direct signs of Luther in the city, but his theology has left a long and stony shadow in the *Georgskirche*, whose monuments evince the Protestant metamorphosis of holiness that we've witnessed up to now. In

The flat farmland of the Rieskrater

lieu of images of saints culled from Christianity's golden age, the church's nave is watched over by a set of shield-like epitaphs—homages to local *Burgermeister* and nobility, heavy with crisscrossed weaponry and facing the world through horned battle helms.

The overt martial, muscular spirit is at first off-putting. But even if it's a nod to the bourgeoisie, it's also a vernacular sprout from the Reformers' teaching on vocation: that service is one's calling and that just and beloved leaders (for these are certainly not revolutionaries) can become, through their patronage, through civic piety, through their support of the church and its ministry, living testimonies to God's preservation of the world. In a way these ponderous epitaphs are relics of the holy founders and sustainers not just of the church but of society itself. The *Georgkirche*'s monuments are not as mysterious nor as transcendent in their greatness as what they replaced. But they consummately show that Protestant shift toward the quotidian as the locus for human holiness.

Still more symbols accentuate what we have witnessed in the lands since Nuremberg. Between the donors' mortuary monuments hang shields of their respective guilds as well. Here saintliness originates not in the purity or supernatural merit of any individual but flows directly from being set apart to do God's work today in various ways. The townspeople certainly did not possess any superabundance of grace. They were sinners just like all the rest of us. But in the crucible of life the dross of sin was minimized, made good by faithful work, and craftsmen—even nameless members of the guild—thus were sanctified and memorialized among the greater saints.

The close marriage of the holy with the elected magistrates contained a danger. It required the constant watchfulness and vigorous independence of the preaching clergy, who were expected to denounce the injustice they witnessed daily—a job that pastors did not always do with stalwart courage. But this was deemed a necessary risk, for Luther saw strong public power as the only antidote to anarchy. Even before the Reformation conflicts erupted into violence, Luther foresaw that without order "men would devour one another. . . . No one could support wife and child, feed himself nor serve God."[4] With such a looming threat the excesses of a few power-hungry burghers were worth the danger.

A familiar light drizzle follows us out of Nördlingen. Just south of town we start the gentle climb out of the crater onto its rippling southern hills.

Although we have Regine's map—the first paper directions we've used since our inauspicious scribblings at Arnstadt—we nevertheless quickly lose our way among the zigzagging forest roads.

As we head generally south, the forest grows ever darker, the hillsides steeper, the ravines deeper and duskier still. We are Hansel and Gretel plying through Grimm's woods, which lurk with unseen life, whose savage sounds are muted by the mossy, leafy litter. And then begins a steady, soaking rain. When our meandering road finally comes to a dead end, we head cross-country, bushwhacking down a shoulder of jutting rock.

At the bottom of our slippery descent, we find two comforting things: a nicely graveled road and a tiny shelter made to order—straight from the Grimm catalogue, apparently. Rounds of wood are stacked toward a steep tiled roof dripping with moss. We light our stove and cook up lunch on the small porch, our mushroom stew adding to the fungal perfume of this fairy-tale forest.

We stop for the night at Neresheim Abbey, where Luther might (or might not) have stayed. It was founded in 1095 by his kindred Augustinian Canons. But soon thereafter some Benedictines acquired the abbey and applied their version of what we might call comprehensive rural development. For a millennium and more it was the monks who colonized Europe's west: clearing forests and planting crops, introducing agricultural techniques as well as bringing God to the uncharted heathen backwaters of Europe. Long hours of *ora* fueled even longer hours of *labora*. The wealth that flowed from the annual gift of the harvest filled overflowing coffers and added to their estates. By Luther's time, monasteries controlled much of Europe's richest land. The material benefits of faith had precedent long before Protestantism.

We marvel at the cloister garden: bursting with lettuces and brassicas, cascading with rainbow rows of fall flowers, whole patches of it spotted with orange pumpkins. There must be monkish wiles at work here, I reason, keeping up this cornucopia. But my eyes deceive me. There is but a handful of the religious left, their numbers insufficient for the work. The complex is now maintained by a foundation and funded by guests and conferences. I do not know who keeps this garden, but I hope that it's a monk who sows his *ora* by night and *labora* by day—the one above and the other below, bringing the two together in this explosion of abundance.

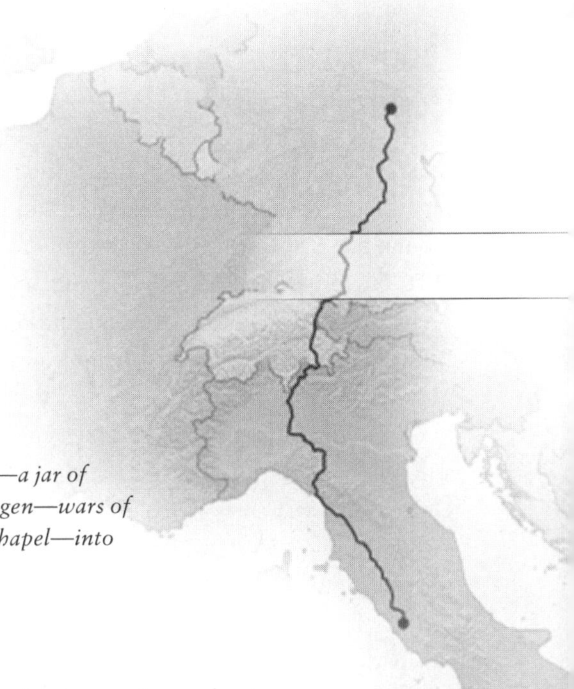

Four

Ulm and the spire Luther didn't see—a jar of interconfessional honey—Memmingen—wars of religion—Genhoffen's mysterious chapel—into Austria with inadequate footgear

As we leave Neresheim, a heavy morning fog settles in, forcing our eyes downward, inward, toward oft-missed minutiae: porcelain gnomes lurk in weedy gardens, Virgins huddle sad and cold in their niches, rose hips glow crimson among scraggly fungal leaves, spiders wait on sagging webs pearled with dew. We walk through misty colonnades of fir, past vacant cabins chock-full of cordwood behind their windows. From a rustic wagon spills forth a cornucopia of squash for the taking; a painted barrel to the side says, "Just drop a coin, please!"

After a time—hard to say how long—the landscape opens up into rolling pastureland, the first we've seen. Interrupted by our passage, some straggling sheep, white splotches in the dim, stretch and yawn their way reluctantly from the dirt. They join their groggy flock staring at us as a single, collective Sheep, blankly chewing cud. In the fog things are reduced to mere suggestions. Against a backdrop of cedars and pines, silhouettes of trees, haystacks, distant onion-domes looming like Oriental minarets, it's as if we're walking through the world of the Bible.

That is, until a strange and rustic apparatus wakes us to a different present. Just outside of Aurenheim, beside the thick woods, a local fourth-grade class (so says the sign) has assembled out of logs a charming *Waldxylophon* ("forest xylophone"), complete with mallet tethered to a string. I whack away with childlike abandon. Later on we cross the Neanderthal Trail, a circuit marked by signs of prehistoric settlement. Transported in my mind I shiver beneath the great ice sheet's moraine, vigilant against saber-tooth tigers, on the lookout for wooly mammoths. In another town we see a parade of vintage cars. Between the petite MGs and patrician Mercedes roadsters hails a bona fide yellow-and-checked New York City Cab, ready with rates from 1970: $1.15 for the first 1/8 mile and $0.15 for each 1/8 mile thereafter. The prehistoric, ancient, and pastoral mix recklessly with modern and Baroque. Buffeted by these unresolved temporalities, our journey has lost its way, not in space but in time.

At Giengen an der Brenz, several signs point to distant Compostella—we're still following the golden shells of the Camino. The medieval guides mention Giengen as a way station. It's on Etzlaub's map too. Luther was probably here.

Some panels along the way tell us of another, less placid face of the historical Camino. As much as the discovery of Saint James's bones in the ninth century, it was the advance and constant threat of the Moors that occasioned this path through Galicia and Asturias. To fund the standoff and the continued slow-creeping *reconquista*, the retaking of Iberia for Christendom, the apostle's newly discovered and installed relics were quite a boon. The steady stream of pilgrim coinage, dripping in from hostels and pious devotions, flowed also into the war-chests of Spain's hidalgos, funding their crusade against the nearby infidel.

We hike almost without rest, as we have quite a way to go before reaching Stetten ob Lontal. Sarah "hits the wall" and forces me to sing to keep her mind from bitter thoughts. I try, but I was raised on National Public Radio, not on pop songs, so I end up humming wordless strains of classical music. Sarah, on the other hand, has hidden in her childhood brain a vast repository of oldies, absorbed while her dad wrote his dissertation. Exasperated at my pathetic grasp of lyrics, an incompetence rewarded by uncontrollable giggling, she takes over—with plenty of musical reserves even several hours later.

Tired from our trudging, and reeling from this additional episode of temporal confusion, we see yet another sign that calls us to the present—and to calm. Written with a marker in bookish letters on a spare wooden board and tied to a spindly tree with a scrap of red twine, it reads: "Pilgrims and wanderers are heartily welcome to rest by the hives." Sure enough, just beyond a little clearing sit stacks of boxes full of bees. The entire scene is generosity distilled: the love of one who concentrates nature's loveliness, sharing the thrumming process with passersby.

At Ulm we reunite again with my parents and our child, who have come by train from Strasbourg. With them we wallow and putter in their hotel room for several hours. All too soon Sarah and I are heading off to stay with Andreas and Carola, pastors in the local Lutheran church who have volunteered to host us. They are slender, keen-eyed, wild-haired, and energetic in the way of sincere devotees of moderation. A former era might have suspected them of vegetarianism. Carola dissolves into the background behind the flinty conversation of her husband. He's a churchman through and through, whose stalwart standing in its history and hierarchy has only sharpened his misgivings. It helps that Lutherans here are in the majority—for self-criticism in churches is much rarer during periods of persecution.

Over our evening's beer and bread, butter, cheese, and ham—as well as the odd olive—Andreas relates his eight-year stint as a missionary in Japan and his slow awakening to its persistent and hardly hidden caste system. Still now, he seethes, while engineers and managers and their dynamic multinational companies have risen to the fore of the global economy, Japan's untouchable dregs fill every menial position and are inhumanely treated by their superiors. It was for him a Damascus road conversion, a cross-cultural conscientization that shook from him his childhood Luther.

Luther? What has Japan to do with Luther? Well, Andreas pressed, had we ever heard of the Sorbs? Of course we hadn't, which proved his point quite perfectly: they've been made invisible, written out of human history. When Luther's father Hans moved the family to Mansfeld, it was to colonize a foreign land, Andreas tells us. Saxon capitalists came to exploit the productive copper mines and cheaper labor of this Slav minority. Luther's education was by paid for by this profiteering. The entire Reformation was built on shaky ethical ground, it seems. Andreas thus understood and sympathized with the notorious Japanese resistance to his Christian faith. It's we who dropped the atomic bomb, after all.

After this unexpected dousing, we're a bit stunned as we head to their guest room. We wonder what parts of Luther's life we can really know, how much we can take him from his setting, how much the unseen structures of the past matter for present regard. These questions are unanswered and seem unanswerable. A couple of years later we learn some details that temper Andreas's outrage. The Sorbs apparently accepted the Reformation happily, not least because it brought them Scripture in their Slavic dialect and thus preserved their language—and much of their culture—from extinction. The first book printed in Sorbian? Luther's *Small Catechism.*

We leave our hosts early the next morning and meet up with the family. Our first task is to buy hiking pants for Sarah, as it's not been summer-warm at all, and she's been wearing thermal tights beneath her skirt almost every day. Task two is for us wander through the old town—or what's left of it. Like Nuremberg, Oettingen, and countless other German cities, historic Ulm was razed during World War II—or rather during a single destructive night. On December 17, 1944, Allied bombs rained fire on strategic sites of the city and on much more, toppling 80 percent of the medieval town.

Most of modern Ulm is a sea of glass and steel. But the city's Gothic Minster (as it's called—technically, it's not a cathedral) came through the war intact with its skyscraping spire still head and shoulders above the city. At 530 feet, it's the tallest church in the entire world. But it wasn't always such a height. When Luther gazed upon its bulk five hundred years ago, the spire was only just begun; it remained unfinished almost until the twentieth century.

Their truncated spire must have been a sore spot for the syndics of the city, who had tithed their *talers* faithfully to raise it. Ulm was a proud and prosperous merchant town, the westernmost port on the eastward-flowing Danube. The frescos on the *Rathaus* (city hall) merge the burghers with the patriarchs, conflating their magnificent metropolis with Jerusalem.

One scene in particular captures the city's notion of itself. Upon a river barge, surrounded by heaving oarsmen, a set of merchants and their wives survey their territory: *Wir Schifters leut sind wohlbestellt; Und uns gehört die weite Welt* ("We bargemen are well commissioned; to us belongs the whole wide world"). Recalling the Doge of Venice's annual marriage with the sea, Ulm stakes the claim on its respective watershed. As La Serenissima ruled the Eastern Mediterranean, so Ulm's merchants dominated the Danube. For us it's a reminder that Luther's world was one of city-states, not nation-states. It was the likes of these proud burghers who took up the Reformation, financially prepared and anxious to assert their will to self-determination.

But even without its heaven-piercing spire, the Minster still burst with bourgeois patriotism. As we circumnavigate its bulk with our family, we marvel at the edifice, its delicate tracery, its profusion of crockets, its forest of pinnacles. The Gothic may have been refined by ethereal imaginations, but it was clearly funded by decidedly earthly endeavors.

We go inside through the side portal and see what Luther might have seen, our eyes wide and necks craned upward in the irresistible verticality of the place—the opposite of bowing. The most interesting elements, though, I find in the choir. Carved in wood dark with age stand two ranks of figures facing each other. On the north side are the lights of classical antiquity: Ptolemy, Pythagoras, Seneca, Vergil, and so on. Opposite them are women who personify the nations: Delphi, Phrygia, Persia, Libya. It's a work of the High Renaissance, imbued with its particular vision of history's progression. These carvings are instances of general revelation—of natural theology—that were later built upon and expanded by Christian truth. And indeed above the choir stalls, scrolled across the architrave in less dramatic bas-relief, are scenes from the Bible and beyond: saints from the Scriptures and the early church set on high to channel the heathen wisdom that rules the stalls below.

Luther mentions none of this, neither the Minster's great and unfinished height nor its artistic synthesis of pagan and Christian wisdom. Exceptionally for our journey, though, he does say something about what he saw, a short tidbit from his late-in-life *Table Talk*. What he most remembers of this testament to God, this towering symbol of Ulm's urban pride, is its echoing dimensions—which for him are not an asset but a liability. The place "is hardly suitable for preaching."[1] Again it is sound, that privileged medium of Lutheran piety, which is most important to him. As if to answer Luther's concern, an unexpected concert begins around us—not of proclaiming voices but of organ pipes. We take a pew and let chest-thumping waves of Bach, Buxtehude, and Arvo Pärt wash over us. Though the pulpit be inadequate, these Lutherans of the highest rank have conceived a sound sufficient to fill the Minster's void with heavenly reverberations.

Our way out of the church is scrutinized by a fierce bronze likeness of the archangel Michael hanging in the vault below the organ, stolid and cartoonish in the way of totalitarian art—and much, much larger than life. Its presence is an ongoing scandal. Conceiving it as a memorial for the city's fallen soldiers of various eras, Nazi sympathizer Heinz Wetzel entitled his sculpture *Attento*, meaning "strive, challenge, protect." For several years in the late 1920s and 1930s, the church's council managed to bar entry to the conspicuously belligerent statue. But after the Nazi ascent to power the so-called German Christians—a group of Nazi-sympathizing Protestants—had their way. The council's scruples were overruled, and *Attento* was installed in 1934 to the tune of the *Horst-Wessel-Lied*, the fascist national anthem.

This leads us, somewhat against our parental protectiveness, to discuss the Second World War with our questioning five-year-old Zeke. He struggles to comprehend what we say about Ulm's bombing, the Nazis and the Jews, and so on. He innocently asks what became of "the bad guy" who led Germany astray, and with some qualms we tell him that Hitler killed himself. It was the first time he ever heard of suicide.

Upon exiting the church, we notice in the rear aisle yet another artifact in bronze that recalls the deeper roots of marriage between faith and the affairs of state. It is the three-and-a-half-ton *Schwörglocke* ("swearing-in bell") that has been used since the fourteenth century to ring the burghers in to their civic loyalty on the *Schwörtag* ("swearing-in day"). Such a ceremony sounds far from evangelical, but it was a widespread practice, particularly among the free cities of the Holy Roman Empire that were anxious to secure the fealty of their citizens against encroaching imperial patrons. In Ulm the burghers gathered before the Minster to recite aloud the oath articles once a year before each other and God.

The issue of oaths became a signal issue as the Reformation spread. For at its extreme the call to civic loyalty alluded to the possibility of violence. It's all well and good to swear in peacetime. But to swear in God's name—as so many did at the time and later would do again during the bloodbath of the Thirty Years' War—is to stamp human frailty with divine imprimatur.

The early Luther had good reason to question such ceremonies, particularly within church buildings—especially since his own oath to God as professor of Bible was to uphold Scripture and not any city. But when so-called radicals, claiming Luther's name, rejected oaths as idolatrous and reserved allegiance to God alone, Luther was profoundly disturbed—along with magistrates of all rank. To forbid oath-taking absolutely, to abolish *Schwörtäge*, was to abrade the thinning fabric of social cohesion itself. And neither Luther nor any great thinker for centuries to come could imagine a public space without God as the glue.

But even if Luther himself was not opposed outright to the mix of religion with certain worldly affairs, neither did he expect from such civic oaths much true faithfulness. "Since the beginning of the world," he cynically observed in 1523, two years before the outbreak of the Peasants' War, "a wise prince is a mighty rare bird, and an upright prince even rarer. They are generally the biggest fools or the worst scoundrels on earth; therefore, one must constantly expect the worst from them and look for little good. They are God's executioners and hangmen; his divine wrath uses them to punish the wicked and to maintain outward peace."[2]

Exiting the Minster in the long shadow of the Nazi Michael, I feel afresh the torn piety of Andreas, filled with godly outrage yet daily surrounded by the trappings of churchly power. There's no erasing the harsh reality of history.

The next morning we say farewell again to our family. It will be eight long days till we see them again and then in a new country—Austria.

It's Saturday morning as we cross the Danube. The Alps are still beyond our sight, but we sense as we amble along the burbling Iller River that the high mountains aren't too far off. Weekend warriors are out in force: a steady streams of joggers, in-line skaters, and cyclists crowd our riverside path. Schools of teenage canoeists paddle on the water below, splashing and giggling in the sun. Once we make it outside the reaches of the city, our trail grows darker. Branches droop and bushes lean. Bit by bit as we advance we are enclosed within a long green tunnel. The riparian forest vibrates with life all around, pulsing with late summer vitality.

Sometime in the afternoon we leave our green tunnel to search for water. As we are walking by some workers' gardens, a beaming seventy-something man accosts us. "Ach! Pious Catholics!" he remarks, noticing my dangling cross. We are compelled not to mislead him and respond that we are pious Lutherans, *lutherisch*, and that we are following Luther's steps to Rome. His sanguine grin grows wider still, and he beckons us into his chain-linked enclosure.

Soon we're eating cakes and refreshing ourselves with lemonade inside the modest summer cottage of Horst and his wife Rosemarie. Horst is short and square-faced, sturdy of build and voluble with his tenor voice. His crew-cut hair stands straight and white atop a well-bronzed face that has been darkened from a summer in the garden. Rosemarie is taciturn but effusive in her smiling, soaking up and reflecting back the adoration of her husband—a tender care that has kept her looking younger than her years. A Lutheran by confession, Horst met and married Catholic Rosemarie. At the time "mixed marriage" was a scandal. They know well how the unresolved strife of past ages lives on to taint an unjust and prevaricating future. Reconciliation between churches, like so many things, begins at home.

As we relax into our chairs, Horst tells his story. It seems half-rehearsed in a way that has made it a life's liturgy of sorts. He grew up in the 1930s in Silesia, and at the very hour of German annexation fled his native Poland, heading west on foot. For three long months he scurried from barn to ditch, stealing food from farms for his provisions, before making it to friends and safety. He was only thirteen years old! The day he retired from his career installing televisions, he threw out his own TV. "Every hour in front of the television is an hour lost forever," he tells us sagely. He and his wife now live for their many grandchildren.

And for their garden. Horst takes us on a grand tour of the precious plot. Save for a few tomatoes, it is given over to flowers: shoulder-high peonies, giant pink anemones, orange marigolds, fluorescent yellow daisies. The rainbow beds are food not only for our eyes: in a sunny corner stands a shock of swaying asters bombinating with bees. The bees are his other children, Horst giggles with his tenor voice. He and Rosemarie eat no sugar at all; they use only honey from their hives to sweeten their cuisine. Golden sunshine, golden flowers—all the work and weather of the year concentrated into golden droplets of delight.

Horst and Rosemarie send us off with hearty salutations, wishing us well for our laborious pilgrimage and for our vision of churchly reconciliation. As we exchange our last farewell, Horst runs in to fetch a one-pound jar of honey; Rosemarie hurriedly fills a sack with freshly picked tomatoes, still warm from the sun. Despite the added heft, their gifts magically lighten our load.

Honey vade mecum in our packs, we head back to the Iller's jungly path. Up to that point we had been driven by our schedule, by our plan not necessarily to shun such interactions but nevertheless to avoid them out of temporal expedience. After our time with Horst and Rosemarie, we resolve to accept such invitations in the future. A pilgrim must make peace with serendipity.

The lazy Iller now runs slightly stronger. Each mile or so, piles of boulders tame the tumbling river. And though it is man-made arrow-straight, each successive cataract reminds us that we're climbing slowly out of Franconia into the Piedmont of the Allgäu. Some sources say Luther walked east from

Ulm to Augsburg before turning definitively toward the south, but there seems no special reason for it. The dotted line on Etzlaub's map leads straight to Memmingen, and we opt to stick with him.

A gloomy viaduct under the roaring Autobahn marks our exit from the overgrown canal. We veer into the outskirts of the city, past movie theaters, supermarkets, rusty bits of shuttered industry. We make it to the center city just in time for Sunday evening mass at Saint Johann's Catholic Church. We're tired and tempted to skip, but our drooping eyes are arrested by a bit of fresco that we might easily have missed. Painted on an oriel beside the church's entry, two blocky angels herald with an unfurled banner that this building is the *Ehemaliger Augustinerkloster*—former Augustinian cloister! It's as glaring as a neon sign to us. Here slept Luther! We duck forthwith into the service, sit quietly at the back, and contemplate Luther's one-time presence during the mass.

Luther had a long and complicated history with Memmingen. The city had gained its freedom from the local lords later in the Middle Ages, and like so many other free cities of the Holy Roman Empire, it quickly joined Luther's movement. The stripping of the Bible from its many-layered glosses led also to great hopes for a new and evangelical ordering of society. Jesus, after all, seems rather to take sides with the world's down-and-out. But the revolt quickly went much further than Luther—and especially his princely backers—had imagined, with brutal consequences.

This is the land of the 1525 *Bauernkrieg*, the "Peasants' War." In Memmingen were written and diffused the Twelve Articles, a kind of late medieval Bill

The Catholic church of St. John in Memmingen is located on the site of the former Augustinian friary where Luther likely stayed the night.

of Rights with biblical backing for each point. Beyond demanding the right of each municipality to elect its own preacher, the Twelve Articles sought also to wrest from greedy landlords the right to hunt and fish, to gather wood, to work less onerously, to be paid more handsomely, and other things seditious for the times.

That world was still ruled by landed gentry, and whereas the cities and their money-making bourgeoisie had won a kind of self-determination, the land itself and its annual stream of revenue remained firmly in the hands of local lords—many of whom were bishops and abbots. When in the wake of the Reformation certain lords got even richer from dubious grabs for this requisitioned land, it is not difficult to imagine the modest dreams of modest people being all too quickly dashed.

At first Luther sided with the peasants—but only tacitly—by chastising greedy magistrates. Share the wealth and spare the whip, he wrote them in his early 1525 *Admonition to Peace*, or God's wrath would rise up against them. And it did. The peasants rose up, hoes in hand, and after a few months of swarming they managed to carry away a startling amount of booty, fueling hopes of ultimate success.

The peasants were wrong to think they had Luther's full support for their premature revolution. In matters politic Luther was very much an Augustinian, who ranked peace and order above a fully realized earthly justice. He put out a second pamphlet later in 1525, *Against the Robbing and Murdering Hordes of Peasants*. The title is unfortunate (and was added not by Luther but by the impresario printers who diffused it), for his chief aim was not just to call down retribution on the rebels for their mutinous violence. Luther hoped even more to insist that the true gospel—in contrast to the so-called Christian message that the peasants called their own—could not come at the point of a sword (or a hoe). Jesus suffered for his witness, and so will all who wield the gospel message. Despite the justice of their pleas, Luther felt the peasants' lack of faith deserved punishment—both earthly and eternal.

This Peasants' War was extinguished with frightening efficiency. Once fully mobilized, the lords' pike-wielding mercenaries hewed the farmers down, thus dousing the briefly kindled hopes for a new organization of society. Within weeks the hundreds of thousands of rebels were either dead or dispersed. There was no longer a doubt as to where the power lay. Now that much of the church's power and property had been confiscated, local magistrates held the reins of public order. The perhaps surprising solution of Luther and company to the flight of local bishops was to invest the secular lords with an emergency episcopal office, a dangerous bricolage of competencies tempered only by the fear of God and the often ineffective threats of theologians.

Compared to the twentieth century, Luther's world was one of glacial pace and almost static social forms. Its people were subject not only to unpredictable plagues and disasters but likewise to capricious princes and invading armies that devoured life and disrupted order like swarms of locusts. The murder rate itself was twenty to a hundred times greater than it is today in Western Europe, and death from sickness, accident, or childbirth was omnipresent in a way that is hard for us to comprehend.[3] It's no wonder Luther reacted so harshly against the peasants' foment—not against their material complaints, which he sustained, but against taking martial justice into their own hands and thereby sowing violence in a world that was teetering on the edge of violence at every moment. Their presumption circumscribed the path to peace and coronated in its place the minions of chaos.

This Peasants' War lived a strange and celebrated life under Communism. While commemorating in 1983 the five hundredth birthday of Germany's most celebrated personality—Luther—the apparatchiks of the GDR wrangled attention from his religious convictions toward his role as precursor to the revolution. Sarah and I have a strange map of Luther's gambit that was printed for this event. It highlights Luther's cities—Wittenberg, Eisleben, Erfurt, and so on—but even more important on it are the battles of the peasants. The mass-martyrdoms of these proto-proletariats are marked by bloody splotches. Even godless Communists could put Christian Luther to work for their millenarian goals, racking up his protest against the Holy Roman Empire, his establishment of the German language, and even his valorization of the bourgeoisie as inevitable and necessary strides in the march toward the German Communist state. In all of this creative propagandizing, however, they eviscerated the man. What is left is but a specter, a mere ephemeral shade driven before rank after rank of history's armies.

I awake completely congested. My nose is as wet and dripping as the clouds above. It would be nice to take a break, but our appointments will not wait. There's no sick day for the Wilsons. With Sarah's encouragement I manage to stand up. Once beyond Memmingen's *Kempter Tor* or Kempten Gate, that day is but a blur: just plodding, plodding, plodding all the way to Bad Groenenbach.

Friendly Allgäuer cows

Wrecked by a mere ten miles of walking, I collapse into our hotel bed. Sarah goes out looking for medicine to alleviate my miserable self. She tells a friendly pharmacist, somewhat unartfully, *Mein Mann ist krank in der Nase* ("My husband is sick in the nose"), and is given a packet of green pills, which she is assured are *pflanzlich*—that is to say, made purely from plant matter and presumably not tainted by evil industrial chemicals. That evening Sarah surreptitiously cooks dinner on our camp stove in the bathroom—fan on, windows open, and TV loud enough to dissemble any odor or noise.

Whether from the herbal medicine, the home-cooked meal, the prayers of some eight hundred Facebook fans, or perhaps the longish walk, I'm almost better by morning. The cloudy sky has lifted too, and we leave Bad Groenenbach refreshed.

Not long after our departure, just outside the forest south of town and among the swells of Swabian pasture, we suddenly glimpse the Alps. There before us stretches the dark dividing line of Europe: distant, toothy silhouettes receding row by row. It will be ten more days before we reach the pass.

With great mountain peaks in the distance, the hills of the Allgäu roll gently out before us. Tawny cows, bred with a desperate instinct for human company, come trotting toward us from the fields' furthest corner just to say hello. Tier after tier of them jostle between each other, finally to stand before us arranged like piano keys. They push their eager muzzles as close to the electric fence as they dare. Then they stare, mooing a half-confused, collective "Now what?" Before their loving large-eyed bovine gaze that promises both nourishment and warmth, we judge that Aaron's folly—to make a golden calf for the Israelites—seems less strange.

Another halo of commerce and industry signals Kempten, the next point on our *Rompilgerkarte*. Like Memmingen, it too joined the Reformation. At least the burghers did, happy as they were to be out from under the town's abbey and its domineering abbot. For the next century Kempten was physically divided between Protestant and Catholic. The Protestants ruled the Imperial Free City with allegiance to the Emperor; the Catholic side remained obedient to the abbot and his wealthy monastery. This convoluted arrangement illustrates the jurisdictional confusion and squabbling that led eventually to outright confessional war.

As reward for its double allegiance, Kempten was doubly destroyed in the Thirty Years' War. This shameful drawn-out affair began and was prolonged by religious concerns. But it quickly defied any coherent confessional program. Swedish Lutherans were soon fighting for the Catholic Cardinal Richelieu and his papal allies. Their goal was to check the dynastic ambitions of the wily Habsburgs and their Holy Roman Emperor Frederick—himself a devout and clever Jesuit-trained statesman whose pious devotion did not prevent him from opposing the Papal States. Both Swedish and imperial forces exacted tribute, leaving flame and famine in their destructive wakes. Kempten's Baroque basilica is appropriately dedicated to Saint Laurence, who was martyred by roasting. And so in utter incoherence Lutheran Sweden attacked Lutheran Kempten. So much for the so-called wars of religion.

Little is left in Kempten that Luther could have seen. Nor could these later conflagrations have been foreseen when Luther walked through this city. Upon what unseen cusps of time do we now tread as we stroll through the square beside Saint Laurence in the warm September glow?

It's market morning as we leave, so we pluck some potatoes, carrots, and radishes from among the picturesque piles of produce. Sarah finds and quickly takes advantage of a special offer on foraged chanterelle and porcini mushrooms. From Kempten we turn to the east, over the Vorallgäu, and back into the basin of the Rhine.

The landscape is exceedingly lovely and oddly lonely—a recurring surprise for us Americans who come to Europe expecting endless built environments. There are villages and farms, of course, and woodlands crossed with paths and roads. There's hardly an acre that's not accounted in some ledger, written in some local planner's record book. But despite this administrative fullness, this ubiquity of possession and management, we see few people and only traces written in infrastructure: hand-hewn stone catchments holding water for lapping dogs, power lines buzzing overhead, Hansel and Gretel cottages clad in the thick thermal armor of wood stacked up to their wide eaves.

Most of the people that we see hurtle past unknowing in their cars, driving us to the ditches and shoulders of the modern world. We see our apparatuses, our productions, but the humans who conceived and made them are out of view, secondary, protected, proxy beings. As traces of human activity cover the earth, our bodies are eerily absent from the landscape of their making. Merely by the act of walking, the pilgrim becomes alien to it all, maintainer of a tradition almost forgotten. A footpath is tradition inscribed upon the land. As new ways of thought and new technologies drive the masses to other means of locomotion and thus to other byways, the old path is grown over. Heraclitus, the ancient philosopher famous for saying that you can't step into the same river twice, was wrong not to extend this insight to the land as well. After five hundred years, you can't step on the same trail twice, either.

At one isolated spot along the empty road, a lonely mare with a flaxen mane trots up to greet us, nuzzling clumps of clover from our hands, its muzzle warm and soft like velvet. It's enough to transport us from this land of steel and concrete and pretend permanence into another world of quicker and more obvious decay. There was good reason in Luther's day to be obsessed with gold, which alone among the elements glittered without tarnish, and with the stars, which turned unchangeably above in their perfectly spherical heavens. Where flesh was animated at all, it was only because of some mysterious spark of life, some vital force keeping death at bay. All things tend toward entropy, as any physicist will tell us. It takes the added energy of love, of art, of imagination and caring to keep not just the sensual joys of a healthy muzzle living but also anything at all—a building, a trail, even a religion—from submitting to inevitable oblivion.

After a comfy night at our inn in Missen, we prepare for the day's exertions by shoveling down great mounds of muesli drowned in yogurt, bowls of fruit, hard-boiled eggs, rolls stacked high with butter, ham and cheese, and many cups of coffee laced with cocoa. Not all our breakfasts are so voluminous or so tasty, but by this point our hunger is practically insatiable.

David from Dallas walks in on us as we swallow our last bites. He saw an article Sarah wrote about our pilgrimage for the *Wall Street Journal*,[4] and since he was already planning to be in Europe, he decided to come and walk with us. A fifty-something guy, he's very tall with an athletic build, ruddy skin, and a full head of whitish hair. He looks like a sometime CEO whose unflappable mien would reassure the shareholders. Just substitute the suit with travel garb from REI, a small backpack, some hiking poles, and a couple of days' worth of whiskers. Together we'll climb over endless swells of Swabian foothills to Scheidegg, some twenty-one miles distant.

We leave along the main street, walking for a ways with a herd of tawny cows and their ambling drover. It's wet again today. Close clouds scud through the scattered pines. Our undulating path is both mucky and wet. We fill the damp hours chatting about Martin Luther and Alexander Men, the Orthodox priest. David seems to be an armchair theologian, even more now that he's between jobs. The gap has given him pause to search for more meaning in his work.

He also tells us with some delight of the astonishing traits of seeds. In a former life he assayed soil, and he once counted in a cupful from the Indiana forest the traces of more than two hundred species. How delightful for us to think that hidden beneath our every step lies an entire forest of possibility: dormant, lingering one more year interred, only awaiting some storm, some fire, some rough beast to dig it up.

A morning filled with climbing and descending hills brings us into Genhoffen, a vestige of a village, built up in the Middle Ages by blacksmiths. The hamlet is a stop on the old salt road, and porters always needed shoes and tackle for their beasts. The site is dominated by what was the blacksmiths' chapel: high-gabled, squat-towered, whitewashed St. Stephen's Church. We eat our pasta and mushroom stew behind a nearby windrow of pine trees. Then we step into an ecclesiastical time warp.

The simple church is a marvel of rustic piety. It manages without costly refinement to articulate the profoundest of truths in the most vernacular of aesthetics. The space inside is simple and cool. Without the slender windows and whitewash it would be a cave. Across the southern wall an atavistic artist has scrawled out the drama of a hunt in carbon black, echoing the drawings in the caves at Lascaux. Stick figures pounce and pirouette, bristling with arrows, dangling with swords, clanging toward bounding beasts heavy with antlers. More inscrutable glyphs are scattered all about: tined escutcheons, herons spitting thorns. We've stepped back into the Stone Age.

Frescoes at the church of St. Stephen in Genhoffen

Elsewhere the walls swim with further symbols ancient and repurposed, images likely transported by a medieval muleteer from nearby Augsburg, Ulm, or Lindau, who rendered them semifaithfully in ochre hues. The building is not Gothic, but its artists have reproduced its elements in childlike simulacrum: lancets, mullions, oculi. Other hands have added to the doodling, affectionately rendering patterns only faintly understood: zigzags, fleurs-de-lis, Jerusalem crosses, crows, chi-rhos, creeping tendrils of ivy across the architrave. The flood of visual trivia transforms the otherwise austere nave into a window upon heaven.

Spread out across the panels of the organ loft and drawn with a more modern hand in strokes recalling mason's marks are the instruments of the passion: the foot-washer's urn, the praying hands of Gethsemane's vigil, the crowing cock, the cat-o'-nine-tails, the crown of thorns, the vinegar-soaked sponge, the untorn tunic, a pile of dice. Above the altar stand more familiar statues of painted wood: patron St. Stephen holds the stones that killed him, pilgrim-robed St. Roch uncovers his plague bubo, and in the middle a wimple-bound St. Anne holds a haloed baby Jesus with crowned Mary.

Hidden among this common iconography, on a folding panel behind the altar, stands an image of an unnamed "Holy Abbot." The bearded monk is clad in a traveler's cloak. In his left hand are a staff and string of beads, while his right hand lifts in trinitarian blessing. Below the holy man's feet a claw-footed and bat-winged dragon spews forth a stream of impotent fire. It could well be St. Anthony, who left Egyptian civilization to battle demons in the desert.

Genhoffen lies at the heart of the Irish mission, begun by Columbanus in the darkest of the Dark Ages. The Celtic monks, armed only with their holy lives and holy words, spread out across these former Roman regions.

Hacking their way through forested darkness, they carried Christianity beyond the Rhine. We must see them, though, not primarily as missionaries or colonists—a contemporary vocabulary that falls short—but as corporeal concentrations of spiritual power, who drove from the vast and trackless wilderness the shadows of the savage and demonic.

The tale of St. Gall sums up in one man this heroic Christian age. According to legend, the hermit was alone in his cave above Lake Constance, warming himself by a fire, when suddenly a ferocious bear made to attack him. The holy man rebuked the beast, which fled into the wood. Not long after, the bear returned, this time not with malice but with a gift: a log for Saint Gall's fire. In payment for this change of heart, the monk gave the bear some bread, thus establishing an allegorical exchange between the wild power of nature and Christian civilization.

Just as we go out a woman heads in to pray. We leave her kneeling, head bowed deep, and silent. Her aging collie waits patiently under the portico. When she exits from her vigil, aware of our keen admiration for the place, she leads us out around beyond the apse to a viewpoint. To the left and to the right, she points, at equilateral angles, lie sister sanctuaries, equidistant from each other and Genhoffen. Within these bounds, she claims, there is a geometry of plenty. "This was a holy site from long before the Christian missionaries," she tells us. "The land here, within this triangle, is more fertile, the climate more agreeable, the population longer lived than without," she adds with peaceful certainty as she sweeps her hand across the green horizon. There's no iconoclasm here. On this ancient holy site, sanctified by the monks, edified by its church, written upon by the faithful literate in mysterious symbology, Christianity does not uproot the ancient spirits utterly but instead channels deep fonts of spiritual power. As Saint Gall tames his bear, the chthonic forces here are harnessed and directed toward heavenly ends.

After fifteen miles (and a few more thousand feet of climbing) we stumble out of the woods at Weiler. We stop by a house improbably ringed by cactus and wonder how such plants survive in humid Germany, when out of the window above pops the head of Rena. She's heard us speaking English and answers us in kind: "Come in, come in. You're pilgrims, yes? Come in and have some tea." She skirts around back and opens the side door. Joined by husband Oskar, we slide in to their kitchen nook as trays of teas and cookies slide before us—hospitality they extend to many pilgrims, they tell us warmly.

Rena is a retired English teacher, dressed in the baggy clothes of a post-professional, her head covered with loads of wiry flaxen hair. Oskar's strongly built and leather clad, looking rather like a biker as he smiles aggressively beneath his thickly mustached mouth. He speaks no English but interrogates us energetically *auf Deutsch*. They're a perfect picture of robust retirement, the comfortable sunset of a middle-class life, full of modest comfort wed to generosity.

The tea and cakes go down quickly while Sarah and I recount for them our journey up to now and elaborate the reasons for our pilgrimage to Rome in Luther's steps. They show us pictures of their kids, who are now spread across the globe—one pressing danger for parents too familiar with foreign tongues and too accustomed to travel.

After slogging a few miles more along a highway, we say good-bye to David at his hotel. He's looking rather pale from the day's exertions; his legs are trembling though his spirits are high. We haven't realized until now how much stamina we've already gained.

A couple miles more for us, then we stumble into the *Pilgerzentrum Scheidegg*. After twenty-six days of walking, it's our first stay in an official hostel, set up by local Lutherans eager to provide a place to passing pilgrims. The simple, modern building is perfectly appointed for its purpose. It's complete with men's and women's dormitories, a common kitchen, a dining room, and ample equipment for washing. It stands beside a blocky Lutheran church whose concrete spire is hung with solar panels. A billboard advertises nearby: "Scheidegg: Sunniest City in Germany, 2007!"

The hostel is tended by volunteers. The current crew is a pair of Dutch alumni of the Camino de Santiago, reliving the epiphanies of the trail. We warm up, dry off our damp gear, take hot showers, and put our muddy clothes into the washer. We get a stamp in our nearly empty pilgrim passports, then sign our names into the register: we are pilgrims #770 and #771, the only ones today. The volunteers serve up spaghetti, which we devour in unseemly quantities.

Sarah and I manage to coax some limited and muddled information from our hosts. They're not religious, they assure us, but they love to walk so as to see the world as it is at a human pace: the ephemeral communities of the trail, the spontaneous friendship and generosity that extends to and is extended from the pilgrims' community. For these modern walkers, who live modern office lives that make the human body auxiliary, walking and its rhythms return frazzled minds and atrophied frames to a former peace and calm. They have internalized the modern pilgrim's motto: "They journey is the destination."

How different from Luther's day! Then the goal was heaven, to glimpse eternity's fleeting incarnation in holy men and women and their relics. A pilgrim hitched himself to the saints and their upward inertia. How odd, too, that now it's these lapsed Protestants—whose churches from Luther onward detested pilgrimage and its implication that salvation was to be sought strenuously and far away—who offer rest for pilgrims, facilitating escape from daily life.

We leave our hostel early the next morning, climbing out of Scheidegg into yet another fog. The clouds condensing on the pines drip, drip, drip upon us. We ascend some logging roads past clicking electric fences and beneath soon-to-be occupied hunting stands. At the top of one particular hill, hunkering vigilant above the pastureland, there stands a lone chapel, a vestige of a now half-forgotten apparition.

Still further up into the dripping pines, a blaring red sign shakes us to attention: *Achtung Staatsgrenze*. It's the border! After twenty-seven days of walking (twenty-two of them under clouds and rain), we've crossed half a country. We take a moment to contemplate our accomplishment, though the setting is not as dramatic as one might hope. There's no fence, no barrier, no clear-cut swath through the forest. A hundred yards beyond the sign is a small abandoned customs office, a prefab box of aluminum and glass. The place is indistinct. What on the modern map is such a solid, almost tangible thing, here on the ground is utterly abstract and insubstantial. A few more easy steps and we leave Germany behind us to enter Austria.

From the deserted border station we climb still higher. The clouds lift and Lake Constance glitters through the trees far below our hilltop vantage. The peninsular town of Lindau sticks out like a ship moored upon its northern shore. That's where Luther would have walked. From there he likely took the ferry to Fussach—at the Rhine's inland delta, visible below to our left—then walked up the Rhine. We can see the same rough trajectory that we will soon follow, fading gradually behind a veil of haze as it enters into the maw of the mountains.

The path down into Bregenz is slick and muddy. We seem to manage without too much trouble despite—according to a few consternated passersby—wearing unconscionably inadequate footgear. At one point on our cautious descent, a winded hiker heading up rebukes us for our shoes: I'm wearing plastic clogs and Sarah, sneaker-sandals. We've received this scolding several times already in Germany, where people seem to regard feet with a sort of fearful reverence, as fragile things in need of sturdy support and adequate armor. Invariably when strangers inquire after our destination, digest the distance, then ruminate briefly on our intervening trials, their shocked gaze descends from our eyes to our feet. When they see our flimsy footgear, their eyes grow wider still with disbelief and reprimand—as if the further the distance, the sturdier the leather, the thicker the sole, the more robust the ankle support must be.

Is this what keeps people from heading out, from going the long pilgrim's distance—inadequate shoes? Who has not heard the occasional walker complain of blisters? What pilgrim returns without tales of podiatric agony? Wear sandals, we say, wide and airy. In any case, our boy and his grandparents are already waiting at the bottom of the hill; a bit of slipping just might speed things up.

Five

Bregenz—little Liechtenstein—fortress Switzerland—some thoughts on translation—rescued—church and charnel house—Bivio's religious rivalries—snow

At Bregenz our journey seems to begin anew: a new country, a visit from our family, and a craftily staged surprise appearance—catching us totally and delightedly unawares—from dear Australian friends who are ex-pats like us in Strasbourg. Zeke is thrilled to have three boys to play with—Aidan, Liam, Christian—and they bring him presents; their parents Phil and Marianne treat us to an Italian dinner. For a couple of days it's almost as if we're at home: together in a comfortable hostel, eating copiously, doing chores electronic and hygienic, strolling about the pleasantly modern town. It'll be almost two weeks—our longest stretch by far—till we see the family again on the other side of the Alps. When we meet again outside Milan, there'll be no more good-byes: they'll be with us all the way to Rome.

Even the weather seems to have taken a more enduring turn for the better: the warm *Föhn* wind is blowing softly to the north, keeping the clouds at bay. Phil walks us a few miles out of town. He pushes our bags all the while in their family stroller—a brief and welcome respite from our burdens.

Our way from Bregenz through the Alps is as simple as could be: up the narrowing valley of the Rhine. Here the storied waterway is neither great nor wild but just a little river meandering between a pair of straight and sturdy levees. Just beyond its muted babble a highway buzzes with a stream of transalpine traffic. The narrow valley teems with agricultural abundance—an entire great plain's worth of villages and farmsteads, as if they had been washed down in torrents from the steep slopes above. Verticality determines everything here: while the frost bites and winds whip across the crests, down below all is warm, wide, mild, lovely, and full of life.

We are entering into Luther's borderlands, where his cultural shadow reaches a diffuse limit. From early on the region has had strong Protestant presence, but the energetic efforts of Counter-Reformation Austria and the influence of the nearer Swiss reformers Zwingli and Calvin have rendered Luther less significant here than further to the north.

After weeks and weeks of Germany, our walk through Austria is shockingly short—hardly more than a day. We sweep briefly along the river-border with Switzerland, then enter our next country: microstate Liechtenstein. This tiny principality, formerly ruled from distant Prague, is a historical orphan, an island in the rising tide of the nation-state. Only by the most arbitrary of historical accidents has Liechtenstein survived at all. Permitted rather than respected, it exists as a reminder that the world was once much clearer in its hierarchies and chaotic in its jurisdictions than today.

When we imagine Germany or Italy, they seem to be such solid things, such natural expressions of geography, of culture, of language. This is exactly how we're meant to think, of course, and it just goes to show how successful nascent nations were at centralizing power and defining their identity. It's easy to forget that "Italy" as such did not exist until 1861; "Germany" until 1870. Before these nineteenth-century consolidations, much of Europe was a patchwork, a nest of petty domains—bishoprics, dukedoms, city-states—each vying for its own interests large and small, and for survival itself. And, after the Reformation, for its religious confession too. In Luther's day, everything was a little Liechtenstein.

If Liechtenstein is a relic of this older political world, it's also a kind of fairy-tale throwback. It consists of but a single, west-facing slope of a mountain and a strip of fertile farmland beside the Rhine. Grain is planted along the river, vineyards stripe the higher slopes; higher still graze cows and sheep on pastures below the gray and craggy crest. The country is still governed by a prince, who in addition to being the executive lives in a castle and acts as seemingly the sole patron of the arts.

Like the principalities of Luther's day, Liechtenstein is hardly independent. It has neither the size nor income to do anything on its own. It imports

Hilltop castle and vineyards in Liechtenstein

almost everything, including its currency, the Swiss franc. And as for national security, it must rest on the fact that its wealth is tied up almost exclusively in art and banks.

We walk into the capital city of Vaduz, which is really just a small town, and to the home of Hartwig and Katharina, doctors of theology and pastors of the local Lutheran parish—a church built to chaplain the steady stream of German immigrants to the underpopulated country. The day of our arrival coincides with their church's "ecumenical" Bible study, and since our journey is about such ecumenical affairs, we are especially invited to attend. The small group, solicitous of their visitors, agrees to speak in *Schriftdeutch* on our behalf, as to us the local dialect is incomprehensible. On the way home, Herr Pastor laments that his own parishioners don't attend—the folks we met are all Catholics. The Lutherans, he says, believe themselves to be biblical by definition, which relieves them of the need to read the Bible at all, apparently. How easily an identity replaces the substance of a movement.

When we return to Hartwig and Katharina's, our conversation over *Brotzeit* is full and refined in the manner of fellow divines and is intermittently kept down to earth by the burbling interventions of their two small children. Our host couple is tired from parenting, from living far away—they're German—and from the isolation of their small country. They feel very much the foreigners that they are.

Liechtenstein is a simple, rustic place, our hosts assure us, despite the colossal per capita income. Many of its few thousand citizens are servants in some way or another to the powerful prince and other magnates who domicile here for tax purposes. In some other epoch, one might have taken comfort in a noble lord, his lofty castle, and his admirable art. But shake a perfectly normal slice of ducal territory a couple of hundred years out of temporal sync, make it very real, and it's no longer quaint at all. It's odd and even creepy.

The next morning, as we walk out of Vaduz in the bright blue morning light, the city is as incoherent as one might expect. The buildings are either rustically stodgy or bristling with the geometrically perfect stone, concrete, and glass of modernity. The glittering stuff indicates unsubtly the world of finance. Liechtenstein is basically a bank. Wealthy patrons roll slowly by in black cars chock-full of the latest Teutonic technology, as silent and hidden behind their tinted windows as is the money in the coffers below. The spotless plaza of the prince's museum is almost empty, yet busy workers mop away dutifully. Upon the hill his palace dominates not in an ostentatious show of authority but with a sort of condescending watchfulness.

The glass and concrete buildings dwindle with each step farther away from town. First clock-towered churches appear, then a picturesque chateau on a little hill ringed by vineyards. Then we reach the Rhine again, still levee-bound but crashing white and almost wild, drowning out all other noise. Beyond the dulling chatter of the river, we walk again on forest paths in dappled shade, in water-cooled breeze—as if in some kind of primitive past.

For a fleeting moment the land is like what Luther might have seen and felt and heard—sandal-clad, tunic-cloaked—walking down his gravel path toward the doleful Alpine peaks. We find a tiny sandbar and wade into the milky glacial water. It is achingly cold. Continuing just beyond, still in our sylvan reverie, we find ourselves standing before the menacing embrasures of a concrete bunker. It's empty and completely overgrown but could quickly be repurposed. Thus, with mute weapons of the past, we are welcomed into fortress Switzerland.

Just up the river our next stop is Bad Ragaz, which was a miserable village shivering in the shadow of the Saint Gall summits until the discovery of hot springs transformed its muddy squalor into a destination. Its most famous sometime itinerant, Rainer Marie Rilke, lived here several summers in the 1920s as he recovered from the heartaches of the war under one of the many roofs of his patroness, the Princess Marie of Thurn and Taxis. That he fell madly in love with the secretary of the telegraph office tells where his mind—and his feet—must have wandered.

The concentration of such leisurely decadence in this gateway to the Alps underscores the great chasm that lies between our own romantic vision of hale mountain air and the contrasting horror of former generations. Mountainscapes and beauty are but recently linked. Contemporary people's fondness for dramatic vistas has displaced a more perduring and pastoral preference for the gentle curves and productivity of fields and gardens. It took the nascent industrial revolution to germinate a fondness for the wild, to hint that nature had limits and that we, too, had lost something in its taming.

Besides the craggy tops, the rumbling glaciers, the inaccessible vales of scree, the Alps' most striking feature is emptiness. From outer space by night they are a curving eyebrow of black, devoid of light. People here may sojourn or drive their flocks or scale a peak or two, but they can never stay the whole year through at any height. This very absence of things human is why Romantics rehabilitated mountains for cultured critics. In town and country, Nature had grown too tame, too sullied by our activity. Wordsworth laments the cancerous growth of cities, "O'er which the smoke of unremitting fires / Hangs permanent and plentiful." The hiker seeking nature "sees the barren wilderness erased, or disappearing." As therapy Wordsworth pointed citified asthmatics toward the undespoiled, rocky pathways of the Alps, "The sky-roofed temple of eternal hills. . . . Bright stars of ice and azure fields of snow."[1] The mountains are Nature's last impenetrable outpost, a place of purity and re-creation of the harried modern self.

In Luther's day the Alps were not on anybody's bucket list. They were a barrier plain and simple, the more quickly crossed the better. Welsh canon and chronicler Adam of Usk, while crossing nearby Gotthard Pass, asked to be blindfolded so as to block the terror from his view. Enlightened bishop and philosopher George Berkeley was similarly unmoved by the eternal snows, which rendered everything around "excessively miserable." To Samuel Johnson they were irritating "protuberances." William Gilpin had a cold financial judgment: "There are few who do not prefer the busy scenes of cultivation to the greatest of nature's productions."[2] According to early alpinist Edward Whymper, even the peasants who called the mountains home lived in fear of their caprice; windows nearly always faced the valley—and not only to block the katabatic currents tumbling from the frozen heights. Adventurer Richard Bangs sums up the sentiments of this prior age: "Mountains were things to avoid, or, if one were a merchant, soldier, or pilgrim, to go around. Mountains, as a whole, were anathema."[3]

All this comes well after Luther, and we don't know where the lowland Saxon might fit on this continuum. The land he found austere, nothing but hill or vale, no good for farming, only useful as pastureland. Yet the walkways he found unexpectedly sure-footed, the houses handsome. Food was much too scarce to feed both residents and travelers, so the guides carried extra in from elsewhere. Perhaps due to this hardship of life, Luther praised the Swiss as robust, clever, honest people, "the first among the Germans." He was surprised to find that in times of peace the local men were not ashamed to milk the cows and make the cheese; apparently they were ashamed elsewhere.[4] It doesn't seem that Luther was terrified like Adam of Usk, but neither does the Alpine grandeur lift his heart like it would that of a Romantic poet. Or at least he made no note of it.

I'm dreamy-eyed when it comes to mountains, and while the pleasures of lowland Germany did not escape me, it's here that our trip finally leaves what seemed to me like its long, damp introduction. To my own ears, tuned by a childhood full of outings in the Cascades and trained by the mystical visions of John Muir, Luther's disinterest in the mountains is conspicuous and frustrating. Perhaps it's fitting that a journey in Luther's footsteps should force me to see the world through his more prosaic eyes. Our trek is not an athletic event where we triumphantly scale the soaring heights, a reality to which I only gradually resign myself. We are pilgrims in a parallel dimension, with different buckets and different lists—a fact that would soon become clear.

Inhospitable rock and ice are far from mind as we plod under the beating sun to Chur, a prominent dot on Etzlaub's map. That Luther came this way is almost certain, for in this neighborhood there *is* no other way. Chur was the capital of an Alpine empire—Grisons in French, Graubünden in German. The prince-bishop grew rich from his monopoly on the passes to the south, a privilege challenged by local burghers who pushed for larger slices of the tariff pie. Later on, as with Erfurt, Bregenz, Ulm, and Memmingen, the region joined the Reformation cause. Tired of prelates and their privileges, the people kicked the bishop out and turned this crossing of the Alps to Protestantism—all the way to northern Italy.

At Chur the modest strip of flat land narrows to oblivion, the once broad valley of the Rhine turns abruptly toward the west. Here the mountains begin in earnest, and the valley walls mount to still greater heights, which press upon the churning river. Now undiked the Rhine tumbles iridescent with its glacial till. At one point an even siltier tributary joins the turquoise flow; the two currents flow downstream unmixed for quite a while until, at last, they eddy into one another.

Despite the airy beauty all around, we're suddenly struck with boredom and melancholy. Trudging uphill all afternoon, our aching feet plod on and on, while our thoughts are carved into a groove. Walking all day long for weeks on end has brought us to a rhythmic, almost contemplative state. And with it comes the noonday devil, a mental sloth that has us yearning for new input, new books, new words and thoughts to spice our repetitious conversations. It doesn't help that Sarah is now sick with last week's cold, and has a couple of blisters, too. She takes one of our green *pflanzlich* pills and slogs painfully on.

Our monotonous ascent ends in Tamins, a tiny village perched upon a shelf above the valley floor. We stay with local pastors Anja and Georg. They're ever so attentive as they feed us well and warmly, wash our clothes, and pull out maps to plan the days ahead. Georg goes so far as to arrange our next night's lodging. Not a hotel seems to be open, so he calls the Catholic priest at Alvaschein—our next stop. The priest then calls a woman from his parish who runs a small establishment, telling her that pilgrims are on their way. Though it's typically her day off, she'll gladly open up for pilgrims—regardless of their confession.

Over dinner in their kitchen's nook, Georg and Anja disclose to us the trials of the Swiss Reformed. Proud holdouts to centuries of energetic Counter-Reformation, they maintain an identity that seems frozen in a steely independence. Each Swiss canton has its own independent church, its own independent synod, and its own unrelated officials—a feisty federality that extends into the structures of the state as well, with which Protestants have historically had tight ties. Catholics have long been marginalized and still must submit each bishop-elect to local legislators for approval. Waves of secularism have hit the church here unexpectedly hard and left most pastors reeling, wondering how their once august and honored institution has turned so quickly insignificant. They're scrambling to regain a lost respect and in the murky process tend to set aside impractical theology for notions with more political pull. You hear a lot about the heritage of Protestantism and its relevance for today. But very little about God.

Shifting to another theme, we learn that Anja's mother tongue is not German but Romansh—a mixed-up child of Latin and an old vestige of the day when each village had a dialect. Our own historico-linguistic sensibilities are muddled by the predominance of print and by the compulsory education that has eradicated so many tongues the world over. Today's linguistic map is political—with hard borders and fixed grammars. Before the printing press and the nationalist ambitions of educators, Europe's linguistic map was rather blurry and undefined—just like its petty principalities. From Norway's northern cape down to Palermo, each village could comprehend the next but often not much beyond.

Luther unwittingly aided and abetted this linguistic consolidation. By translating the Bible so lovingly into the language "of the mother in the home, the children in the street, the common man in the market place,"[5] Luther ensured that from church's pew to school's desk it was his Saxon German that became the verbal instrument of choice. When religion was a set of rites or a dramatic reenactment of eternal truths, a bit of Latin learned by rote sufficed. Comprehension was less important for the masses than the public act. But the reformers' insistence upon mental apprehension and their encouragement of schools to facilitate it meant that the days of many dialects were numbered. When printers printed, preachers preached, and teachers taught, they needed a common tongue—a *lingua franca*, so to speak.

That Luther himself did not envision such an outcome is quite clear. Which is why he insisted—as many of his heirs still do today—that each pastor master the biblical languages in addition to Latin. Luther's hope was not that his own *Lutherbibel* would become the standard text but that each and every preacher would, like a good Renaissance humanist, go straight *ad fontes*, to the pristine ancient sources, and translate a local Bible for their village, town, or crossroads—or at least be capable of doing so.

Alas, this vision was never more than a dream. The world never ceases to place such high hopes in the clergy, nor does it ever cease to be disappointed. This optimistic humanism soon foundered upon all-too-familiar cultural lines. Though the linguist pastor remains the ideal, reality is far behind.

Warm beneath our down duvets, we slumber late; Georg and Anja are much too kind to wake us. We must be off, and quickly. The sunny forecast is holding for the moment, but not for long. Snow and frost are predicted in three days' time. While Anja packs some sandwiches, I look over the maps one last time with Georg. There's a tricky bit of pathfinding ahead involving a certain church and a railway station. From there we'll start our ascent up the *Alte Schin*—the old toll road that Luther would have taken—to our hotel at Alvaschein.

We are genuinely sad to leave Tamins so soon, perched on its little shelf above the crashing river, the panorama of the Alps scrolled across the horizon. But we walk hurriedly toward Thusis, our final gateway to the true high country.

It is well-nigh teatime before we pass the aforementioned church and arrive at the train station above Thusis. We're obviously late. But even now there's no sign of the *Alte Schin* in sight. We were supposed to find a well-marked sign. In the muddled hurry of our departure and our harried walk, we must have missed something far below. Perhaps we were distracted by the views, for all around us rise great mountains—cones skirted with conifers and topped with rocky summits. It would have been easy to miss a little sign.

We turn back around and head toward the church again, rehearsing where we might have erred. After at least a mile, or maybe two, we both conclude that this way can't be right either, and we are fast running out of daylight. Who knows where our trail begins; and even if we find it, several hours of ascending await us along the precipitous *Alte Schin.*

I snap some photos of the pretty church, especially beautiful in the evening light, then we practically run back to the station—which we now notice is completely girded to the eaves in a cloak of carefully split firewood. Thusly warned of the encroaching cold and frantic to get somewhere fast, we follow a promising path into the woods. A couple of discouragingly dark switchbacks later, haunted by increasingly insistent visions of shivering sleepless through the Alpine night, we're startled to our senses by encroaching footsteps.

A pair of fifty-something ramblers, faces ruddy with both effort and vigor, come bouncing down the track swinging baskets full of *Pfifferlinge* mushrooms. They are the very picture of mountain hale and hardy: their eyes are bright and faces gently wrinkled in the way of those who often squint and laugh. The woman, Trudi, is plaid-shirted and jeans-clad, with a head of well-tended but windblown salt-and-pepper hair. Gaudenzio's permanent grin is half-hidden by a voluminous white horseshoe mustache. They live the outdoor lifestyle to which so many urbanites aspire but cannot buy with gear and mini-breaks.

The pair greet us with a radiant gentleness (not failing to appraise our footgear) and ask after our destination. Their faces quickly flip from angelic delight to a kind of parental dread. "Oh, no! Alvaschein is miles away. Hours!" erupts Trudi in motherly distress. "And it's not on this trail. You're nowhere near the *Alter Schin*, and even then . . . it's a whole day's walk! Perhaps along the road . . . but the tunnels! You'll never make it before dark." A brief consultation with taciturn Gaudenzio (whose name means "I rejoice"), and the magnanimous pair begins to escort us to their waiting car.

Sarah and I hem and haw between ourselves along the way. Our goal, we had imagined at the outset, was to unite Erfurt and Rome with our feet, to reconnect the cord that had been severed by the churches' subsequent divisions. It seemed so symbolically wrong to take a ride! I'm distressed by the scenic losses too. Now, for me, is where the real adventure should begin, where the climbing and the vistas fill both lungs and eyes with health and loveliness. The *Alter Schin*, we've heard, is so *wunderschön*, so marvelously beautiful; besides, it was almost certainly where Luther walked. What treachery on so many accounts! At last arriving at their car, we both reluctantly relent and pile our packs beside the fragrant sacks of mushrooms in the trunk. We ultimately conclude that if God sent us these angels to the rescue, we shouldn't begrudge the help. But we feel like we've cheated. It won't be the last time.

The car tears up the highway at a speed that is both frightening and fantastical. After so long traveling at foot-pace, it's nearly breathtaking. We ask about the trail we're in the process of bypassing, the *Alter Schin*. Trudi assures us that it is indeed a beautiful walk. The path was constructed by the *Säumer*, Gaudenzio chimes in, the sturdy guides who packed the goods and chattels over the Alps upon their horses and mules. While the highway we now hurtle up follows a narrow gulch beside the river, first on concrete pylons, then through well-lit tunnels, the medieval road climbs high above this deep and turbulent gorge. At times it's carved directly into the precipitous slope; at one point it goes through a hand-hewn tunnel one hundred yards long. I can well imagine off-season drovers hacking their treacherous way through solid rock with pick and hammer at cathedral speed.

A mere ten minutes later (rather than the threatened eight or ten *hours* on foot) we're crunching up the gravel drive of a rustic hotel, all dark-stained wood with windows flanked by red shutters and cheerful flower boxes. We say a somewhat sheepish but sincere farewell to our benefactors, and they deflect the thanks and praise upon their car, their "mule," they joke. They are our *Saümer*, Gaudenzio proclaims with a mustache-hidden grin and a deep historical bow, patting his metallic beast of burden.

The pious parish lady contacted the night before is standing in her door to greet us. She's somewhere north of seventy, with hair that's short and curled and dyed a reddish brown; her hands are swollen with hard work and arthritis.

The hotel is almost as tired as she is, its ambiance half-oppressed not by lack of cleanliness but lack of activity. The season is nearly over, and we are her only guests. We mount the musty stairs and plunk down on stale sheets.

Perhaps because we're not nearly tired enough, we again begin to lament, to try and come to terms with our betrayal. To travel one needs more than a horizon; one also needs a path. Now that the older ways are less traveled, and roads for cars the norm, it's walking that's contrived. We need only to imagine, by contrast, the human scale of Luther's world to see how today's mistake was well-nigh inevitable.

Partly. For it wasn't incapacity or fatigue, weather, or even poor directions that drove us into Trudi and Gaudenzio's car. It was, above all, time. We have appointments in Milan, in the Apennines, in Tuscany. We've booked our discount tickets out of Rome. No room for error is left. It is the unrelenting clock that broke our intact chain of steps from Erfurt.

While we had begun our trek as historical re-creators, we were in truth, step by distancing step, walking away from this dubious conceit. Our magnanimous modern *Säumer* simply made obvious yet another trench between an elusive past and the efficient modern landscape. In another sense, the swift rescue carried us toward a more practiced and less rigorous aspect of Luther's own walk. For us to get to Rome today we could go by bus or train, by car or plane, by bike or even boat for most of the way if we wanted. All of these modes could be completed on surfaces of such consummate smoothness. This is the normal way, the path of least resistance. Luther walked not because he could but because he had to. How accurate are we in our re-creation if we, unlike Luther, take the least convenient mode of transport?

While our disappointment settles in, our anxiety, on the other hand, lifts. Looking at our schedule for the days ahead, we realize that sticking to it would be painful, if not impossible. So Sarah and I agree—mostly silently—to take it easy over the Alps, enjoy the scenery, stop and see the sights that come. The clement weather is still holding, but for how long?

Walking the next morning from our forlorn *pension*, we're directed by our aged hostess toward the church in the neighboring village of Mistail, where our path picks up again. It is both ancient and sublime, she tells us tiredly, as if it's been a long time since she's ventured so far.

Fresco of Christ with the evangelists in the apse of St. Peter Mistail in Alvaschein

Half an hour later we walk into the sanctuary of Saint Peter's. It is the opposite of Baroque; any grandiose campaign to conquer the affections is refreshingly absent. At first it's all austerity and simplicity—great white-washed blanks, prepared for the spiritual projections of rich imaginations. But gradually a thousand subtle details begin to shine beneath the faded frescoes. High up in the apse Christ reigns as *Pantokrator*, Lord over the universe, his mandorla ringed by angelic evangelists, each identified by the customary ox, eagle, man, and lion. This throne hovers atop a colonnade of twelve apostles, each distinguished by his emblem: St. Peter bears his key, St. Jacob holds his staff, St. Bartholomew displays his flayer's knife, and so on. Each face is stoic within its nimbus, like icons of the East—the resurrected retinue of God's celestial court.

A triptych panel opposite depicts St. Gall exchanging food for wood with his familiar bear. Beside him a towering mitred bishop asperges a kneeling knight. On this side of the nave Jesus is not so mighty: the scourged Christ stands among what at first seem to be the instruments of his passion. But they turn out to be a field full of farmer's tools: reapers, scythes, rakes, yokes, dibbles, working tunics, a butter churn. It's an eschatological outcome; every last sword has become a ploughshare. Christ's mightiness has drained away, giving bounty to rustic peasant folk. Here is no philosopher's deity. Here is a helper in the very stuff of life.

What is otherwise a chilly refuge on the pathway to even chillier climes above embraces the pilgrim in eternal verdure, where the waning sun cannot dim the life flowing down from heaven. This vitality has crept up into the beams above, which squirm with painted coils of creeping ivy. It is the opposite of suffocating; other than the benches and the images, the space is empty. "Here is a place where the Holy Spirit has room to breathe," says Sarah, relieved that the place has not been colonized by the Baroque. So we stand and sing our customary morning prayers. Refreshed, renewed, and slightly chilled, we leave the church beneath the watchful gaze of St. Christopher, child in arm, fish at foot, patron saint of travelers.

The chapel has still another window to the past—and toward eternity. As we walk around the back we spot a gated lean-to set into the church's wall. Peering into the shadowy shed we see an entire cord of bones, neatly stacked beneath a pyramid of skulls. It is the parish charnel house! Such morbid features emerged from mere necessity: when a churchyard's graves were full, the warden had to free up space for new remains. But the practice stuck from deeper supernatural preoccupations. Nearness to the church and to the relics held therein gave protection from evil spirits, devils only recently—and barely—tamed. The bones were kept together in waiting for the resurrection, ready to be reanimated, as prophesied by Ezekiel, at God's trumpet call.

But habits cannot long remain without still greater meaning. What for us are grotesque signs of a distant mortality were for medieval minds the opportunity for salutary contemplation. You see it often in the portraits of the era: a skull and crossbones sitting at the feet of powerful nobles, as a *memento mori*, a reminder to the faithful that the pleasures of this life are fleeting and that death, that great equalizer, will soon take us all away. We should fix our eyes instead upon eternity. A wooden sign leans against the bones, giving voice to this muted tradition: "What you are, we once were too; what we are, you too shall be."

The later Luther might have been inspired by such a sight—but not as the occasion to contemplate mortality.[6] For him such symbols were but poignant goads to rebuff the devil's threats with sanguine life and hearty work. But the early Luther would likely have been terrified—not just of death but of the unbearable and unflinching judgment of Christ that would come after.

Until we too gaze unflinching at an entire cord of bleached bones—stacked either for the furnaces of hell or as benign reminders of a yet unrealized resurrection—we're not fit to wear the cowl of a medieval monk.

Our way from the sanctuary is lit now by pearly autumn light and accompanied by the muffled roar of the tumbling, bluish Shin River on its way to join the Rhine. Soon we also hear the steady mechanical hum of Swiss infrastructure. Penstocks plummet from invisible reservoirs far above turning whining hydroelectric generators, the wires of which buzz and crackle. We cross the river beneath the swaying cables of a river dredge that is scraping up the pebbly bed. These rocks will soon be mixed with cement and steel, only to be piled up somewhere else against the crumbling mountains whence they came.

From the river we climb an old path, now through forests, now atop the glacier-polished rock that is chipped away in places to aid the footing of former mules. It's steep enough to warrant frequent rests; now freed from hurry we happily indulge. Aromatic pines mix with thick-barked tamaracks. Above us rise green meadows dotted with sheep, while further still the bald summits loom.

A sprightly sixty-something woman, squinty-eyed and tanned from time outdoors, stands along our path picking crimson pea-sized fruits. When we ask her what they're for, she says they make a medicinal compote. Scanning us quickly from feet upward, her eyes note our light equipment and then linger on the sky above. She spurs us onward with grandmotherly concern. Lenticular clouds begin to form their frosty caps upon the summits, and high above them glitter icy cirrus streamers. Stratospheric sun dogs twinkle, goading us to hurry. The balmy *Föhn* wind cannot hold back winter for much longer.

At the village of Salouf, a cheery round of hunters dressed in drab wool flannels drink to their collective kill. Just beside them on a trailer a massive buck lies peaceful on a bed of fragrant boughs, its ten-point rack five feet across. In its mouth they've stuffed a torn-off branch of pine as a ceremonial last meal, a purported courtesy that is tempered by the puffy tongue lolling grotesquely to the side. The men are hushed in beery satisfaction, mighty Nimrods holding court. Above them on the lintel of the inn, a painting of St. George slays his writhing dragon.

That we are on the ancient road is confirmed by the succession of crosses and steeples and shrines and sanctuaries, strung as beads upon a necklace, marking the way from village to village, hilltop to hilltop. The modern road is distant, deep below, piercing dark, damp tunnel after tunnel, while we walk high and in the light.

All signs now point to a change in the weather. Before we come to Tinizong, the morning's cirrus have bloomed into a menacing wall of clouds. The village houses are built for any onslaught, squat chalets weighed down by roofs thick with tons and tons of greenish gneiss, ready for their load of snow. Sometime in the afternoon a hiker's signpost says that we're still six hours from Bivio, and I know from hard experience that Swiss estimates for hiking times are not to be made light of.

We hem and haw again about whether to go on or to hitch a ride up to our hotel. We're still not over our recent pilgrim treachery. When we walk into town and see that the bus will come in half an hour, though, the decision is almost made. The chain has already been broken, so it's easier to relent this time. On the bus we go. Up and up we wind, past lakes, past lonely huts, past clumps of thinning evergreens, beside the fading green fall pastures to Bivio.

The town is also known as *Stalla*, for the stables sheltering beasts of burden and for the inns harboring *Saümer* and their clients. It's a tiny village, probably not much larger than in Luther's day, perhaps two hundred souls to serve the transalpine traffic. A few very old buildings, as advertised by dates carved into thick stone lintels, are still standing. One harks back to 1591, and others, though probably much younger, seem older still: the whitewash flakes, the shutters crack, the wood is almost black with stain and age. If even possible, they are squattier and more stalwart than their siblings down below.

One more premonition greets us on the short walk to our hotel. Clouds of smoke, reeking with the mechanical scent of diesel, billow from a sizable garage. Inside, a mighty orange snowplow sputters to life, groggy from several months of summery reprieve. At first sight Sarah bursts with laughter, managing to get out between the giggles, "I don't think we're going to make it!" I try to hold out the possibility. We've got warm clothes, and I've gone running in colder temperatures with lesser shoes, I think. I say. I protest.

Around the plow huddles a confabulation of mustachioed men in coveralls, tending to the plow's assorted rattles and nobs with hieratic dedication. One portly fellow in thick aviator glasses sees us pause and look and mentions with a knowing grin, head nodding toward the truck, "She's sleepy." Like the woman earlier in the day, he scans us from toe to head, stares at our insubstantial shoes, then looks toward the greasy clouds above. He then offers us an obvious and cautionary interpretation of his smoking, growling oracle: "Tomorrow, snow."

We stop for dinner at a restaurant advertising *ragout de marmotte*, marmot stew. These furry mountain rodents stock up bulging layers of fat to fuel their hibernation. Once they fall into their wintry sleep, the locals go out looking for their holes and gather their torpid bodies in sacks, rather a harvest than a hunt. Intrigued, we ask the waitress if it's any good. She deftly steers us away. *Molto di grasso*, "Lots of grease," she says apologetically.

All is snug and warm in our attic rooms at the Old Post Inn. We spend the evening reading through a musty local history found lying in the lobby, *Bivio und das Bergell*.[7] It is lovingly produced and simply told, embracing rather than suspecting the legendary. One need not go all the way to Saxony nor to the pope's Rome to find traces of religious strife; one finds them even here in these isolated Alpine heights. Luther, who traveled through this hamlet with such traceless silence, seems to have left behind him a wake of spiritual unrest.

As Grubünden's burghers kicked off the yoke of Chur's bishop and adopted the Reformation, age-old intervillage rivalries took on a confessional bent. At first, according to our homespun chronicle, Catholics and Reformed got along quite fine, sharing Bivio's Saint Gall Church in almost perfect harmony. But the edicts of the Council of Trent and the creeping Counter-Reformation finally made their way up and over the passes from the south. In the year 1631, Father Rafello, a fervent Capuchin from Lombardy, arrived in Bivio and vigorously preached his partisan convictions. So offensive was his message to the Reformed that the local guides, well versed in ropes and knots, lashed him to a mule, led him as far as Bernina Pass, "warned him energetically with rancorous words never to return, then so terrorized the beast that he galloped toward the south at a furious rate."

This fate was not confessionally one-sided. Just down the valley in Marmorea, the Catholics had again regained a foothold when a Reformed zealot, Pastor Gian Agitta, showed up from Zurich. The villagers of nearby Tinizong, notably its women, were so incensed by his brazen profanation that they formed a mob. Armed with pitchforks, shovels, sticks, and stones, they "chased him like the furies beyond Septimer Mountain." In thanks for their courage, and "to this very day," our storyteller notes, "the women of Tinizong are allowed to sit on the right side of the [Catholic] church."

These smoldering indignities, first petty, then more grave, were fanned from year to year until Protestants and Catholics grew to hate each other as fiercely as rival gangs. Catholics heckled Protestant sermons; old Protestants from Soglio and Bivio "would empty the ash from their pipes into the holy water stoup" outside the Catholic church. Such constant desecrations came to an end only when the Grisons council at Chur intervened, allowing the Reformed to build their own sanctuary. This was all well and good except for the bell tower, to which the Catholics remained stubbornly opposed. "Only after numerous clashes and obstructions, in which many pistols were fired," did the Protestants get their bells—one hundred years later!

All of it seems so petty, almost comical: toothless codgers, no dignity left to lose, no life left to preserve, dumping ashes in their bullies' holy water; main-street showdowns, pistols blazing over the erection of a steeple. Though Bivio is but a village, the *Bergell* but a passage on the way to places greater and more important, such open confrontation between confessions is repeated all over Europe in ten thousand little villages and greater cites too.

Upon waking very early we shove aside the towering duvet and stumble to the window to glimpse our fate. The morning dawns just as predicted: snow, great white tons of it, everywhere: piled on rooftops, blanketing the forests, shawling up from below, still tumbling down in huge, wet flakes. Spread out beneath our third-storey room, the huddled village is completely covered. And there's no sign of it abating.

Early winter hits Bivio Stalla.

At Bivio we're just over one mile high, 5,800 feet. On a fair summer's day—days like we've had the whole week previous—it's a balmy six-mile stroll through flowering meadows beneath the green and sheep-shorn slopes to cross the Alps. But looking up into the blackness, we're more threatened than delighted. Somewhere up there, almost half a mile above, swirling in the winter storm, grumbling with nascent avalanches, lies Septimer Pass—Luther's way over the Alps, and what we thought would be ours too.

I suppose we could have continued, turned our walk into an ordeal, frozen some toes, eaten some limbs, and provided occasion for a rescue more dramatic than that of Trudi and Gaudenzio's. But we're still in our much-cross-examined sandals, for goodness' sake, which have finally reached their climatic limit. In another century we would see the *Saümer* milling about below, fitting tack and bridle to their horses. They would be unfazed by such a flurry and probably chuckling quietly—as had our snowplow men—at their anxious clients, who would be staring silently at the growing piles of snow. But both they and their infrastructure are no more; the refuge at the pass, once well stocked with warming wood, has long been taken down. All this makes our choice depressingly simple. We'll take the PostBus, not over Septimer at all but over nearby Julier Pass.

So with a disappointment just slightly shy of crushing, we climb aboard the yellow bus and into its cabin-comfort and plush fabric seats. It's our third ride in three days. Our broken pilgrimage, our historical re-creation, such as it is, creeps slowly up the hairpin turns. The summit of the Alps comes and goes in a moment while we stare out the windows in silence at the treeless expanse of swirling snow.

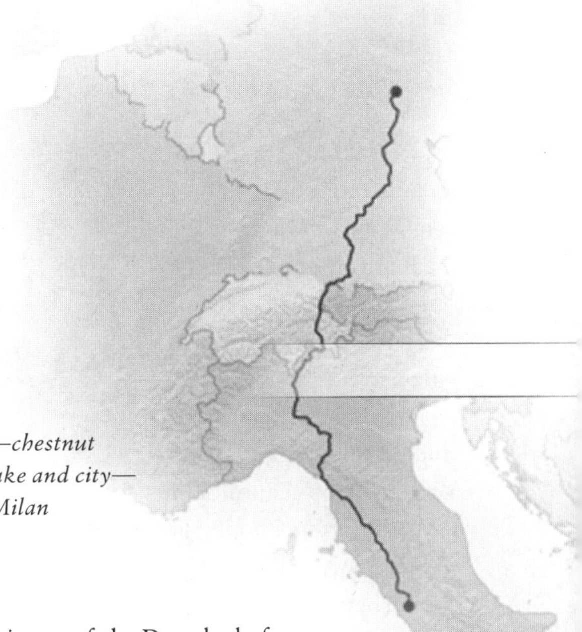

Six

Into Italy—at home in Chiavenna—chestnut groves beneath the Alps—Como, lake and city—sidewalks end—unfashionable in Milan

Our bus briefly crosses into the drainage of the Danube before climbing another, lower pass into the watershed of the Po. Then down we plummet into realms now named in Italian: Viscoprano, Stampa, Soglio, Dogana. Precisely at the border of Italy, as if divinely ordered, the sun rips through the clouds, unveiling the toothy Bregaglian Alps. Just minutes later we step off the bus in Chiavenna, and all of a sudden we're wandering stunned among chattering marketers in a balmy valley. Winter rages on the peaks above while summer sizzles here below, bathing us in warm Italian benediction.

It's difficult to describe just how high and craggy the mountains are—absolutely beetling over us. Necks crane. Long shadows are always present. Far above, itty-bitty cars zigzag along endless switchbacks. A crashing river splits the town. Scrappy buildings perch above the rapids, which mute the gentle noises of the town. In the distance a barely perceptible rainbow stands between us and the threatening peaks.

Some sort of procession is on the move. Platoons of men dressed casually in jeans and fleece march past us down the street, their round and ruddy faces glowing beneath distinctive green Tyrolean hats. Emblazoned pennants and banners hang from tall standards, which bob and sway to the slightly off-tune brass and drums of several high school bands. It's a parade of local Alpine clubs headed toward an inaugural mass, where a priest will bless the contenders for tomorrow's mountain-running championship. This is unmistakably Italy, in its hale Alpine flavor.

Chiavenna is a border town, and like so many other crossroads it has lived a liminal life, tied to both sides of the Alps and the successive powers that controlled the passes. Like its neighbors to the north, Chiavenna was quick to join the Reformation. Throughout the sixteenth century, the protected valley provided refuge to a long list of Italian dissenters: Agostino Mainerdi, Pier Paolo Vergeri, Scipio Lentolo, the anti-trinitarian Camille Rente, and future Heidelberg professor and Augustinian Canon Regular Girolamo Zanchi, who was pastor of the Reformed church here from 1563. The Alps, as with most imagined barriers, turn out to be a fruitful crossroads of ideas, where the practical necessity of intercultural encounter fertilized both mind and spirit.

Luther may have stayed on "Augustinian Street" in Chiavenna.

Wandering around Chiavenna in search of signs of Luther, we find little here that's very old. Ice and war, flood and fire have done away with almost everything. We spot a few remaining walls of an abbey-castle, destroyed in 1525. Luther would have seen it standing. The *Via Degli Augustini* seems more promising still, as does the thick, bulging rampart that lines its length. Indeed, here once was an Augustinian monastery. Behind the bulky wall lies the church of San Lorenzo, some parts of which were built in the Middle Ages. Luther could certainly have slept here.

He also could have seen the church's oldest treasure: an unbroken chunk of soapstone six feet across, artfully carved into a baptismal font. A frieze in bas-relief encircles its octagonal edge, and on it are carved cartoonish scenes in the uncomplicated naturalism of the Romanesque. First there are the fitting baptismal scenes: a godfather presents a child; an acolyte carries the paschal candle; a priest reads the liturgy from a book held by a deacon; a prelate in a pointy pileus hat carrying a processional cross leads still more clergy swinging smoking censers. To these obviously sacred scenes are added three profane figures: a blacksmith hammers steel before his forge; a guard pokes his head out of a tower; a gallant knight upon a horse holds his hooded falcon—atypical additions to a baptismal parade. But on second thought, they're not. That age did not divide such spheres so neatly. The noble and the serf, the craftsman and the burgher, all process toward the font together. The ritual is the glue, the common act that binds them all together, where they covenant with God and with each other to be fruitful and to multiply in vigor, in honor, and in virtue. An unbroken stone depicts unbroken Christendom.

The unexpected snowstorm has blown us into town a full day early. We call the man with whom we have booked a room and explain to him our predicament. He's very understanding and excessively apologetic that he cannot take us in tonight at his tiny inn. All this is on the phone in struggling pidgin French-Italian; we've reached our linguistic limit. He insists we come to his home address. He has a plan. We see him from his courtyard bounding down the stairs, telephone in hand, talking animatedly. He has some friends, and they have a room to let—just opened, too new to have been advertised. He herds us down the street into his waiting car, and we zoom uphill to our new quarters.

Emanuela meets us at the door, wiping hands upon her apron. Middle-aged, of middling height and build, she has waves of well-kept auburn hair bouncing above a tanned and smiling face. Her eyes shine bright between the crows' feet of one who constantly smiles. Her movements are both quick and calm, and never stop. We speak to her in French, which she recalls from deep schoolbookish depths and pronounces with the delightful staccato cadence of Italian.

She ushers us in and introduces us to her assembled brood; they lift their eyes willingly and unquestioningly when Mama blocks the TV's soccer game. Sixteen-year-old Sabrina dips her head demurely when presented as a laureled Latin scholar. Two younger sons—perhaps less lettered, or at least more interested in sports—are English students. Mama lays it on thick: here are two Americans with whom to practice. Off to the side, a wavy-haired thirty-something neighbor, Clemente, looking rather like a beached surfer, sits in his wheelchair; a car accident, he explains quickly. He's not related but this seems to be his actual family; he's an unofficial son. He had a Cuban girlfriend once, he says, so we speak to him in Spanish. Emanuela's husband Stefano softly descends the stairs from above. He is taciturn and tall, his dark hair close-clipped, and fashionably casual in his sweater, jeans, and Birkenstocks. He apologizes for his rough but ready German.

We barely begin to explain ourselves, stringing together a broken tale in several tongues. We don't really know Italian, but mixing French and Spanish with a clichéd singsongy lilt seems to work surprisingly well. We mention that our son is adopted, causing eyes to raise and hearts to warm. It turns out that two of theirs are adopted as well. As we begin to talk theology and church history in relation to our trip, a look of elated expectation grows upon Mama's face. When finally we mention Martin Luther—and that Luther likely passed through their very own Chiavenna—Emanuela gasps with excitement. Clapping hands together, she ushers us above to our apartment: "You're tired, you must rest and clean up. But you will join us for dinner, yes? I'll come get you when it's ready. Or come down when you are ready. Come down. You are at home." We rest as instructed and catch up on our various online chores—reporting to the world at large our disappointing bus ride over the Alps.

After a while Emanuela calls us down, and we take our places around a large round table that is crowded into the kitchen. Clouds of steam billow from a large bowl full of *gnocchetti* as Mama stirs in handfuls of grated cheese, globs of butter, and sprinklings of herbs. Surrounding our main course are wooden platters strewn with more blocks of mountain cheese and tiled slices of *bresaola*, a dry cured beef cut almost paper-thin. With our plates loaded with these local specialties and our glasses filled with wine, we begin to eat and drink.

"Do you like the *bresaola*?" Emanuela asks. "We would have had more but we didn't know you were coming!" We confirm, and truthfully, that all is perfect—to which she affirms that the most important thing is "fellowship, not formality!"

"Welcome, Americans!" continues Mama, hands outstretched. "I'm very happy that you are here with us. Because," she continues over pouring wine and clinking plates, "it is important for us to open our hearts to every person." She gushes, gesturing wide again, then touching her heart, "Your visit is an enrichment for me and for my family."

"Yes, yes," says neighbor Clemente in Spanish. "I must say that it's a pleasure to meet new friends, from the United States." Gesturing upward with hands and eyes, he warmly exclaims, "May God bless us tonight!"

Mama then looks expectantly at daughter Sabrina, who quietly whispers "Hello" while looking away and covering her mouth. Then to son Giacomo, *Inglese! Inglese!* ("English, English!"), after which he stutters the same embarrassed and robotic "Hello." Mama pushes him to practice some more, but he demurs. "Sabrina," he says, pointing toward his sister with his eyes. "She likes school. She likes to study."

Trying a different tack, Emanuela decides to get us talking. "Say something about America. Is it beautiful to live there?" We hem and haw as only academics can, saying that our country is so big, so varied in climate and geography, in demography as well, that it is difficult to summarize. Clearly this is too vague. Clemente pushes in Spanish, "Why is New York called the Big Apple?"—a pressing etymological question to which we have no ready response. "Why not check Wikipedia?" Sarah, a New Yorker herself, suggests. Some Americans we are.

We ask about Italy, renowned for both its Catholicism and now for its very low birthrate. "No, not Catholic!" insists Emanuela. "People here are mostly consumers. They buy beautiful things. For them children are too expensive." And she looks around admiringly at her little flock, almost three times larger than the national average. It's clearly a sore subject, and Mama starts talking about to their recent mission trip to Peru, life there among the poor, the charity they offer.

Then we turn to matters more apropos of our visit. While we were upstairs resting, silent Stefano did some research. "I read a lot. History, church history especially," he tells us diffidently.

"*Sì, sì.* My husband is an amateur historian!" bursts Emanuela with uxorial pride. I mention that my degree is in church history, to which she proudly effuses, "What luck we have you two here."

"This valley was Protestant in the sixteenth century," Stefano continues. "Chiavenna was under Switzerland, Graubünden—*Griggioni* in Italian. It was both Protestant and Catholic. The churches too were either Protestant or Catholic, or even shared. Many Protestants came to Chiavenna from Florence and Modena as refugees." He shows us a book from his personal library, *The Reformation in the Valley of Chiavenna*, paging through and pointing out all the references to Luther.[1] He seems very well informed, though he struggles to express it in his rusty German.

"A month ago my wife and I were in Volkstein, in the Groedental in Tyrol with the Jesuits," says Stefano. "Our friend is a Jesuit. Now he's a guy who has learned a lot of history, a *lot* of history. . . . He talked a lot about Luther."

"*Sì, sì*!" exclaims Emanuela in Italian. "I see all these books that Stefano reads, and I got interested too. Just a few weeks ago we also went to a different conference, given by a priest from the diocese of Como. He talked for three hours straight about Martin Luther, his life, his conflict with the church. To me it was like ten minutes because I found it so interesting. The life of Martin Luther was *bellissima. Bravissimo! Bravissimo!*" she adds with waving arms. "The priest, he put Luther's life in its historical context. And he told us, too, what the pope had done to him."

Stefano adds while looking down and shaking his head, "Yes, the mistakes of the popes . . ."

"He talked about everything in that period, the Reformation . . . *Bello, bello, bello! Interessante.*"

What luck we have had, in our first foray into Catholic Italy, to come across a pious couple eager for confessional reconciliation. "It's not so often," says Sarah, somewhat surprised, "that one meets an Italian who knows about Martin Luther, and also likes Martin Luther. Usually they think we're talking about Martin Luther King Jr."

After her own recent and positive encounter with Luther, Emanuela asks us to articulate something more: "Say something about the meeting of all the churches."

"Yes," adds Clemente. "What do you think about the union of all Christians? For there is only one God. We can't construct a united world if we ourselves are not united. Are we far from achieving this?"

I respond (in French) with a packaged answer that is very theologically correct if not terribly illuminating: "It's something we must hope for, but which only God accomplishes."

Sarah echoes my caution (in her own less-than-refined German): "It takes lots of time for the churches to do this, because the Catholics treated the Protestants badly, and the Protestants treated the Catholics badly. The first step is to confess the truth, to say what has happened. And then we must decide together that this was good and that was not. We must apologize and forgive one another. And we must learn to speak well of the other. So often we hear only evil things about the other."

Stefano translates for the rest, while I affirm, "We must first have reconciliation, make apologies for all the wars, for all the dead, for all the struggles of the past."

"*Certo, certo*, of course, of course," they nod in a kind of reticent deference to our diplomas.

"*Geschichte*, history. *Human* history!" laments Stefano.

But our insistence on academic truth-telling is not nearly ambitious enough. Stefano dodges all our caveats: "We still hope there will be a coming together."

"We're a fast-moving people," says Clemente. "We are Italian! Hot blood, you know."

With these fiery, happy, polyglot words, we retire and reflect upon an evening full of marvels. Lutherans and all Protestants love to take the upper hand, to fixate on the unresolved transgressions of the past, to obsess about ongoing privilege and abuse. It's easy for us, for it's our script. And indeed, for many Catholics as well, especially those most invested in Catholicism's structure—much of which took form after Trent to resist and attack the Protestant cause—no quarter can be ceded.

In Chiavenna, the much-fought-over borderland, we can glimpse the squabbles of the Reformation in their setting—battles, political and confessional, imbedded in a world of princes, emperors, popes, bishops, and all their interwoven privileges. Living among the crumbled ruins of papal anti-Reformation politics, the local faithful see the justice of what Luther and so many of his Italian sympathizers sought, for which so many were driven to exile and of which today's Italians were so long deprived.

Our insistence upon reconciliation as a first and necessary step was also part and parcel of our northern, Protestant heritage. Emanuela, Stefano, and their clan offered us another heartfelt, modern Catholic way: why not get together first, and then as feuding sisters and brothers begin the process of truth-telling. It is already happening. Here in Italy's gateway, a faithful Catholic family has learned of Luther from a sympathetic local priest. Confessionalization, it seems, is crumbling before our very eyes.

In the morning as we pop in to say farewell, the entire family, all six of them, is assembled formally upon the couch under Mama's iron wing. Emanuela makes a solemn announcement: considering the trials of our journey, the ardor of our quest, the righteousness of its intent, they are firmly refusing any payment. We try to object and gesture to the many mouths to feed and children to educate. Think of the poor in Peru! But our protestations fall on deaf ears. We're as moved as they are and part under a joyous seriousness and renewed conviction: that we are truly brothers and sisters *now*, not merely great and future friends.

At Stefano's suggestion we hike first along the *Sentiero del Giubileo*, the Jubilee Path (established for a pilgrimage in 2000), then the old *Via Spluga*—a continuation of the route that crosses the Alps at Spluga Pass. We'll contour our way just above on the steep western slope of the Val de Chiavenna.

We are now one day ahead of schedule for a change, and after so many weeks of German rain and then Swiss snow, we grow drunk on the luxurious

Stony landscape above Lake Como

sun. The frost of yesterday lies in a different universe, while we walk through a balmy dreamland. To our right raging falls tumble down from unseen snow, while to our left towers the serried, snow-dusted ridge of the Bregaglian Alps. The chestnut forest is as lovely as can be, glowing and dappled with golden light filtering though the leaves. Upon the thick and spongy duff the spiky chestnut husks pile up, splitting to reveal the shining shells within.

Now that we are further to the south the buildings are spared the worst of frost and damp, and there is a proliferation of ruins. Countless shelters of stacked stone stand roofless, filled with trees, open to the weather. Are they a hundred years old? A thousand? Even the roofs, where they are maintained, are made of stone—not delicate slate but slabs of rock inches thick, tons and tons of them shingled atop massive timbers. They're covered with lichen and moss and seem to age with geological rather than human time.

Our trail traverses hamlet after nearly abandoned hamlet. In one particularly rustic village peppered with such ruins, we meet a rare resident, an older aproned woman with a bent back and a wizened, weathered face. *Bello, bello!* we gush, gesturing with appreciation at the beauty all around us—the sun, the mountains, the waterfalls, the chestnut woods, the old houses built to last. She looks blankly all around, frowns, gives a nonplussed shrug, and replies with a single adjective of her own: *vecchio*—“old.” One can well imagine the toil it is to clean and to heat the houses and to chink the walls, how damp and chilly and relentless it must feel in the depths of winter, beneath the constant shadow of the peaks. What’s charm for us is to her a curse. Perhaps she pines for a daughter far away in Milan, who seldom visits but stays safe and comfortable in a modern apartment, surrounded by insulation, heat.

Out of the woods and down a silent, sunny street we greet another lonely soul. This seventy-something bids us to his roadside stoop with a wave of a hand and mutely offers us a seat. His body is slight and over-clothed, his face broad and weathered like that of so many mountain people. His bright eyes shine with a watery shade of blue. But his most conspicuous accouterment is a white handkerchief around his throat. When we take a seat beside him in the shadow of his house, he rasps a greeting, lifting the veil to reveal his weeping stoma. Hearing that we are walkers come from afar, pilgrims, out on a warmish day, he jumps up spryly, disappears into his open garage—cluttered with many decades of unfinished business—and returns with bottles of beer for us all. Between his airy Italian and our incomprehension, there’s little to say as we sip our draughts, but it doesn’t seem to matter. He’s happy for a bit of company. As we sit in the shade, the brief moment expands to fill the hours, the days, perhaps eternity with fellowship.

Here on the northern rim of Italy we’re at the edges of a life displaced and out of sync. Everything is as it used to be, though now overgrown by the decades and the centuries. Five hundred years ago, the general population was an order of magnitude smaller, but the countryside was fuller than it is today. Along the road we walk would have rolled a steady stream of carts and commerce: barrels of wine, sacks of stiff dried stockfish, entire convoys of salt. In the backdrop of the nodding columns of mules jouncing down the cobbled path, the drab masses hoed their hardscrabble life from the plunging slopes.

We walk for miles and miles along terraces of dry-stacked stone, up cantilevered steps and stiles. These steep mountainsides have been made flat at great cost and effort. But what once was heavily cultivated is now completely overtaken by the forest, left to be broken apart by bulging roots before tumbling to the valley below. But nothing, even winsome contemplations of decline, could dampen this, the most glorious and picturesque day of hiking we’ve had so far.

A nice place for a picnic overlooking the Valchiavenna

A bit further on, where the valley takes a turn to the west and the Chiavenna River empties into the Lago di Mezzola, stands a chapel set deep beneath the mountain wall. It is dedicated to San Fedelino. To enter we climb a couple of steps and then descend into a damp and dusky cave-like sanctuary lit by feeble candles. It is rather like a tomb—and with good reason, for here we find the remains of its eponymous patron, a Roman soldier converted to Christianity, who, facing persecution, was chased long and hard. His pursuers finally caught and killed him on this spot.

After this somber meditation, we try to find an exit from our chapel's holy promontory. We follow a promising path for few minutes and end up at a dock. To our left is the lake; to our right a vertical cliff several hundred feet high. Perhaps there might be a ferry to round the point, but there's no sign of anything and no schedule posted. We backtrack past the chapel and beyond and find ourselves below a slope of car-sized boulders. There seems to be a path picked through the rocks, marked by bright red points of paint. And so we start to climb. Up and up, impossibly up, until again we enter into the regal groves of chestnut trees. The sun on their upper leaves glows yellow-green in the evening light.

Atop the dizzying climb, sweaty and winded, we come across another chapel. What a prospect for our prayers! The summits to the north tumble down, their snows spent, to meet the balmy forests of the south. From our chapel-outcrop, the whole horizon unfurls from left to right like a blessed scroll with a gospel message: Now you are in the south. The dark gate is past. Warmed by the setting sun and buoyed by the vista, we gambol down our darkening trail.

After a night near the water's edge in Dascio, we head out to catch the morning ferry. Long ago we'd decided that it was neither safe nor advisable to walk along the shores of Lake Como. This is a great shame, as the scenery is grand, the weather clement, the people warm and friendly. But try as we might, we could find no proper way to walk. There is a path that winds among the hilltops of the northern shore, but following it would add days of tiresome ups and downs. So in lieu of roads or circuitous scenic routes, we went the way of many a medieval monk and took a boat. Unlike our passage in a bus over the Alps, this is a shortcut we had planned. While a pilgrim was supposed to walk, it seems as though the occasional ferry was permissible.

And a good thing, too. From Dascio to Sorico the lovely terraces and cobblestones and chestnuts continue, and from there it should have been a quick and easy walk along the water's edge. But all the way to Gravedona we're forced to scurry along the lakeside highway, darting along the shoulder, hearts thumping from adrenaline. There is frequently no sidewalk, and the traffic is truly terrifying. At one point we climb over a fence into an active construction site along the water—an improvement in our safety. To walk from here to Como on the road, tackling tunnels and unending streams of motorists, would be suicide.

From the dock at Gravedona we board a hydrofoil and are soon racing across the lake. A foaming wake extends behind in broad bubbling curves, while an Italian flag flaps vigorously above the prow, wetted by leaping sheets of spray. Sprawling villas basking in the autumn sun go by; just beside them crowd ranks of cramped apartments scrambling for their prestigious place on the steep shoreline. An instant later, so it seems, we arrive in Como, a drained swamp gridded by the right-angle minds of Roman engineers.

Still vibrating from the ferry's rumbling diesel engines, we pump our way quickly through the town, stopping only to admire the cathedral—which

Luther likely saw, with some puzzlement perhaps. For in place of the usual guard of bishops and saints, the bronze portal is watched over by a pair of pagans: Pliny the Elder and Pliny the Younger. The marriage of classical wisdom with Christian truth is as ancient as theology itself, though seldom so overt. These famed natural philosophers, uncle and nephew, here ward off ignorance with the sound foundation of reason. In buildings we have already seen—in Ulm's choir first of all, a work of similar vintage—philosophers sing in antiphon to their biblical compeers. But here it is less the harmony of human thought than the buzzing of local pride that installed such heathen paragons. The Plinys are from Como.

We may be uncomfortable nowadays with such admixture of local politics and orthodoxy—at least when done so overtly. But not so for historic Como, where church and city seem in patriotic competition. Buildings encroached and practically devoured the cathedral, and the city hall overtook it in size and luxury. Then in a gesture of ambiguous significance, the city hall donated the highest stones of its spire to the church. For in generously providing the tower's building material, the very mineral stuff of city power now sits atop the church.

We walk quickly to get out of Como, past the Renaissance piazza, all scrubbed and gleaming marble, down scruffier alleys, scarred and patched by constant renovation. Our path takes us under the Roman triumphal arch, black with soot and sprouting everywhere with weeds. Just beyond, we leave the crumbling historical dreamland and enter the creeping sprawl of greater Milan, still twenty-five miles distant. We sleep lullabied by the white noise of traffic.

The next morning, just two days after the snowstorm of the Alps, we feel no less out of place as we start to walk across Milan. We hike on highway shoulders and ephemeral sidewalks, squish through empty catchments, skitter across bawling traffic circles as menacing as any mountain cataract, as enervating as any airplane runway. Comically jaunty crosswalk signs picture obviously running children, an older brother dragging his harried, pony-tailed little sister. What are they running from? Or to?

The pedestrian does not so much cross Milan as wade against its mighty currents, its haphazard development, its cracked sidewalks, its disappearing rights of way. The metropolis looks oddly familiar to us Americans. If one wished to replicate the experience, it could be done by taking the commuter train to West Orange, New Jersey, then trying to walk back to Penn Station—possible, perhaps, but equally insane. Here, it's as if Cousin Vinny had taken all the chaos and anarchy of his Jersey childhood and re-created the nostalgic scar. Here is Europe's most American city—hardly a resounding compliment.

Walking across the sprawl, I wonder if the powers of chaos have not triumphed over order. For a built world overlain by conflicting ideologies cannot hide its incommensurate visions for the pace and quality of life. The contradictions are painful to both foot and mind. The greatest monument we see all morning is a circular parking garage: pure in form, glittering in execution, and futile in intent—for there is no center, no evident purpose for its location. And yet a stylish orange walkway extends from it across a thicketed ravine, and at the end a bank of automats, both to pay for parking and to dispense breakfast.

The aural assault approaches intolerable, and Sarah and I soon find ourselves practically running, driven by reptilian panic past miles of gated lots, grass-crumbled asphalt, yards enclosed by threatening spikes and warning signs to *attenti al cane* ("beware of dog"). And to stamp it all we pass a shop completely dedicated to weights and measures, as if everything that is meaningful needs a number.

I search my maps for an alternative to this aggravating route. Finally, at Cantù, San Pietro of Verona comes to our aid, rescuing us from exurban darkness. This thirteenth-century Dominican was murdered by Milanese Cathars for preaching against their heresy; the billhook that did the deed lies in a nearby church's reliquary. A short pilgrim trail commemorates his flight. Just a jog to the right, a plunge though some brush, and the harrying roar disappears. Nature asserts its own soothing order. We are hikers once again.

How relaxing it is to walk beneath the chestnut trees and beside the gentle clacking of the drying corn, to stroll twenty feet deep in an ancient rut, and not to have to struggle against the currents of modernity. Spotted saffron butterflies flit among the bushes; patient caterpillars munch away the undersides of leaves with blunt strokes, leaving behind a popcorn palimpsest. Even now along the less-traveled streets, the creepers creep, the climbers climb, the roots flex concrete-breaking racemes, the lizards scurry furtively from crack to crack. And in a cemetery the stones and photos are cold and dead, yet real flowers bloom. The constant tenderness of the living, rather than the monumental memories of the dead, keeps the morbid place alight and colorful.

Late in the afternoon we reach a nondescript geographical location called Seveso, about halfway between Como and Milan. At some point it surely had a more distinct identity, but now it is a train stop and a home to many large parking lots. It's here that we've arranged to meet my parents and our son.

Team Wilson left the day before from Strasbourg in the camper. After a night at a rest stop near Gotthard Pass, they should now be somewhere near. Right on time I get a text message from my dad. They are parked nearby. But where precisely? I try and call, but just when we begin to talk the line goes dead. Out of credit. We'd bought a card two days ago in Chiavenna, but perhaps that call to a foreign number ate it up. Or is it my dad's phone that's dead? I send a text of our coordinates. Nothing. We begin to panic. Somewhere here among the tarmac and rail yards is our dear family, sitting in a camper, waiting for news.

We plop down on a curb to regroup. Beside us is a car dealership—they surely have a phone. While I stay outside and wait in case my text goes through, Sarah heads inside with my father's number in hand, pleading apologetically to the secretary. In a panicked pidgin she sputters: "*Scusi, no parlo italiano. Telefono no funciona.*" This seems to have them intrigued and not a little startled. She asks again more urgently, gesturing wildly with her hands like an Italian: "*Telefono? Due minutti? Francia—salti!*" She shows some coins, indicating willingness to compensate them for their trouble. Recognizing Sarah's evident discombobulation, the secretary says, "Ooo-kaaay, *calma, calma!*" and hands over the phone. Soon she has my parents on the line but then comes running out to me, almost screaming that we need the coordinates of the GPS so they can find us. She stays out to watch the bags (and for my possibly arriving dad) while I run in to give him the numbers. It turns out that they're only half a mile away. Reunion assured, we thank the receptionist profusely, and she waves off our renewed attempts at compensation.

And so it is with heightened relief and comfort that we finally reunite, parked beside the railroad tracks, hugging and chattering about what's happened since we parted in Bregenz. It's hard work traveling against the grain, trying to walk while everybody else is driving. To coordinate the two is even harder. But now we'll have our family with us nearly every night from here on out. They will follow us and carry our heavy things. And when there is no inn—or no room—we two can doss down in the camper.

Stocked well with food and water, we park among other RVs in a nearby lot designated for that purpose. We cook some pasta, eat some cheese, and drink Italian wine. While walking through Seveso, we'd seen a secondhand shop and bought a giant plastic T. rex for Zeke. He's thrilled and slightly frightened by it, but he's even more excited by all the TV he can watch while Farmor and Farfar are driving. We relax in familial fellowship, then settle into our mobile bed, crowded but calm. Very calm.

Screeeeeech! Just as we are nodding off to sleep, a ruckus arises from our nearest neighbors. First we hear some animated shouting, then silence, then more screeching tires seem to carry the conflict away. Relieved that it's all over, we peek outside our curtained windows, then lie down again, alert. Only minutes later the screeching rubber returns, this time closer. Our now panicked five-year-old begins to cry. We hear a thud followed by the shatter of breaking glass. Now Sarah and I are wide awake, barking orders: "Zeke, lie flat!" "Dad, drive!" Conscientious Zeke in the bed above the cab worries that he has no seatbelt, but now's not the time to explain. My dad fires up the little diesel, and we drive away in haste. A couple miles down the road, we pull into another lot—this one full of tractor-trailers and retirees, it seems. Perhaps this one will be calmer, we hope. And it is.

Only partly rested, in the morning we resume our urban scramble where we left off—beside the car dealership, along the train tracks. Despite all the concrete, there's no environment more abstract than a modern city. By comparison, even the most Baroque of monuments is a pillar of clarity. For to interpret the city's forms and eruptions one must become an archaeologist of the imagination. Today's Milan is not a city at all, historically speaking, but just a sprawling urban area. As such it testifies less to the immense effects of the machine age than it does to what the human mind resorts to when given large enough tools and the freedom to use them. What we get reveals the novel and hubristic assumption that the land itself can be circumscribed and cut up according to our own quadrilateral rationality.

And what a strange rationality it is. I keep wondering why that sidewalk ended at the border of Varedo, why the ditch is the only place to walk along the Viale Brianza in Gattona, what perverse incentives have caused the most populous region of Italy to be the most inhumane. To ply these roads, one ought to hang up the footwear of the pilgrim, don the metal jacket of a car, and contemplate the arbitrary nature of what purports to be urban planning.

We stop for lunch in what seems to be a very local joint. It glitters with that superficial splendor that quickly fades beneath fluorescent lights. Its cluttered counters are pressboard covered with Formica. The signs, fridges, and napkin dispensers are freebies from the cola and the ice cream vendors. A television blares above; gambling kiosks beep and blink below. Fat men, bald and dressed in fleece, chitchat over beer and coffee at the mirror-backed bar. We eat a *piadina*, a kind of baked sandwich using pizza dough in place of bread.

Block by gradual block, the ideological confusion of outer Milan resolves itself into something more comprehensible. Apartment buildings swell in size; sidewalks stop disappearing; bicycle viaducts tunnel under *superstradas*. Instead of homespun cemeteries, there are now mall-sized mausoleums lined with row after row of red brick silos, warehouses for the dead. An endless stream of cars go in and out to pay—and pay a lot for—their respects. Forests of construction cranes spin on spindly legs, nodding to their mounting concrete creations, growing Babels in this, a modern Mesopotamia. Then at last—dwarfed in canyons of skyscrapers and concrete, drowned in the sputtering exhaust of a river of cars and buses, ears assaulted by the swarms of scooters—we reach downtown.

The streets are packed with particularly natty fellows and elegant ladies dressed up to the nines. We've stumbled upon the last day of Milan's renowned Fashion Week. This year is the rebirth, apparently, of crochet—the bulbous yarn kind made by grandmothers. We see lots of it, in infinite variety and color, dotting shop windows along our route. Surrounded by the well-dressed crowds, we suddenly feel very out of place. Sarah and I look at each other in our polyester shirts and zip-off pants, backpacks dangling with sink-washed socks. Until now all these practical things have been our comfortable companions. But here they jangle upon our dusty frames with an almost audible dissonance. In not one single way is our garb, our mien, our path *à la mode*. Even Grandma's ugly afghans would, apparently, have been better.

As night approaches, we reach Milan's huge Gothic cathedral. Before it in the open plaza the city's din is diminished, the skyline hidden, leaving the

Basilica of Saint Ambrose in Milan

pilgrim in a temporal eddy. The recently cleaned façade glows a hue of ivory. It may be Gothic in form, but it is certainly Renaissance in detail: gone are placid Marys and languorous apostles of the north. Here the heroes of the Bible are poised in pregnant motion, like so many togaed Telamons bearing the church through history with muscled ease, contrapposto. Luther would have seen none of these, for almost all of the church's forest of statues were put up long after his time.

Since we're on a Luther quest, we head to the only "Augustine" on our map. It's a tiny thing, a small chapel on a narrow lane made even narrower by cars parked on either side. An inscription above the door in Latin capitals announces: "Here the blessed Augustine, called to the light of faith by Saint Ambrose, was washed in the heavenly waters." The heavy oak doors are closed, so we can only speculate. Luther stopped here, we imagine—we hope—to pay homage to his order's patron and, in particular, to that patron's baptism.

It's almost completely dark when, hurrying to our hosts, we stumble upon St. Ambrose's actual church. It was here that this aristocrat, courtier of the emperor himself, was seized by public acclamation into the office of bishop. It was here as well that with his honeyed tongue he wooed the up-and-coming rhetor Augustine from his Manichaean follies. Nothing of the original is visible, but the present brick building was rebuilt upon the classical foundations in the eleventh century. We don't linger, as it's almost Italian dinnertime, and we have to make it to the home of Eric and Valentina.

I found Eric's blog online while investigating routes through Italy. He hiked the Via Francigena from the French border, not just to Rome, but all the way south to Brindisi, the port from which the pilgrim boats used to leave for Jerusalem. I wrote to him about our walk, and he immediately invited us to stay with him and his family in Milan.

Eric is an American married to Valentina, an Italian. They have a burbling son just shy of two years old. Both of them are journalists who cover various Italian matters, mostly business. But Eric's first love is walking, and he knows what pilgrims need for food: quantity. They feed us piles of pasta and pour cascades of red wine, while we complain—perhaps too much—about our harried, almost comical crossing of Milan. I mean, who walks across Milan? They understand our troubles all too well. Milan is big and fast and noisy and frenetic. The two of them feel constant pressure to move and perform. It's a common joke that even Milan's old *nonne* vent to their hairdressers about how stressed they are.

In addition to having walked the length of Italy, Eric has trekked to Compostela, too. Having a small child has put his trail days on hold for now, but it seems from his far-off, placid look that he's a bit envious of us. Someday he will hit the pilgrim path again; someday he will don his pack and shed the superfluities of life.

Eric interviews us about Germany, about Luther, and fills us in on the Via Francigena, which we'll be following from Pavia south to Rome. Eric's pilgrim ways are agnostic—the same as most other pilgrims in our Western world. It's no longer Christian piety that calls people to the Caminos of the world but a perception that modern life is lacking, a suspicion that our day-to-day lives partake in but a portion of reality, that to encounter the world, as well as the human spirit, one must face an unknown road and set off for a distant goal. Our purpose is not so existential, but neither can Sarah and I claim, though we walk in pilgrim Luther's steps, the motives of his age. We go not, as Luther did, in expectation of a trial, in hopes of penance, into imagined floods of cleansing saintly blood.

We ask Eric and Valentina about Italy's Catholicism, a question clearly higher on our seminary-educated minds than theirs. They answer with near blankness. For them it is a cultural relic whose morals have left a heritage of mixed worth and whose ecclesiastical machinations make Christian faith difficult for many people. The corruption of a few bishops—as with other politicians—and their connections to the mafia are open secrets. Some résumés are enough to inspire several Dan Brown sequels and to fuel the hungry fires of conspiracists everywhere. Valentina sees this sort of nastiness all too frequently in her line of economic journalism. For our secular hosts, the need for Martin Luther is still quite present: not as a theologian or Christian thinker but as a personification of the ongoing need for ecclesiastical reform.

For centuries certain Catholics have chafed at these unspecific criticisms, for they negate the good the church otherwise has done. And as Luther generalized about his Catholic enemies' ills, so Catholics have perennially made Luther a scapegoat for all ills and a stand-in for heresy itself. We can understand the vitriol, even if it's wrongly placed. For here in Italy lived and grew a flourishing Western Christianity, with armies of saints and courts full of bishops and cardinals. We can see their virtues and devotion transformed into platoons of statuary. In a world where it was one of a very few functioning institutions, the church beautified and comprehended this world and depicted another, better life to contemplate and look forward to.

Full of pasta and tips for the weeks ahead, and radiant with wine and pilgrim camaraderie, we retire to a back room of Eric and Valentina's flat. There between crisp cotton sheets, we rest contentedly, happy in the thought that tomorrow we'll leave behind the tangle of Milan.

From Eric and Valentina's home, it's a short and noisy walk to the *Naviglio Pavese*. The old canal—and the path alongside it—will take us straight across the plain of the Po to Pavia, the old capital of Lombardy. The rumble of the metropolis is slow to diminish, but nature soon regains a foothold. The canal itself is choked with reeds, and the path we walk on is half-strangled with encroaching shrubs. Abandoned warehouses, having lost a few tiles to the crackling frost, then a few beams to creeping rot, now slump into the loam—more victory for natural forces.

As the city fades from view, a novel rural landscape appears. This is rice country, at least since the late fifteenth century when Ludovico Sforza discovered and promoted this grain's cultivation, taking full advantage of the swampy surroundings. Canals were carved, ditches dug, dikes levied. The enterprise was still young when Luther walked through. It's harvest time. The paddies of rice are drained and dry. Yellow stalks, their reedy bases stained by many months beneath the flood, bow beneath their heavy sprays. A creeping combine scythes its way through a field, stacking straw and blowing chaff behind.

Come quitting time, a steady stream of joggers, cyclists, and in-line skaters dutifully do their cardio. It's quite an impressive crowd for such a flat and monotonous footpath, until we realize that there's nowhere else for them go: it is the only surface free from cars for miles around. It's a lesson we ought already to have learned and which will be repeated again and again. Italy, like America, is a land of the automobile. By merely walking we have left behind the quick and easy way of glass and metal and all its infrastructure—that ubiquiscape of global commerce, its ceaseless movement unstopped by any weather.

Once, just once today, does the far past insinuate itself—a distant Renaissance façade, the Certosa di Pavia, a Carthusian monastery. Did Luther stop there? Say his prayers? Have a meal?

The monotony that is so convenient for machines is brutal on the body. Sarah suffers her worst blister of the entire trip. And I mistreat it with a searing, alcohol-soaked thread. To forget the pain and tedium, as well as to prepare us intellectually for the weeks ahead, Sarah starts reading Dante's *Divine Comedy* aloud. We limp our way into Pavia in a spitting rain.

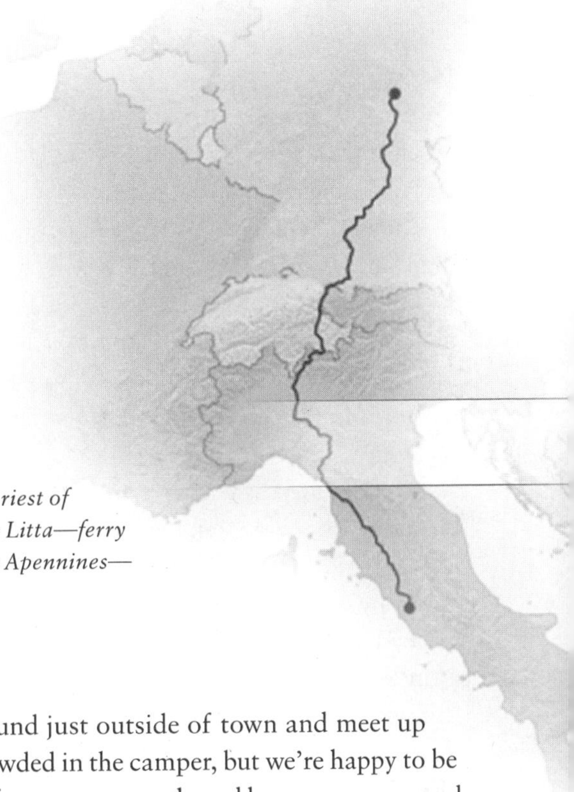

Seven

Augustine's mortal remains—the priest of Santa Cristina—the mayor of Orio Litta—ferry across the Po—Piacenza—over the Apennines—scatological issues—marble

We take a city bus to a campground just outside of town and meet up with our family. It's stuffy and crowded in the camper, but we're happy to be together. This will be our pattern from now on—a hostel here, a campground there, our nights divided between our tiny mobile home and pilgrims' lodgings.

As we bus back into town the next morning, the driver refuses to take our fare. One must buy the tickets at a kiosk, he claims, much to our confusion. The night before we had no problem paying on the bus. We ask where such a kiosk may be found, and he points us to some vague point down the road. So we just get on, thinking that surely he must not care if we pay or not in such a ludicrous situation. But we are wrong. As he pulls away from the curb, he whips out his phone. A few stops later, no fewer than six underworked and consternated transit police get on board. Their coffee break, perhaps, has been annoyingly interrupted. We look around, wondering why they're here, until we slowly realize they've come for *us*.

They swagger down the aisle with a gruff show of "What's all this then?" We attempt to explain in our sham Italian how we had paid the driver the night before and that this driver here refused our money. We'd gladly pay, we say, and try to pay our fare to them—and mortally offend by the evocation of a bribe. They quickly realize we're hardly crooks, just novices, and insist that we descend and buy a ticket at a kiosk. They herd us off at the next stop and point us toward a newsstand where we can buy our ticket. Standing on the curb, we see the chattering pack pull away in the bus paying us no heed at all, satisfied with a job well done. We only had one more stop to go anyway, so we ignore them too and continue on foot toward the tomb of St. Augustine.

Though there is no evidence one way or another, we are bold to assume that Luther walked through Pavia. It would have made sense, at any rate. As longtime seat of the Lombard kings, it was then much more important than today's sleepy almost-suburb of Milan suggests. But more important for us and for Luther, it harbors the well-traveled remains of St. Augustine, patron of Luther's order and the single largest source for the reformer's famed theology of grace.

To claim for Luther the mantle of St. Augustine is nothing special. The bishop of Hippo was and is the single most important theologian of Western Christianity. Medieval thinkers of all stripes claimed Augustine as an authority. So broad was his influence, so diffuse his patronage, and so reliant were all medieval theologians upon his corpus and looming holiness that it is an exceedingly delicate matter even to know what may have qualified as "Augustinian" in the late Middle Ages. Historian David Steinmetz claims at least five valences to the label "Augustinian," the broadest being "the theology of the Latin West in general."[1]

The multiplicity of his sway is complicated still further by the sheer breadth and comprehensiveness of Augustine's own activity and reflection. Just as there are now many historical Luthers, there are as well many Augustines. There's Augustine the anti-Manichaean, arguing against those who would damn all things physical; Augustine the Neoplatonist, filtering his reflection on God through a mystical renewal of Classical philosophy; Augustine the anti-Pelagian, resolute against those who claim the perfectibility of human desire; Augustine the churchman, opposed to Donatist schismatics; Augustine the architect of the Western collaboration of church and state. Within this panoply lies the evangelical Augustine, the theologian of grace. Luther's Augustinian order certainly had no monopoly on its patron.

In the textual confusion that reigned throughout the rise of Western Christendom, moreover, Augustine's writing itself was as obscure as his later influence was clear. After the various sacks of Rome and Carthage, Hippo and elsewhere, manuscripts and transcriptions flew about willy-nilly—randomly copied, haphazardly summarized, cut apart and reassembled. Scholars are still finding lost letters in obscure archives. That is to say, today we have a much more comprehensive view of Augustine, theologian-saint of late antiquity, than would have had a scholastic of the Middle Ages. Such a scholar knew Augustine less as a person than as a collection of quotes assembled from canon law—more precisely from the *Corpus Iuris Canonici*, a collection compiled first by Gratian in the eleventh century. Context, so vital for our own historical consciousness, was conspicuously absent. Augustine was often just a blunt authority.

This skeleton of Augustine's corpus was beginning to take on a bit more flesh by Luther's time. Complete books of the church father—rather than mere isolated quotes—were among the first incunabula. It seems from Luther's notes that he had ready access to the complete and scholarly edition that was published in late fifteenth-century Venice.[2] The establishment of the Augustinian orders, both Canons and Regulars, and their deep engagement in parish life led to a renewed appraisal of Augustine as a pastor who cared for troubled souls.

Particularly important for Luther was the interpretation of Augustine offered by an obscure Erfurt predecessor, Jordan of Quedlinburg. Drawing from a broader collection of Augustine's writings than typical for the fourteenth century and from the so-called Rhine mystics, Jordan developed instructions on preaching, confession, and what we would now call pastoral care or spiritual direction. These documents were essential for the structuring of Luther's inner and outer life in the Erfurt monastery. Many of Luther's objections to the practice of penance—particularly that it inadvertently fostered spiritual vice rather than promoting virtue—can be found already in Jordan's oeuvre.[3] Luther's Augustine was less the champion of church authority and more a font of pastoral wisdom.

In his 1545 "Preface to Luther's Latin Writings," the aging Luther described his basic Reformation discovery in familiar terms: he was struggling with Paul's epistle to the Romans. What's not so quoted but equally important is that he reports checking his new insight against Augustine:

> At last, by the mercy of God, meditating day and night, I gave heed to the context of the words. . . . There I began to understand that the righteousness of God is that by which the righteous lives by a gift of God, namely by faith. . . . Here I felt that I was altogether born again and had entered paradise itself through open gates. There a totally other face of the entire Scripture showed itself to me. . . . Later I read Augustine's *The Spirit and the Letter*, where contrary to hope I found that he, too, interpreted God's righteousness in a similar way, as the righteousness with which God clothes us when he justifies us.[4]

Justified by faith, but also verified by Augustine, Luther's Reformation could proceed.

We're on our way to see this Augustine's remains. His bones, venerated in his home of Hippo, were evacuated with North Africa's Catholic priests who feared of the bones' desecration by the ruling Vandals, who were partisans of the Arian sect. For two centuries the bones lay safe in Sardinia, only to be overtaken by the Saracens, who conquered the island as a stopover to newly occupied Iberia. Luitprand, the wealthy king of the Lombards (712–44), paid the colossal sum of sixty thousand golden crowns to ransom them. After

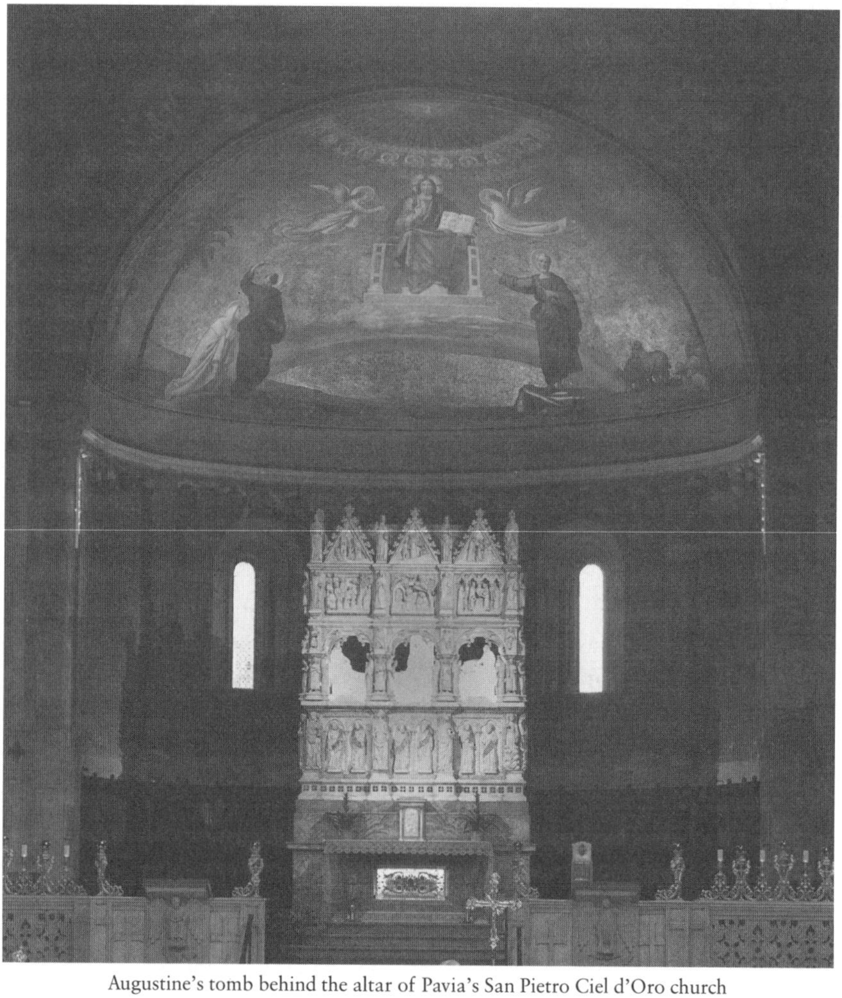

Augustine's tomb behind the altar of Pavia's San Pietro Ciel d'Oro church

a journey across the sea, the relics landed at Genoa to huge ecclesiastical fanfare and made a swishing-robed and crozier-nodding procession through the Ligurian hills, across the Po to Pavia. Here they lie at final rest, tended by Augustinians in Saint Peter's of the Golden Ceiling.

We peek our heads through the doors of the old and run-down-looking church. There beneath the coruscating apse, embowered in a spiky Gothic sepulcher, surrounded by gold-framed panels of glass, the citizen of heaven holds his earthly court. Morning mass is underway with the faithful filing forward, so we must keep a polite distance. We pay our silent respects from the entryway and set our course again toward the south.

From here to Rome we'll follow the Via Francigena, the "Way of the Franks." Based on the tenth-century itinerary of the English bishop Sigeric the Serious, it starts in Canterbury. Though the route has authentic pedigree, in truth it's Italy's answer to the success of Spain's Camino de Santiago. It's not the way that Luther went, precisely, but it's close enough—and more importantly, it's been set up with walking pilgrims in mind, something not to be discounted in car-dependent Italy.

After the heavenly sights and holy contemplations of the church, the atmosphere that meets us outside is noisy and polluted. Under the blanket of fog that's settled atop the Po, we walk through traffic out of town. After Germany's scenically routed Jakobusweg, we are at first perplexed when the very officially blazed Via Francigena takes us around a highway's cloverleaf interchange. It's wide and lightly traveled, so it doesn't seem unsafe, exactly. But it's jarring nonetheless. There's little else that can make you feel as small and slow as walking up an exit ramp.

At last we reach the countryside, leaving the paved *Via Cremona* and descending into the fields of rice-stubble. Our route zigzags on dirt roads lined with ditches ten feet deep—drained now for the harvest. The yellow mantle goes on and on, broken here and there by crops of poplar pulpwood trees, green-leafed still and waving in dark patches on the horizon. Beyond silos and mills, the shallow depression of the Po lies covered in haze to the south.

Around midday, at the very moment we begin to think of lunch, the Trattoria San Giacomo appears, almost in the middle of nowhere. A sandwich board out front advertises a *Pranzo di Lavoro* ("workers' lunch"), which seems like a perfect meal for a couple of hungry pilgrims. Ten euros will buy each of us a starter, main course, side dish, wine, and coffee. The New Jersey connection we sensed in Milan rings true again as the hostess leads us through the modest entrance into a labyrinth of halls, all billowing with starched curtains and kitsch, full of chattering *lavori*, then finally seats us in a distant room. Servers whisk in plates of *bucatini* with *salsiccia piccante*, asparagus risotto, then roasted guinea fowl. All this is washed down by a flagon of effervescent table wine. Only the stiff espresso and our postprandial march keep us from falling straight to sleep. It's the first time in quite a while we've taken such a midday pause. There won't be many more of these: as the autumn days grow shorter, our distances get longer.

Across the fields later in the afternoon, Santa Cristina and its church stand out distinctly. It's not the greatness of the old building that is most apparent now, but the scaffolding. Two tall cranes tower above.

Our guidebook tells us there's a pilgrim hostel here, so we circle around the church knocking on doors. We finally raise a harried and disheveled priest, who hastily shows us a spartan room above the parish hall, furnished with two creaking metal beds. Passing us the keys with no ceremony at all, he resumes his frantic chores. Below our window we watch him watering the plants, chattering on his phone. A parish lady drives up and talks at him for some time; he listens in patient silence; heads nod, then she drives away. When I go down to offer our donation, he's in his kitchen slurping down dinner while half-watching the TV. At some point he races away in a sputtering car, says mass, visits Mama, buys hardware—who knows? His seems a life of perfect self-effacing service. A bit too much of him seems missing.

We eat with our family in the camper, calm and relaxed among the trucks in the parking lot out back and free from the cares of our host. The town is tagged with the most evocative graffiti: a jilted lover has proclaimed her love for "Giorgio," then added accusations against his breach of faith, in many iterations, on many walls. It's certainly not art, but it's refreshingly frank.

Church bells wake us promptly at seven. As we buy our morning bread, we show our pilgrim passports, and the baker gives us a discount! It's the first such perk we've had so far. And then we're off into the settling fog. Fall is in the air, just barely. Hunters stalk the fields, dark silhouettes with shotguns akimbo and dogs snuffling through the stubble in search of gleaning birds. Motorbikes buzz invisible circuits somewhere in the distance. It's Saturday morning.

The past struggles disjointedly to assert itself against advancing modernity. At Lambrinia the medieval Church of San Antonio is stranded between rivers of traffic, an island of antiquity awash in the mechanical flow. At one point we come across a real castle, a kind of noble manor house, the Castello Procaccini. The eighth-century tower of Luitprand, Augustine's usher, is now enclosed in eighteenth-century elegance. Then there's another crumbling villa that can't keep it together either; its rusty gates and walls of disintegrating bricks guard another monument to a world that's gone, whose extravagance we can no longer afford.

On another bump above the plain stands Orio Litta. Again our guidebook gives a phone number for pilgrims to call; a chirpy voice tells us to meet her at the big church. Just as we arrive, an energetic parish lady of nondescript middle age drives up and shows us to the pilgrim quarters. The one-time monastery has very recently been remade into a public hall. Rollaway bunks and beds enough for dozens are filed away in a back room—an optimistic or premature gesture. Today we are the sole visitors and have the run of the pilgrims' penthouse suite—a drafty room in a tower beneath massive beams and terra-cotta tiles stacked so loosely we can see the stars between them.

After a chilly night, persistent knocking at the door awakes us. Dragging ourselves up, we are greeted by a cheerful mayor, an indefatigable fifty-something waif in baggy jeans and a puffy orange vest. He makes a point of personally greeting all the pilgrims. Finally noticing our still disheveled state, he tells us that he'll meet us in a few minutes. Dressed and properly breakfasted with the family—who've parked just below our window—we head out to a more formal civic reception. For the mayor and his couple of colleagues, we stitch together a broken quasi-Italian summary of our ecumenical quest. We're the first Lutherans he's ever met! We snap some portraits for the record. In light of this hearty greeting, the ongoing divisions between Lutherans and Catholics seem absurd. How can there be conflict between parties who don't know the other exists?

To cross the Po we've called ahead to Danilo, owner of the one-man one-boat *Transitum Padi*, the Po Crossing. There is a footpath we could follow over the river on a bridge, but it would add at least a day. Besides, a ferry is more authentic and certainly more charming. We arrive at ten o'clock sharp to hear the distant whine of a motor. Clanking down the metal ramp onto the floating dock, we see Danilo's boat skimming toward us upon the glassy calm. The Taxi Sigerico, named after the English bishop whose logbook inspired the Via Francigena, pulls in before us with the watery equivalent of a screech. Out bounds Bilbo, an affectionate and damp-smelling mutt, followed by his hefty master. Danilo, dressed in baggy sweat clothes and plastic clogs, helps us into his little boat.

At the crossing of the Po River near Calendesco

We race across and down the river. Bilbo's friendly ears and lolling tongue flop in the wind. Riparian woods, mere smudges suggested by the fog, peel by. Our white wake bubbles up in long, slow, dissipating curves. With the same shocking rapidity we experienced in the bus a week ago, we seem to arrive almost instantaneously. Bounding Bilbo leads the way up and over the levee, then down to Danilo's riverside hospice.

Danilo is innocently proud of what appears to be a sinecure and gives us a tour of his generous compound, a rambling assembly of brick and arbors gathered picturesquely about a tree-shaded terrace. It abounds with signs of its significance and exudes an ahistorical pride of place. He shows us a true impression of the aforementioned Sigeric's foot, a miraculously enduring remnant of his tenth-century crossing. A wooden placard advertises the distance to Rome (352 m), Santiago (1,240 m), and Jerusalem (1,842 m). It's as if this very spot had been a pilgrim crossroads since time unknown. Rivers being meandering rivers, this is manifestly false. But we get into the charade with Danilo and ooh and aah over the dubious relics. His guestbook, entitled evocatively in Latin *Liber Perigrinorum* ("Book of Pilgrims"), plays the part of ancient archives, though it dates no earlier than the 2000s. We patiently page through the signatures and comments of his illustrious guests: a minister of culture, a priest, a senator, and even our recent friend Eric with whom we stayed in Milan. We pay our fare, get a stamp, then resume our trek to Calendesco.

We seem to have left the rice behind, for fields of tomatoes now surround us. A creeping tractor sprouting impossibly long and spindly arms—like some sort of arthropod—sprays a sterile-looking field. We walk by foamy mounds of surfactant, toxic signs of the tractor's recent passage. A few fields beyond, a skeleton crew harvests truckloads of tomatoes by machine. It doesn't seem particularly efficient, as thousands upon thousands of tomatoes are squashed upon the ground. The rest are gathered first into dump trucks, then poured into trailers still more cavernous, which lumber away to be pressed into Italy's famous purées and sauces.

It's difficult to envision an Italy without tomatoes or the Po without its rice, but we must. Herbicides and trucks aside, Luther would never have seen these crops at all, which were imported from the recently discovered Americas and other far-off places. Neither would he have seen corn, tobacco, squash, peppers, sunflowers, or even potatoes. (Imagine eating gravy with crushed peas, and you'll have a better idea of Luther's German cuisine.) All these staples, which seem so deep and indelibly rooted in Europe's cuisine, came from afar, and relatively recently.

Our walk among the crops comes to an end as we crawl our way with traffic through the miracle miles of Piacenza. It is a sensory cacophany: the dull roar of the *superstrada*, the tearing of the tires, the reek of gasoline and exhaust, the clanging of scrap metal, the silence of abandoned warehouses, the half-finished hulks of concrete housing, idle fleets of factory-fresh automobiles, the mute microwaves pulsing from the cell towers. A sign announces that here the Romans fought with Hannibal's advancing armies, though this information is easy to miss beside the much larger and more familiar advertisements for McDonald's, Blockbuster Video, and Burger King. It's the background noise of global capitalism, the economic pressing of the landscape into a familiar and infinitely reproducible mold.

Once in Piacenza proper, we can more easily see the old stuff. A renovated building highlights a former elegance with a "truth window"—exposing half a marble arch. We pause just briefly before the fissured brick façade of St. Hilary's. Its triple bays, arches, and spiraling pilasters make me think of Venice's Rialto. It's a lone pulse of calm in a town that's otherwise buzzing with backhoes, piled with sand and stone and empty sacks of cement. Renovation is in full swing for this, the oldest Roman town along the Po. On the far side of the city stands a monument to the city's Roman heritage: a copy

Amid this visual chaos near Piacenza is the sign for the Via Francigena, our route through Italy.

of the Capitoline wolf suckling twins atop a pair of pillars. In case we didn't get the reference, a bar just opposite, The Romulus and Remus, lets us know just who the twins are.

The friendly mayor in Orio Litta told us to ignore the guidebook's suggestions for Piacenza and head a couple of miles out of town. We are to knock at the door of San Lazzaro. This we do, and just as promised another parish lady, almost a copy of the previous, emerges and entrusts us with the keys to a hostel down the road. We see the tiny metal plaque declaring the Ostello San Pietro, crowded beside the busy highway. It's a remnant of brick opposite a supermarket and its sprawling parking lot. The hostel has been recently renovated—including a washing machine!—and is absolutely void of guests except for us. We eat with our family in the camper parked across the street, then return and close the shutters, hoping they will dull the highway noise.

At Piacenza begins the *Via Emilia*, an ancient Roman road running ramrod straight from here to Rimini, on the Adriatic coast. It's the route that Luther would have taken through Parma, then Bologna, before crossing the Apennines to Florence. It's where we part from Luther for a couple of weeks—as much for safety as for scenery. Perhaps it does exist, but we can find no continuous walking route along his probable path. So in place of Luther's trail, we'll follow the Via Francigena, which goes further to the west, mostly through Tuscany.

Having learned our lesson about scheduling in the Alps, we decide at this point to skip some flat and less interesting terrain to gain a couple of days more to cross the Apennines. Since taking the bus in Switzerland, we feel that we can cheat here with a mostly clean conscience.

Luther's Via Emilia is now a *superstrada*, still as straight as in his day but eight lanes wide—rather like the New Jersey Turnpike. We're glad that we decided not to walk this way, just as a New Yorker would prefer not to walk to Philadelphia. We hurtle down the asphalt in the camper, past a couple of exits, then head up a little ways into the foothills.

We resume our walk at Costa Mezzana. It's a drizzly, cloudy day—a farmer's blessing, a hiker's purgatory. We spend it rounding, mounting, and descending swells of green and red, our feet maddeningly weighed down by sticky gumbo clay. Shelters here and there are stuffed with hay, dry and safe. The smells kicked up by the rain are soothing and pleasant: wild mint, tangerine-scented cypress, rose, oregano, all mixed in country potpourri. From the grapevines, their leaves reddened by the autumn cold, hangs shriveled fruit, leftovers from the recent harvest. Pressed cakes of must, great purple wheels of empty skins and stems, rot pungently here and there in ditches.

Our fog-foreshortened vistas and our bogged-down feet come to an end beneath a solitary oak looming over a grassy hillside pasture. Hanging from its trunk we find, encased in a plastic envelope, a "Wanderings Book," a sort of hiker's register. It asks all passersby to share their thoughts. Sarah writes a brief entry. A few days later we get a response on our blog from Carolina, who wishes us good luck. She longs to make a pilgrimage to sacred sites but can't do it yet. So in lieu of trekking off to distant places, she converses this way with pilgrims near her home.

For a dreary spell we follow the Taro River, dredged almost to death by a cement factory and littered with scrap and sorted piles of fill. We dart across a terrifyingly narrow bridge at Fornovo di Taro, wincing as the trucks tear by and throw great rooster-tails of water from standing puddles. On the other side, we climb again into the clouds. Just before we stop for the night, we see in the gloaming a thousand gentle lights, dim glimmers glowing in a hillside mausoleum. Here as in Milan, Italians prefer to inter their dead above the ground.

There's no hostel where we stop, somewhere near the road to Sivizzano, so the family picks us up and we drive a ways up to a parking spot for campers.

My parents have prepared a big dinner of spaghetti. We eat it perched above a pleasant view, then sleep away the blustery night. In the morning, they drop us off just where we stopped the night before and head off to Parma to pick up my older brother Jed. He's flown over from the States to walk with us for a few days.

At Bardone, in the shining morning light, we find an ancient-looking Church of the Assumption, by far the biggest structure in the hillside hamlet. It's a sturdy, blocky building of Romanesque geometry, with little for ornament save the side door's lintel, where a cartoonish madonna and child are accompanied by an adoring saint. The sign outside says that the foundations date from the seventh century, the nave from the eleventh.

But the bulk of it, the same sign tells us, was reconstructed in the seventeenth century "to meet the liturgical demands of the Counter-Reformation." This meant, practically, the suppression of side-altars and their attendant masses for the dead—practices heavily criticized by Luther and his reforming colleagues, both Catholic and Protestant. The Council of Trent, both in response to the criticisms of the Protestants and as a result of its own internal reforms, had influence even here, an isolated village of the Apennines. So though the church is almost ancient, it also bears the signs of Luther's historical passage.

Hilltop villages like Bibola are a common sight throughout the Apennines.

Now that we've climbed up and out of the river bottoms and their attendant industry, we can escape the mental clutter of modernity and breathe a more ancient air. Mycological damp, fungal forests wet with decay. Hillsides leap upward on densely forested slopes, just now tinged with the autumn's orange and yellow. Here and there a string of terraces is holding back the hillsides. Around us spreads a smattering of hilltop villages, cascading roofs of red protruding from the forest. Stone walls, stone roofs, stone stairs, stone tower, stone pathways—the mountainsides dug up and stacked again in harmonious simulacrum. It's urban planning in three dimensions.

Today's walk is punctuated by such villages. One after another passes by, each built of beige stone, each overseen by a church's tower—sometimes toothed, like an ecclesiastical fortress. War seems a theme. The hamlet of Terenzo is tiled with memorials to the dead. Native son Antonio perished here for the Duke of Parma, defending local honor against usurping Charles V, Luther's adversary. Another plaque relates the gory death of Renzo Marubi, "bathed in his own blood" in another universe, at Selenj-Jar on Hitler's Russian front, January 16, 1943. More than sixty boys from this little wisp of a crossroads fell in the First World War, eighty in the Second—all martyrs to a now defunct martial spirit.

The trail here is as hilly as any we've seen so far, even in the Alps—and much rougher, too. It seems hacked into the hills by churning feet. We climb up channels tossed full of stones, through head-high ruts overarched by bushy arbors, down plunging stream beds that must be torrents when it rains. It really is the old, old path, hopping from village to village, church to church, monastery to monastery, crawling at a slow and contemplative pace from high place to high place. At Cassio we rest a moment in the minuscule Piazzetta del Pellegrino, the Little Plaza of the Pilgrims, another reassuring sign that we follow in the steps of many generations heading toward Rome. Over the course of centuries, the trickling traffic has left a geological mark.

With my brother Jed in the camper, we are now six! A pilgrim hostel is a must. We call another number from our guidebook and reach another lady with a set of keys in Berceto. She lets us into a huge, shuttered dormitory that dates from the time when each diocese had its own seminary. There are thousands of these mothballed buildings moldering throughout the Catholic world. This one is made yet more pathetic by an overgrown schoolyard, paean to the virile men shooting baskets and scoring goals in huffing respite from their studies. Our hostess marches us along what seems like miles of dark and musty halls into a somber room of soaring height. There in the feeble glow of our bedside lamps, we rest in the inner darkness, two breathing beings in that dusky cavern of bygone possibility.

Today we'll cross the summit of the Apennines. We eat an early breakfast in the camper with the family and are on the trail by seven thirty. Brother Jed is exhausted from his jet lag and won't join us quite yet. It will be a long day, and arduous.

Whereas before there were only hints, now it is undeniably autumn, chilly and damp as the sky lightens to the east. We climb up paths carpeted with fallen leaves, pointillist patterns in the squishing mud. Mushrooms of all kinds tumesce around us: little pink parasols, long white caps, tawny brown types fit for Alice's caterpillar, odd and disturbing ones dripping with black ooze, storybook red-and-white-flecked amanitas—the first of their kind we've ever seen. Sagging bushes wet our legs, drops of water trickle down into our socks, cold creeps down toward our toes. Scrubby pastures higher up are white with dew, almost frozen. Then we emerge from the forest into a fog swirling about the Apennine crest.

A herd of feral horses mills across our path, grazing protectively about their many foals. They are dapple gray, their markings blending with the drifting clouds. We clamber through some bushes uphill to circumvent them, slipping quite a lot and soaking up more dew. The vigilant and skittish horses watch us warily. Finally we come to a treeless ridge. We assume it's the crest, but we can't see much beyond our noses.

We stop for a hot coffee pick-me-up at the nearly derelict Passo della Cisa. It's off-season, and only one of the many houses and bars is open. There's a chapel too, dedicated to Our Lady, for the protection of travelers. Almost all of the traffic now rumbles hundreds of feet below, tearing through the mountains on a four-lane tollway. A little ways beyond the real pass, we see the *autostrada* far below: a stream of cars and trucks emerges from one mountain, hovers on stilts above the gorge, then disappears into the belly of the next, ignoring the terrain as best it can. There's no need for the old pass anymore, except for a few locals and some tourists. This once workday stop is now scenery. Bypass is the byword.

For all the stone-cold mountain architecture, unquestionable signs of the south appear. Clearings in the forest reveal terraces of olive trees, ripe with little green fruit; rosemary blooms in glowing cornflower blue; grapes hang from scraggly vines; whiffs of mint and oregano float through golden atmosphere. We see wild plums the size of blueberries, brilliant rose hips, wild geraniums, borage. It's not agriculture but gardening. Here there is no economy of scale—and no likely possibility for it with the land so steep. Poor folk live wholesome, timeless lives, embraced by fresh air and sunshine.

Or maybe not. A garden-gloved woman, bright eyes shining under her broad straw hat, bends over, trimming her garden. She shouts some muffled instructions to her husband, headed to town in a tiny hatchback. As we get close, the muffled words resolve themselves. The pair aren't hardy locals scraping by at all. They're English ex-pats! Retired from soggy Britain, pensions trickling, they've come to clear away the centuries of neglect and reinvest the hollows with their habitation.

The afternoon passes like a sylvan dream. The endless ups and downs have taxed our already depleted reserves and lulled us into a kind of trance. For hours we plod slowly through a fairy-tale scene of horses, chestnut forest, over stone-arch bridges spanning burbling streams. The fast-approaching darkness shakes us from our soporific haze. Our waiting family is likely worried. We end by running down the hill into Pontremoli.

We stay with the Capuchin brothers in their nearly empty cloister. The prior himself receives us. He's large, bearded, and bear-like in his brown habit. In a resonating baritone he queries us in perfect English about our trip so far and its greater purpose. Of Luther he confesses to know but little, though any effort to bring divided churches together gets his approval. He served for thirty years in Turkey, he tells us, and witnessed unfettered fellowship of Christians there who would be divided elsewhere. Perhaps, he opines, such spiritual vigor and robust life together might return to his native Italy once the church has definitively lost its privileges. Appropriate words from a mendicant. Finally, he asks whence we walked today. When we say Berceto, he gasps, then chuckles at our youth and audacity. But Rome as a destination seems to him quite sane.

The only road out of town is busy and narrow and has not a single provision for pedestrians. Our guidebook suggests we take the bus instead of walking—advice which Sarah and I summarily dismiss as both paranoid and lazy. At first there is a tiny shoulder, but even that concession soon runs out and is replaced by a large and looming retaining wall. There's nothing left to do but flatten ourselves against it, trying to be as thin as possible, and hurry. Garbage trucks and delivery vans hurtle down upon us with the frightening speed and disregard of people perennially late for their appointments; they make up time at our expense.

It seems like an eternity, but after a terrifying half of an hour we veer off the *strada nazionale* and enter a lovely countryside. The crystal-clear autumn light glitters on a million dewdrops. Fields fill with blue borage. At Virgoletta—hardly more than a presumptuous path hemmed in by houses—the blazes of the Via Francigena send us plunging under vaults and through inside-outside colonnades. It's another 3-D town. Around several more bends, we come out beneath the buttress—several stories high—of a city that covers an entire little hill. Flapping along its wall in the midday sun are the T-shirts, sheets, and towels of laundry day.

Everywhere the grapes are coming in: picked in the leafy vine-lanes, piled high in plastic buckets, bouncing down pockmarked paths on tractors and in car trunks, and finally ranged under roadside tents to be sold by the hundredweight. Swarms of bees slurp the juice dripping from the plastic pallets. Wafting up from unseen cellars into the alleyways rises the tart aroma of fermentation.

We end the day as we began, pinned to the side of a busy highway by rush-hour traffic. On our way into Aulla we spot our white whale of a camper in a supermarket parking lot. Memories of the morning's trauma in mind, we decide to hitch the last mile into town with our family. After eating a dinner of fresh porcini, Sarah and I sleep in yet another empty monastery.

Jed has recovered from his travels enough to walk with us today—a rather short jaunt up and over a ridge to the Mediterranean. As we climb in the cool morning hours, though, our thoughts are far from sunny pilgrim-pure. Jed—who has accompanied Team Wilson for two days now—reveals the hidden dramas of RV life. All has been well hidden from us by my magnanimous parents, who don't want to burden us with their hardship. The addition of Jed to an already crowded crew has not just heightened tensions but, even more exasperatingly, taxed the capacity of our vehicle's plumbing. The camper now has . . . issues—far too many of them, in fact.

To this surfeit is the added inconvenience that northern Italy seems to have entered the tourism off-season. The usual abundance of facilities for RVs has proved—one after another—to be completely closed for business. What ought to have been a rambling ride through the scenic countryside has instead become a frenzied search for the camper equivalent of a bathroom.

It all seems so absurd and scatologically funny from the outside. But it is a real dilemma. My scrupulous father has been forced into a life of petty RV crime. After reasonable—and even beyond unreasonable—efforts to find a legal dumping site, he spotted a German couple parked in their RV beside some railroad tracks, looking like they'd just concluded some sort of maintenance. My dad pulls up beside them to ask after their solution to the waste problem. After a quick and conspiratorial palaver with these fellows in frustration, he takes out the brimming "pot" and dumps it between the rails. If a pair of law-abiding Teutons can be brought to such delinquency, my dad too can make this closest possible approximation of the spirit, if not the letter, of the law.

It seems that certain locals are also less than entirely legal with their waste and even less thoughtful about its disposal. During our ascent into the Ligurian hills, just far enough out of town to be inconspicuous, we find a truckload of garbage: busted blocks, shattered glass, kinked metal, and disintegrating rubber have been dumped atop the forest litter.

But it can't suppress the overwhelming pleasures of a mountain stroll. Purple cyclamens dangle, propeller petals reaching back as if in a dive; ants tumble into their conical caverns; dappled green lizards scramble across the outcrops; gentle trickles seep across our trail; crimson berries of the strawberry tree shine like miniature setting suns. Pomegranates, red and waxy-ripe, droop from scrubby trees; olives go from green to black. Brilliant green stick insects, patiently awaiting their prey, pose on leaves in plain sight.

Just below Ponzano Superiore, a pen of repurposed bedsprings corrals a lonely dun-hued jenny and her devoted colt, who nuzzle our friendly hands over their ersatz enclosure. The pair waits and stares, glum and scolding, as we walk on. At the top of our climb, through a low saddle, we see for the first time the hazy darkness of the Mediterranean Sea. Container ships large as city blocks slide into the port of La Spezia far below.

We meet the family at Sarzana's railway station. After the recent trials of "the pot," today has not been easy for my dad. The GPS, or "GP-Stupido" as my mom now calls it, has led them several times astray. Most recently it had them turn into the station's busy parking lot, where they were blocked by a very low bridge. Honking cars crowded behind as he backed into their consternated ire.

And to add insult to this latest injury, the toilet already needs another service. "We're transporting poop all over Italy!" my mom exclaims, only half-jokingly. Here under the many eyes of town, even the tracks are off limits, so we must go straight. Like many nations with dreams of order, Italy has a comprehensive website to locate rest areas for campers. It sounds so nice and easy, but the system is far from transparent—especially if your Italian is iffy. We finally manage to find some dump site coordinates for the GPS and head out with low expectations.

Our satellite-powered cicerone gives us a very full tour of workaday La Spezia. We bypass all the historic sites and stick to the well-trafficked roads. I suppose that from a certain point of view, it's a more honest way to see a city than through the recommendations of a tourist brochure. Much bombarded by the war, La Spezia is grubby in the way so typical of ports—and of Italian cities in general. It's monopolized by cars and parking lots, fences and strips of dusty greenery. The soothing lap of the sea lies well beyond the towering containers, the colossal ships and cranes that load them.

After twenty minutes of blind and stressful obedience to GP-Stupido—and many suppressed expletives—we find ourselves before a moldy pre-fab sentry box and a decrepit gate. We pay our fee and enter into a ramshackle enclosure full of German, Dutch, and French retirees enjoying the bright Mediterranean sun about their RVs, their picnic tables set out upon the weedy broken asphalt. In one shady corner of the compound whirrs a rank of vending machines. In the other is our destination, a black and yawning hole that would finally accept our accumulated waste. The whole crew erupts with cheers.

With "the pot" properly evacuated at last, we find a place to park a bit nearer the old town and treat the crew to a celebratory meal out: grilled bream, wine, and tiny Ligurian olives. We have a very grown-up talk about our trip since Milan, discussing how to better manage all of the various unresolved . . . issues. Everyone leaves the restaurant in much better spirits.

We menfolk (Zeke included) spend the next day at the laundromat and in the internet café, eating pizza and our newfound favorite, a chick-pea pancake called *cecina*. Sarah and my mom take a women's day out, heading northward up the Cinque Terre coast to visit Portofino.

The next morning we start walking from where we had stopped, the railway station in Sarzana. With Jed along we're three again. As we leave the city behind, the morning's views are filled with familiar villages hovering on their hilltops, fortifications cutting crisp and scenic silhouettes. The light is hazy from the nearby sea and softened further by plumes of smoke rising lazily from smoldering brush. The fall harvest is on. Orange nets are spread beneath the olives trees like carpets. Gardens bloom with bright red clerodendron and flaming callistemon.

By midday we reach the remains of Luna, a Roman city-port that in its heyday boasted fifty thousand residents. That makes it larger than any city of Luther's Holy Roman Empire. Its riches were quarried from the hills above: marble of the purest grain, the kind that could be found throughout the classical world. Save a few bollards of rubble and mortar undissolved by the centuries, there's hardly anything to see at all. And it's been that way for a very long time. When Sigeric the Serious of Via Francigena fame walked by in AD 990, the city was already gone.

Thanks to modern archaeological interest, Luna is more visible now than ever. Bleached columns have been dug up and pinned together, like fossil bones of some extinct species. An info panel pictures the oval amphitheater as it used to be, with seating for seven thousand. Now only its topmost bits are sticking up, flooded by the earth, lapped away by sedimentary waves. Given enough time, every building is a sand castle.

Carrara marble is still the region's source of wealth. We can see the white scars clearly on the mountainsides above, and the zigzag roads that crawl up to the working quarries. From those peaks originated not only Michelangelo's David but works as diverse and far-flung as Rome's Pantheon, Siena's Cathedral, Washington's Peace Monument, and Abu Dhabi's Sheik Zayed Mosque. At one spot near Pietrasanta, we hear the whine of electric grinders through some bushes, then spy a sculptor in his studio *al fresco*, chipping out the right eye of a massive bust. The cope and coif suggest a cardinal; the rectangular beard a Babylonian king. Elsewhere we pass barnfuls of half-finished statues, littered among unworked blanks and chips and other lithic scraps. All these wonders and many more yet to be conceived are present within the hills above.

A yard full of marble blanks near Carrara

At one point we walk by the modern harbor. Giant cranes heft hunks of marble into waiting ships. Yards are stacked high with boulders waiting in the queue on pallets marked with their weight in tons. What doesn't make the grade is used for lower applications. It's aesthetically confusing to see the stuff of fine statues dumped into the sea as a breakwater or crushed into a chunky ballast beneath the railway tracks. Even the highway is lined with opalescent curbs cut from the stuff. What elsewhere becomes art is here the very infrastructure of life.

We bypass the upland route in favor of the seaside strip, anticipating fresh air and the soothing lap of the waves. We are disappointed. It is an unswerving swath of pavement lined by the weathered, low-slung buildings so typical of beach towns and cluttered by an excess of billboards, wires, and signage. A barrier of discount hotels and palm-thatched tiki bars guard the precious strand. It's the off-season, and the summer cottages are shuttered, their awnings withdrawn. Changing huts are empty, the deckchairs folded and stacked and secured against the winter storms by rope. We manage once to find a narrow entry to the deserted beach. There we gaze out over the gray sand to the gray sea beyond, little waves lapping dully beneath a gray sky.

We've arranged to stay at a hostel on the shore, still imagining some vague and fabled Mediterranean charm. Again, disappointment. The place is a blocky mass, intimidating and institutional, rather like an American federal building. In the weedy courtyard stands a crumbling dais, and in the center of it an empty flagpole—for what purpose I can only guess. There doesn't seem to be anyone else here besides the lethargic receptionist. Our first room reeks of urine. After we complain, we are reluctantly given another. This one merely smells of bleach.

The saga of the camper continues. The water tank and "the pot" are fine for a change, but the hostel receptionist, the noise, and the signs all warn us against parking along the marble curbside. So we are forced to drive many miles to find a proper campground. Once we arrive, my stoic father, at his linguistic and bureaucratic limits, absents himself for a calming walk. Mom cooks all of us some pasta, and after dinner my dad drives Sarah and me back to our antiseptic perfumed room. So much for the glamor of the Riviera.

Several days ago we got a message from Alberto, the head of the Via Francigena project at Italy's Ministry of Heritage and Culture. He somehow found our blog and wanted to warn us of an upcoming "problem" in Pietrasanta. A few days later he sent us an updated map of the path to Camaiore. We looked at his "solution" and noticed right away that it is not just many miles longer but also adds several thousand feet of climbing. We can't really figure out from what he's written what exactly the "problem" is, so we simply ignore his help and plow ahead.

Where the circuitous detour veers off, we persevere down a well-marked trail and quickly find ourselves hemmed in by insistent briars. More obedient souls might have turned back, but the recent paper signs stapled to the trees like blazes lure us on. The path itself seems legitimate, but the forest has all but overgrown it. We long for a machete to hack the grabby tendrils that turn our trail into a gauntlet.

Many pricks and gashes later, after much time lost extracting carnivorous spines from our (miraculously unshredded) clothing, we emerge into the calmest of clearings, a very beacon of occidental order and civilization. It is an olive grove covered in green nets. The owner looks up, unsurprised, from his vigil over a pile of smoking brush. He sees our bleeding legs and rewards our trespass with good humor, directing us down the driveway to the road.

In repayment for my parents' fortitude in the face of Italy's infrastructure, we insist on treating them to a proper hotel in Camaiore. It is dainty and adorable, complete with headboard cherubs, faux Tiffany sconces, and billowing drapes—a mother's paradise. My dad, true to character, is more fascinated by the novel air-conditioning installation. Zeke, who has grown weary and testy from the pent-up anxiety of camper life, is delighted to bed down with Mama and Papa. Come morning we are all in better spirits.

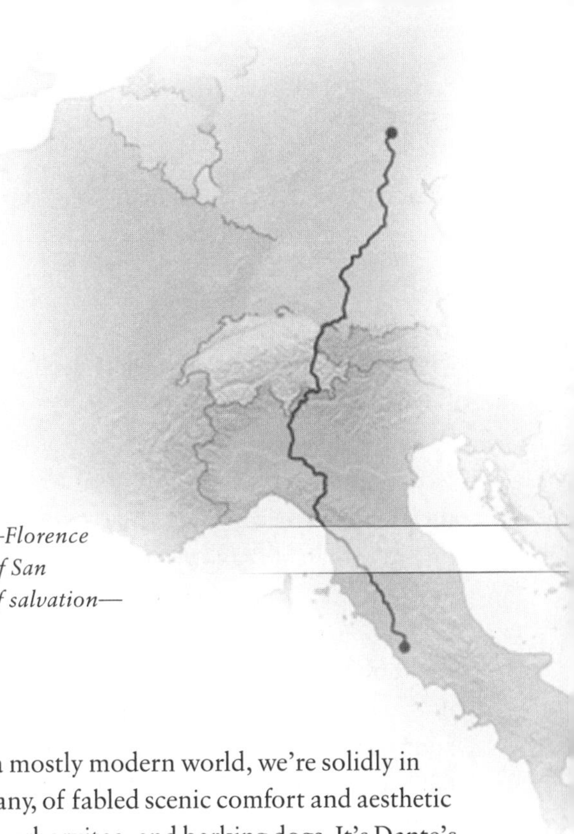

Eight

Lucca—new wine in old Tuscany—Florence through Luther's eyes—souvenirs of San Gimignano—Siena's architecture of salvation—up with Dante, down with Luther

After many days walking through a mostly modern world, we're solidly in the old country again. This is Tuscany, of fabled scenic comfort and aesthetic repose. Our path is lined by shrines, arborvitae, and barking dogs. It's Dante's native land as well, and we see, in Piazzano, a Ristorante Dante. Just beyond we spot another restaurant, this one much more sumptuous, advertising itself ironically as Purgatorio.

It's cycling country too, it seems. The peloton of the Giro d'Italia went by just days ago: graffiti painted on the road cheers mutely to the absent cyclists. At the height of the day some locals beckon us into the bar of their soccer club. The low-hung ceiling buzzes with fluorescent lights; a freezer hums insistently in the corner, empty but for half a dozen well-branded gelati. The room is full of stiff old guys with wispy hair confabulating over drinks; their cardigans are loose on the shoulders and tight around the belly. Our hosts treat us to some cold beer, and while I sip I notice hanging on the wall a kitschy, poster-sized portrait, drawn in pastel chalk, of Italy's most fabled cyclist, Fausto Coppi. He's mounted on his baby-blue Bianchi and carrying a victor's bouquet. I praise the likeness, and by revealing my (slight) knowledge of Italian cycling, I make fast friends with one stocky, glossy-pated patron. To hearty, beery salutations we take up our backpacks and press on.

Not long after we are striding along the *Fiume Serchio* into Lucca. Our path is lined with poplars. Their soaring branches wave in the breeze in their characteristically melodramatic way, swaying across the autumn sky with a calming shush, shush, shush.

"Well, Prince, so Genoa and Lucca are now just family estates of the Buonapartes."

This phrase, the opening line of Tolstoy's *War and Peace*, exhausts our collective knowledge of Lucca, one of Italy's most famous city-states. Even this tiny tidbit of trivia we only know second-hand, being students less of Russian literature than of *Peanuts* comics, which mention Tolstoy's long-winded work as a joke. Italy's landscape is so littered with greatness that I suppose we can be forgiven. But for over five hundred years Lucca's strong city walls prevented its wholesale destruction, even amid the maelstrom of Italian politics. Its institutional integrity was more fleeting, as it was conquered and controlled and bought and sold between a multitude of powers, from the Guelphs to the Ghibellines, Pisa to Bavaria, Genoa to Bohemia. But commercial republics, unlike their military counterparts, have flexibility enough to bend all ends toward profit. While the brawling state triggers reprisals and resistance, the arms supplier benefits from both.

We meet up with Team Wilson in a huge parking lot north of town. Today they've put Jed on the train to start his homeward journey. They're full of bonhomie and happy tales of their easy day of tourism. The trials of camper initiation seem to be fading, the possibilities it offers opening up. We all then meet up with Jonathan and Marian, old family friends who live in Geneva and are working against nuclear proliferation with the World Council of Churches. They are on their way south in their own camper and will walk with us for a couple of days.

We enter Lucca together through the northern gate, under the attentive watch of Mary. Our hostel is nearby, a room in the sprawling and off-season-empty San Frediano. Though we're not walking in Luther's steps here, we are reminded of him nonetheless, as this building was at one time the home of the Augustinian Canons, Luther's ecclesiastical brethren.

On the plaza just outside our hostel, there are images that remind us of Luther's theological afflictions too. A glittering medieval mosaic of a faintly Byzantine air fills the gable of San Frediano's church. Angels to his sides, Christ rises triumphant from his tomb. He is draped in billowing blue upon a throne, his right hand raised in blessing, left hand guarding the book of life. His face is stern, his nostrils flared. Unlike the madonna that guards the city, this Jesus is decidedly unmoved and unmoving. He looks down upon his subjects from eternal placidity, blessing with one hand, judging with the other. It's a vision we've seen all along our way and one that much vexed Luther.

We leave Lucca in Jonathan's company. Marian will drive their camper and see some sights with my parents and Zeke. We exit beneath the star-canopied gate of San Gervasius into the headache-inducing buzz of modern Italy and its cars. Along our exurban itinerary, the odd quince tree sags under its fragrant fruit, while the occasional field is full of cardoons—sprays of light green sticking out from their protective paper tubes like creatures from Dr. Seuss. We apologize repeatedly to Jonathan for the uninspiring scenery, assuring him, truthfully, that it has been much lovelier elsewhere.

The past works its way to the surface nonetheless, temporal intrusions in a sea of erosion. We eat our lunch upon the steps of a bronze-doored, ablaq-arched church of Saint James, built for pilgrims such as us. Just past Galleno, we leave the road for a precious couple of miles and walk on aged cobbles past medieval milestones, over wooden bridges, then through a sandy upland filled with blooming heather and dotted with dwarf pines. The mind deals easier with cliché, and it's with silly relief that we finally glimpse a postcard Tuscan scene: tufts of Aleppo pine, rows of pencil cypress, tawny villas circled with vines. Rosemary and thyme scents saturate each breath with evocations of elysian fields. The sun sets softly, a golden orb behind benignant, puffy clouds.

Marian and Team Wilson park our twin campers beside a field near Ponte a Cappiano—a town that warrants its name, for it's made up mostly of a covered bridge and the attached apartments. We cook our pasta, drink our wine, and conviviate much too late into the night.

Early the next morning, this time in Marian's company as well, we set out from the bridge and walk beside canals on levees. At Fucecchio we cross the Arno under a statue of Saint Christopher. When Luther crossed this river upstream at Florence it was not so drained and diked as it is today, and the swampy wetlands would have swarmed with mosquitos. Florence and its environs were known for infection and the evils of "damp air," as former generations called it, and Luther says that it was there that he and his companion got infected with the ague, possibly malaria.

This episode, one of the rare actual anecdotes from his journey, played a special part in the later erroneous dating of the trip. Because authors since Johannes Cochlaeus in the 1520s had assumed that Luther went to Rome to oppose the merger of his strict Augustinians with the less strict, there were few dates left that fit with Luther's certain whereabouts. The chronological key was this very sickness, from which Luther claims to have been healed by eating pomegranates.[1] Since pomegranates are ripe only in the fall, that little fact sealed the date at 1510, and so it was believed throughout the twentieth century.[2]

At San Miniato Basso, we get a coffee with Jonathan and Marian and await the arrival of our family to take them back to their van. It's a stop on the path we might have forgotten but for the strange and flying-saucer-shaped concrete church next door to our café. It's hard to say what opaque visions informed its architect. But more curious and revealing still is a bronze bas-relief memorial of John Paul II set up at the church's entrance. It lovingly recounts various miracles attributed to the former pope, who in 2010 had not yet been canonized or even beatified. Yet streams of light flood his likeness; seraphs flock about him; behind him a whole conclave of cardinals votes for his elevation. What perfect union of ecclesiastical administration and divine command! It shows powerfully the deep residue of ritual, the comfort in a sole figurehead and a clear hierarchy. Captured in this triptych is a miniature of the universe itself: holiness above, people below, and in-between the inspiring, mediating figure of the (not quite) saint. It also shows that the people of San Miniato Basso canonized John Paul long before the cardinals did.

Another message here is clear: John Paul is in himself a demonstration of truth personified. There is no abstraction, only incarnation. Beside such honest materialism, Luther's airy gospel seems such a wispy thing: that Christ himself came down to earth, that faith in him alone will save, that our actions here count less than an eternal calling. Though Luther insisted that Christians carry out God's deeds on earth by fulfilling the necessities of life, there's an abstraction in this stance that elides the overt goodness of a saint.

After our farewell to Jonathan and Marian, we strike south again. This time—as if to be expressly unfair to our recent companions—we immediately enter more postcard-Tuscan hills. Throughout the afternoon all is gentle and benevolent—until half a mile before our scheduled rendezvous with the family. There our bucolic country track is blocked by a clamor of signage and fencing: *Vietatto!* Danger!, says the sign, promising with little icons all manner of gruesome demise for those who trespass. We look a bit closer to see what all the fuss is about: power lines downed, it seems, and by the looks of it, none too recently. We're atop a rather steep ridge, its sides full of further fences and hedgerows. Brambles abound. There seems to be no timely alternative, so we ignore the surfeit of warnings and scale the fence. We walk on a bit and finally encounter the toppled power pole and a black snake of a wire stretching across the ground. It's quite clearly been disconnected, but we take no chances, stepping daintily over it to the other side of the enclosure. There we scale another fence, walk a few more hundred feet, and see our son running toward us from the camper.

Mom and Dad drop us and Zeke at the train station in Castelfiorentino. Their camper blues are completely gone. They've been with Zeke to visit nearby Pisa and its beloved leaning tower, whose popularity proves that imperfection is more interesting and enjoyable than pristine beauty. They're heading to the hills above the Arno for a brief pause from pilgrimage duty and to see the famous sites of Fiesole. Sarah, Zeke, and I are leaving the Via Francigena's hilltop ramble and taking the local train to Florence for a day—to rejoin Luther's steps ever so briefly.

Our tour of this jewel of the Renaissance is preposterously short. It's a rest day for us mostly, so we lounge about our hotel until nearly noon, editing photos, writing for the blog, reading and playing with our son—who's chary of the hotel's mascot, a squawking, finger-munching parrot. Zeke is also rather fascinated by the presence of a "second toilet"—the bidet—and incredulous of our explanations. When we tell him we're off to see the "sights" of Florence, he asks—reflecting with beautiful transparency the preoccupations of camper life—"the dump sites?" That's all he'll remember of Italy, we fear.

We meet up with our friends Paul and Melissa, who have just arrived from Minnesota. Paul's the one I hiked the Pacific Crest Trail with, and we've dabbled in many less involved adventures since. They'll be with us for a few days. After only occasional company in Germany, people seem to come out of the woodwork now that we've reached Italy. Today they have a reservation at the Uffizi Gallery; apparently one is needed if you don't want to stand in line for hours.

The Florence Luther saw was one of the greatest cities of his day. Though it had fallen somewhat from its high medieval splendor, it was still more populous than Rome—by quite a bit—and much wealthier too. Centuries of prosperity created fertile ground for lavish spending on the arts, which have become the chief attraction of the town since Northern Europeans started coming in big enough numbers to call it tourism, starting in the seventeenth century. But we Luther pilgrims set aside the aesthetic opulence and tour instead the humbler places Luther mentioned.

Perhaps eschewing such dainty luxuries for the eye is proper for our quest. Shrouded in his habit, Luther seemed blind to Florence's attractions—or at least he mentions nothing of them. And so we hurry through these illustrious streets, alternately with jaws agape, then eyes downcast so as not to notice what we're missing. Dodging cavalcades of tourists, we battle our way across the Arno on the Ponte Santa Trinita and enter the plain Piazza Santo Spirito and its eponymous church.

Here we have one of the scant pieces of real evidence for Luther's entire journey: his name is written in the church's register. He preached for his brothers and said a mass at one of its thirty-eight altars. Nothing more is known.

Santo Spirito is an austere building on the outside—just a massive expanse of tan stucco. Inside it is a different story, conjured by the genius of Brunelleschi. It is an earthly, not a heavenly church: the Corinthian columns

Luther said mass at Santo Spirito in Florence.

and semicircular arches keep the viewer's eyes on the ground. The nave is lined by altars, each one a minor patron's jewel, an artist's commission. Such were the economics of religious orders of his day, Luther's included. Their revenue depended on the constant recitation of private masses for the dead. Some of these altars Luther may have seen, while others were completed hundreds of years later.

The church still belongs to Augustinians. A young and bearded, plump and cowled friar greets us at the church's welcome desk—it's more of an art gallery, anyway. We introduce ourselves as ecumenical ambassadors of Luther, linking Germany to Rome with our steps. He embraces our quest with warmth and volubility—seldom, perhaps, do visitors have a spiritual goal—and insists we call him Ivan. He is a pilgrim himself, he says, and has walked to Santiago de Compostela (long ago, judging by his Friar-Tuckish frame). He's familiar with Martin Luther too and has no objection to him or his theology at all. "Luther was," he tells us with a mischievous twinkle in his eye, "a good Augustinian." He then takes out his wallet and hands us a calling card, wishing us well and asking us to keep him updated of our progress.

We receive his token with a dazed confusion. From Chiavenna on, all of our confessional expectations have been upended. It seems to be here in Italy—here where Luther met his fiercest resistance, here where popes and cardinals, vicars and theologians sought to reduce to nothingness the threat of Luther's message—that he now has the most attentive ear. It's as if a hunger for some parallel movement in the church has grown by the Reformation's very absence. Reform, it seems, and even the Reformation itself are now more interesting to Catholics than to their Protestant counterparts.

From Santo Spirito we push across the Ponte Vecchio against a still more seething mass of milling visitors, who bray their pleasure at the booths that line the bridge, shutters open, hung with candy and cheap trinkets. I can well imagine a disillusioned Luther, feet bare upon the icy stones, making his painful way from shrine to shrine to do his penitential duties, while surrounding crowds clinked their meager coins into predacious purses, leaving their costly votive, taking away a sham memento of their priceless voyage. There was no reason not to spend their money. Medieval pilgrims routinely left a will and testament behind, a tacit admission that they might never return. In such a case the purse, whether tiny or large, had no need of returning full. Why not exchange the filthy lucre for the holy things of faith?

Today's visitor is more aesthete than pilgrim. But aesthetic tourism also has at its base a kind of journey of initiation—for art is more than form and skill, and viewing it is a practice imbedded in a certain reading of history. "The Renaissance" is a term of later invention and problematic pedigree, and for modern historians bent on progress, it superseded the "Middle Ages"—a label of similar vintage full of sometimes tacit, sometimes overt anti-Christian polemic. It supposes a "rediscovery" of classical antiquity disabused of accumulated ecclesiastical glosses. Its foil—the superstitious devotion to the ritual and control of a hegemonic church, an oppressive communitarian intolerance for individual differences—is a gross simplification of what for many centuries, for millions of people, over an entire continent was their principal vision of reality. But Neoclassical bridges, harlequin cathedrals, and spindly Tuscan columns are more than a rebirth of Arcadia. They are the competitively pious expressions of fearful believers before a mighty and exacting God. We may doubt their inner convictions, but let us for a moment see ourselves surrounded by the stone-hewn prayers of earnest Christians, quaking before God's judgment.

Walking by the Uffizi, we wave a symbolic hello to Paul and Melissa; the line does indeed snake far out the door. We lament what we are missing: Fra Angelico, Botticelli, Bellini, da Vinci, Titian, Michelangelo, Caravaggio, the whole catalogue of Italian and other masters. I visited once just after college, but it is Sarah's first time here, and passing up one of the greatest troves of Western art is painful. It's like going to Paris and skipping the Louvre, a sacrifice only endured by our single-minded dedication to Luther's steps. We push through the Piazza della Signora with its Davids, Neptunes, Laocoöns, and further hosts of hewing warriors, through the Piazza della Repubblica and its trumpeting victory arches, then past the ostentatious Cathedral of Mary the Flower (made up of white-and-green Carrara marble) with its prodigal façade.

Agape and exhausted, we at last arrive at the Ospedale degli Innocenti, the other sure and trusted Luther site. The building is quite lovely and simple, as well as pleasingly proportioned—just as one would expect from Brunelleschi, again the architect here. Chatting locals and tired tourists sit upon the steps below the loggia. The carved white cameos—on blue backgrounds just like Wedgwood china—in the spandrels are populated by "innocent" infants wrapped in swaddling clothes, indicating the building's original purpose: an orphanage. Today it's a museum.

Luther the mendicant notes nothing of all this art but reserves comments for a singular, practical element. An orphan's fate in Luther's day was grim—grim enough to pique the Christian conscience of the city's wealthy guilds. If stricken by war, famine, or any other penury—significantly a lack of dowry for girl babies—the poor of Florence and its countryside had the option of depositing their infant in a basin at the orphanage door or possibly in a rotating foundling wheel. They would ring the bell and run away, hoping for a better life for their offspring. It seemed a marvelous invention to Luther, who must have been all too aware of the grisly alternatives in his age of shocking infant mortality.

Luther praised the Ospedale degli Innocenti, an orphanage in Florence.

That's it for our whirlwind tour of Florence as seen through Luther's eyes. We pick up our bags at the hotel, then take the train back to Castelfiorentino and meet my parents. We park in a well-lit lot near the station, where Zeke and I run around sword-fighting with bamboo sticks. Our sleep is interrupted at one point by the serenades of drunken soccer revelers. We hear on the morning news that Italy just beat Serbia.

Now with our friends Paul and Melissa, we resume our walk at the tiny crossroads of Coiano, where we stopped two days before. Around and among the Tuscan hills we wend on terra-cotta lanes dampened by the dew, beside long tiers of vines fading into the mists, through orchards of olive trees, past comfortable villas topped with sightly belvederes: an entire ensemble of blurry assurances that the good and tranquil life can still be had. It is the fertile land of Bacchus and Minerva, a pleasure dome of rustic, wholesome hedonism, slumping into nature's generous arms.

One might think from reading certain winsome books that enchanting ruins in their scenic vales are hard to find, but they certainly are not. All around are happy carcasses of villas for the taking, being slowly crushed by encroaching shrubs. The world they represent is long gone, now serving as mere mental retreat from far-off lives burnt up in cars and wasted away in cubicles or harried ragged by play dates and fund-raisers. Pleasure here is squeezed directly from modest hardship—the pure liquid joy of the vine, the unctuous blessing from the hardiest of survivor plants, effervescent wine and flowing oil transforming the Mediterranean scrub into radiant health. Paul and I pass the hours afoot playing benevolent tycoon, amassing fantastical swaths of deserted Italy, rebuilding with grunt and grit the life so recklessly abandoned by the locals.

Acre after flowing acre, grove after fruitful grove inundate our imaginations. At one point we walk by a sheepfold. The guard dogs, a pair of wooly Maremas looking like miniature polar bears, ought to have barked us away. But instead, as if charmed by our fantasies, they abandon their flock and give us a damp and nuzzling welcome. For some certainly irresponsible distance they trot along behind and about us, snowy spirits of assurance: you, friends, are welcome. Beside one vineyard tinged with red and ripe with desiccating grapes, we flush a pair of ring-necked pheasants. They scamper reluctantly before us, the protective male flashing crimson wattles, his drab mate always a few steps in advance.

Caught up in our Italian dreams, the weeks of German weather a distant memory, Sarah and I had forgotten about the very existence of rain. All too predictably the black clouds mount; now comes a drizzle, then a downpour. Paul and Melissa are better prepared than we and loan us one of their umbrellas. Crowded beneath, we walk toward San Gimignano.

If rural Tuscany is a land of scenic dreams, San Gimignano is its capital. The hilltop town is a veritable forest of towers, whose quantity and teetering height stem from transparent competition between medieval clans. Once the tower fad set in, an absurd escalation began, each family piling up stone upon stone, storey after storey, to outdo their neighbors and their rivals. The competition went completely savage, fueling generations of conflict: a higher tower permitted bombardment of inferiors, literally keeping rivals down. We can well imagine the world of family feuds, vendettas, duels, petty slights, and rock-hurling anarchy, a starkly graphic and uncensored vision of unbridled discord. The towers, many of unsound frailty, once numbered in the seventies; some rose over two hundred feet and swayed dangerously in the *tramontana* wind. Not surprisingly, only a dozen or so survive.

The pouring rain lets up a bit as we amble past the fleets of idling buses in the parking lots below. Up and through the western gate, we enter into another town-turned-museum. If tourism saved the village from utter collapse, it's also frozen it in preferred medieval form. Just like in Florence, we jostle through the crushing swarms of sightseers—among whom we don't count ourselves, rightly or wrongly—promenading down the cobbled streets with sentimental delight. Encroaching shops sell their chintz, their harlequin gowns and semiprecious jewelry, their impressionistic canvases of the idyllic countryside thickly laid in oils. Fine ladies beneath straw hats greedily eye the cavernous urns roughly painted with bunches of turgid grapes, swirling vines, benign insects; the less well-off opt for plates with the skyline of the city itself, in case they forgot where they bought it. Homemade chocolate, spinning stands of postcards, ice cream, windows full of brightly colored bags and sandals and other simulacra you can take home to your air-conditioned friends in far-off places. A cornucopia of trinkets made locally, made globally, but mostly made in our imaginations.

It makes me think of Vierzehnheiligen and its row of booths peddling their mementos. Here it is a different kind of beauty to be sure, but the business of souvenirs, of selling memories remains unchanged. Stripped of the evocation of salvation, these secular relics weigh down and do not lift up the soul. The industry of remembrance, founded on the fear of forgetting, has turned the picturesque into picaresque.

There is so much effort, so much money spent simply to re-create an imagined reality. Luther came to loathe pilgrimages and not only because he thought that trusting in relics was false teaching. The deeper problem was the wanton diffusion of human energies, the spreading thin of charity at great cost and risk and much to the loss of one's neighbor. The critique still holds, to judge by today's village-turned-amusement-park.

As we exit the trappings of the city, its shapely profile again comes into view. Set among the vines and groves its tawdriness melts away. We meet Team Wilson at our bed and breakfast—generously arranged for us by Paul and Melissa. My dad has rustled up some local olives, Chianti wine, and substantial steaks as well. Paul and I are so eager to man the grill that we defy the rain and hunker under our umbrellas over the fire, choking on the fumes, seasoning ourselves with beefy incense. We feast upon our lovely dinner and end the epicurean day by watching the sun set and the stars rise over the handsomely lit town upon the hill. San Gimignano is best seen from afar.

Sarah and I leave the others behind the next morning. We say our thanks and farewell to Paul and Melissa, who are headed elsewhere to hike and relax.

For the morning at least, Tuscany smiles on us again, soft skies, rolling hills, and joie de vivre vineyards accompany our path out of San Gimignano. The town's signature towers slide behind the hills, only to reappear smaller and more charming the farther away we get. By afternoon we're back in the workaday world, walking on a valley floor in the dusty, indiscriminate landscape of postmodernity. A few remains of other eras indicate our geography; otherwise we could be almost anywhere that light industry rules. Monasteries and churches mix with manufacturers of fine bathroom fittings. Boxy factories are fenced by rows of waving cypress, like in Roman frescos. In Colle di Val d'Elsa, our route takes us straight up into a hilltop town and the Middle Ages, around obelisks raised to the dead of the World Wars, then along miles of pavement lined by parking lots, tiny shops, pizzerias, and gas stations.

Abbadia Isola ("Island Abbey")—a hamlet we might have missed by blinking, even at a walking pace—was once a great Augustinian monastery, perhaps of Luther's observant strain. His brothers passed their years here pacing around the cloister beside the black basalt church. A chief part of their mission was to care for passing pilgrims such as us, come from afar to see the wonders of the way, to end up at the heavenly ports of Rome and Jerusalem.

Just beyond a few more rust-colored fields, past a pen of snuffling, spotted pigs, we climb to another hilltop town, Monteriggioni, a little huddle of houses and greenery within a set of medieval walls. It has all the historic charm of San Gimignano with a fraction of the crowds. We absorb the historic calm, sitting on the brick terrace, browsing the shops. They also proffer honey and candles, but somehow less offensively. The city is mentioned in Dante's *Inferno* (Canto 31) but only to help the reader visualize the barriers that separated the layers of hell.

Still intact city walls comfort us with the illusion of continuity and harmony, muting the volume of all the battles raging within—think of San Gimignano's rival towers. To extend the image to the realm of institutions, the so-called seamless garment of medieval Western Christendom was also rife with factions and internecine disputes, conflicts hardly hidden or denied. Italy itself was split for centuries between the Guelphs and the Ghibbelines, the one in favor of the pope, the other for the Holy Roman Emperor. It was a lasting feud—and hardly a religious one—with certain cities allied against others; and within cities guilds took sides against their rivals. In time these parties split into further factions. In all-Guelph Florence, the Black Guelphs sidelined Dante's White Guelphs for a time, sending the poet into exile. Somewhat later on, similar conflicts, always over revenues and jurisdictions, brought France as well into the fray. At one point, during what is referred to as the Western Schism, there were three popes. The Reformation was hardly the first split in Christendom.

The striped piers and inlaid floors of Siena's cathedral, Santa Maria Assunta

Dante certainly had no qualms placing his own Pope Boniface VIII in the *Inferno*. There among the fraudulent, in the Malebolge of the simoniacs, Boniface is implanted, flaming feet upward, punished for using his spiritual jurisdiction to gain gold. Dante called into question the wisdom of Constantine for the "dowry [he] pressed upon the first rich Father," that is, the pope.[3]

In the face of all this intrigue, we can hardly blame Luther for insisting that it is God alone who is the mighty fortress, not any earthly edifice or ecclesiastical hierarchy.

Sarah and I leave Monteriggioni well before dawn the next morning, and by noon we see Siena from afar, lorded over by two rival towers—the church and city hall competing with each other for dominance and prestige. On the right stands the black-and-white-striped belfry of the opulent cathedral; on the left, the slender Torre del Mangia high above the Campo, its limestone crown a white torch blazing bright with civic pride.

The closer to the city we get, the more we hurry, carried along by the increasing traffic. Almost running and out of breath, we reach the city wall.

As we plunge toward the city center, the terra-cotta of clay buildings gives gradual way to stucco and dressed stone. The streets grow narrower and more crowded till finally, squeezing through a narrow portal, we are released upon the spacious Campo.

After a couple of weeks apart, we're back in Luther's tracks and will be all the way to Rome. Luther would have seen this very piazza, almost as it is: its top-heavy tower, its brick pavement, its crowds and markets. He might have wondered (as the city's councilmen would have hoped) whether, perhaps, it was as great as Florence. Or perhaps he was unimpressed. There is no record of his stay.

With expansive breaths we take in this spacious wonder of civic architecture, a semicircular piazza paved with brick, gently sloping down toward the city hall, rather like an amphitheater. Here is a proper stage for the drama of a city, its loves and losses, its triumphs and revenge. After the morning's brisk walk, we're much too early for our scheduled rendezvous. So we lie down beneath our hats upon the sun-warmed bricks, lift up our feet upon our packs, and fall asleep.

For a minute or perhaps an hour we rest there, basking in the autumn light. Eventually something blocks the light and the heat. A cloud, perhaps? The tower's shifting shade? We both sit up to see if we should move, and standing there grinning above us are our friends Paul and Melissa! We had no intention of meeting up again, but here they are after their vineyard tours to see some final sights before going home to frigid Minnesota. We shake ourselves awake and exchange hale greetings, happy to have their company for the afternoon.

Our family soon arrives on foot (the camper is parked outside of town), and we all head out together through the maze of streets toward the Duomo—another sight that Luther would have seen. There before its bulk, we are collectively gobsmacked by luxury, the sheer plenitude and preciousness of its decoration. The church is not as large nor even as delicately ornate as its northern European peers; but whether through the shining opalescence of the marble—in multiple colors—or the life-like dimensions of the statuary or perhaps the glowing colors of the tesserae, the edifice is the product of a wealthier and more sensuous civilization.

After the blinding brightness of the façade, the softer splendor of the interior is still yet more sublime. Pensive popes peer from each and every corbel of the architrave; each spandrel sprouts another bearded magistrate in his pallium. The color is stunning: skies of lapis lazuli, magenta mantles, viridian serpents. Our eyes zip up the piers toward the starry vaults; high up in the cupola unedited expanses of gold leaf glow in the dim. And only when our necks have tired do we discover beneath our tramping feet acres of inlay—not mere checkered bits of mosaic but wide expanses of cool marble snaked with outlines of queenly ladies and cogitating syndics. Old Testament sagas are drawn out in stone the color of cream and rust, like classical myths upon Etruscan pots. It is breathtakingly decadent.

After the first rush of pleasure has run its course, the intellectual plan of the cathedral comes into focus. Here is the whole medieval synthesis writ in stone! At the door we march upon Hermes Trismegistus, symbol of human wisdom and reason, of the general revelation accessible to all rational souls. Down the aisles the sundry sibyls of the nations carry this primeval wisdom to the furthest corners of the earth, from Persia all the way to Phrygia. As we enter the nave, secular history rolls out. Siena's emblematic wolf—suckling city founders Senius and Aschius—is encircled by the mascots of her allies. Just above lies a great rose emblem sealed with the eagle of the Holy Roman Empire. (Ghibelline Siena stood for emperor Frederick Barbarossa against the pope-supporting Guelphs.) The next grand panel is an allegory of Fortune and Wisdom, where pagan Socrates is given the emblematic martyrs' palm as his reward for dying for the Truth.

All the general revelation of the nave is built upon in the transept by the special revelation of God's word. Several busy scenes set forth the history of Israel (with a preference for battles and gore): Judith hacks away in hiding at the head of Holofernes; a grand hexagon beneath the dome portrays Elijah's many fights with Ahab; just before the altar spreads a bustling tapestry of Moses hurling commandments and idol calves. There's just one scene from the New Testament: Herod flees while the innocents are slaughtered.

All this harmonizing of sacred and secular makes me think again of Dante and his vision. One must be wary of perfect theories, argues physicist Marcelo Gleiser, for they are easily destabilized. For all we may now love of the beauty and integrity of that great medieval synthesis—with its place for all of knowledge, its dispensation of epochs, its future secure in a lofty blue heaven—when Luther walked by, it was about to crack.

For there's a single figure who is conspicuously absent from the pageant: Jesus. There is a tiny figure hosting the Last Supper behind the altar, and a couple of stock scenes from his life are carved on the pulpit, but otherwise, nothing. One could say that more visual representation is unnecessary, that Christ is truly present in the drama of the liturgy, in the mass, in preaching of the Word. Or perhaps the liveliest details of Jesus's biography defy artistic speculation altogether, our attempts to freeze his living presence in paint and stone are ever inadequate. But I doubt very much that this omission is so calculated.

All along the way since Pavia we've been reading aloud local hero Dante's *Divine Comedy*, and we've had much occasion to reflect on how his high medieval vision might relate to Luther's reform. Dante's chronicle of the soul, much informed by his reading of Thomas Aquinas, is a thing of perfect beauty. It presents us with a system so virtuous, so complete, so aesthetically dazzling as to hide its inner recipe for despair—at least if you were Luther.

Dante begins his privileged tour at death's door, descends through limbo, then spirals into hell through ever more foul fields of vice. At the cold, static bottom stands Satan, frozen and unmoving, the opposite of God's fiery dynamism. Dante then ascends through purgatory, witnessing sinners being purged (hence the name) of vice through painful refinements fit for every sin. And then, finally, Dante bounds up the glorious spheres of heaven to the empyrean, that sphere beyond all spheres that surrounds and fills all beings with the streaming light of God's unending vitality. Thus, in crass simplicity, is Dante's architecture of damnation and salvation.

After centuries of neglect and even disdain from humanists and enlightened thinkers, certain theologians of the past century have tried to revive Dante's vision. They do so for good reasons: its coherence and its harmony, its beauty and, therefore, truth. And right they are in many ways, for we throw away such architectonics to our great impoverishment, as if we—with our great science, our purported knowledge of the psyche, our probings of the atom and of the furthest reaches of the universe—have somehow created a superior vision for humanity, a vision less tainted with superstition. But this is not the case at all, for it's still our minds that decorate this scientific artifice with adornments of meaning—just as Dante did the philosophy his world gave him.

But the very movement of the *Comedy* itself—tracing the soul's path to paradise through the cultivation of virtue over vice—had come to a kind impasse in Luther. We may attribute Luther's difficulties to an overly scrupulous conscience, as many biographers have done, asserting that the overwrought monk couldn't get it into his obsessive skull that God was full of grace toward him. Fifteenth-century theologian Gabriel Biel, the crowning figure of scholastic theology in Luther's day, insisted that the very existence of a path toward salvation at all was ample demonstration of God's magnanimity toward sinful humanity. God in his freedom could have sent us all to hell without injustice, but instead he gave us Christ, the church, and the sacraments as channels for his grace. Biel recognized as well that different people had different capacities, that some were more capable of availing themselves of these means than others. Here again God's generosity intervened: grace was sufficient to make up for any deficits in ability.

Next to this late-medieval theology, the *Via Moderna* as it was called, Dante's grace is more expansive still. His *Comedy* is utterly saturated with it. God initiates and fuels the upward journey of the soul by shining with irresistible beauty. The white-hot illumination of his light works dynamically without stop or alteration to draw the host of the elect toward heaven. There's no lack of grace at all in Dante's vision.

What is missing from the *Comedy* is the same as what's missing from Siena's cathedral: Christ! Dante's Christ is floating in the apse of heaven: he has already come to earth, and now he's gone. Christ has tipped divine history from sin to grace and now rules in judgment from afar. Here on earth humanity is left to plow through vice to virtue—with lots of help, of course. Christ is doing all, but in a distant, celestial fashion. He is the highest light whose radiance illumines all things and refines away the evil. But while the celestial Christ, font of wisdom and forgiveness, draws us toward his very being, *he* does not *descend* to our level. It is always *we* who must move *upward*—always upward—toward a holy God.

Well before the indulgence controversy, Luther was at work reversing this direction. In a letter to his Augustinian brother George Spenlein, Luther wrote in 1516:

> Now I would like to know how it is with your soul, if it has at length learned to despise its own righteousness and seek comfort and joy in Christ's. For, at present, the temptation to rest in one's own works is very powerful, especially with those who long to be good and pious. They are ignorant of God's righteousness, which has been so richly bestowed on us in Christ without money and price, and try to do good of themselves, till they fancy they can appear before God adorned with every grace. But they never get thus far. You yourself, when with us in Erfurt, suffered from this illusion, or rather delusion, and I also was a martyr to it, and even yet I have not overcome it. Therefore, dear brother, learn Christ and Him crucified. Praise and laud His name, and despairing of self, say to Him, "You, Lord Jesus, are my righteousness, but I am Your sin. You have taken what is mine, and given me what is Yours. You have assumed

> that which You were not, and given me what I had not." Beware, my brother, at aiming at a purity which rebels against being classed with sinners. For Christ only dwells among sinners.[4]

The most important point for Luther—one he draws from Augustine and from Paul—is that it is *not* our sinlessness and virtue that permit Christ's presence with us, but it is rather our need precisely *as* sinners for his redeeming presence that summons him to our midst.

But with a distant and always-beckoning Christ, Dante's God—and that of much of the medieval tradition—no longer made his special way down to earth but ever calls us up through refinement, burning off our dross, shaping us to Christlike dimensions. This stairway to salvation so fatigued Thérèse of Lisieux that she longed for a holy elevator. In many details, especially the acuity of insight into the human condition, there's little difference between Dante and Luther. But in orientation and direction, the two systems could hardly be more opposed. As Dante's Christian climbs up to heaven, Luther's Christ hurtles down to earth.

It's a fault that contemporary Catholic theologians have sought to remedy. Indeed, that there are these two strands (at least) in medieval theology—the *Via Antigua* and the *Via Moderna*—is now acknowledged, an understanding utterly absent when Luther was tried and judged for heresy. The 2013 statement of the international Lutheran-Catholic dialogue, "From Conflict to Communion," points to Luther's formation in the mystical tradition of the Christian West, which drew upon Bernard of Clairvaux as interpreted through the Rhenish mystic Johannes Tauler. It's recognized now, as it was not then, that Luther's piety was derived from a legitimate, minority tradition of his day and was therefore not a novelty. But such cool heads did not rule the day, and flaming polemics on both sides came to draw the era into its own form of self-destructive purgatory.

After such lofty thoughts and inspirations, we drop quickly down to earth. We say a second good-bye to Paul and Melissa, then go looking for the Augustinian cloister where Luther would have stayed. Considering its size, the building is less difficult to locate than to identify. On the Prato di Sant'Agostino we find a large ecclesiastical shape, but there's no hint of any Augustinian connections. Parts of the building have been repurposed: windows hang with co-ed laundry, and an inscription above the porch reads "Collegio Tolomei." It's a middle school named after the classical geographer. Every door is locked.

But it's Luther's cloister, all right. Over much of its expanse little seems to have changed since he stayed here. It's a solid mass of undecorated brick, made all the more austere by comparison to the gaudy cathedral. Inside, if we had entered, would have been a historical blank. The interior was gutted by fire in 1747 and rebuilt in flamboyant Baroque. Luther's passage, too, seems to have gone up with those flames.

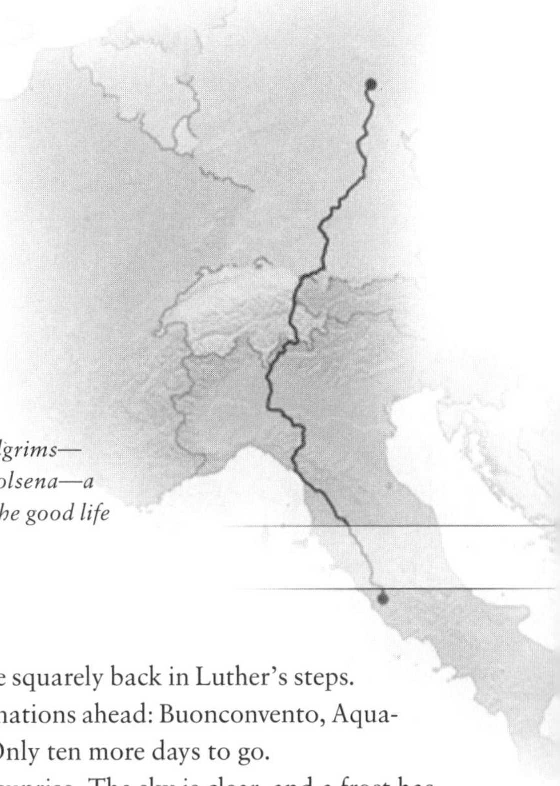

Nine

A soupçon of volcanic ash—fellow pilgrims—fortunati!—the Papal States—Lake Bolsena—a real Roman road—Etruscan caves—the good life with Mary Jane

From Siena all the way to Rome we're squarely back in Luther's steps. Etzlaub's map names for us the destinations ahead: Buonconvento, Aquapendente, Montefiasconi, Viterbo. Only ten more days to go.

We hurry from Siena well before sunrise. The sky is clear, and a frost has settled; we pull on gloves and hats. Siena's skyline is visible in the distance well into the morning, its many towers casting shadows across the brown fields, plowed and loamy, darkened with damp. We can't keep from looking back to admire it again and again.

The vistas here go on and on and on, sharpened by the crystalline air, broken only by occasional and scrappy vegetation. Gentle hill and gentle vale, all cultivated to harmonious effect, extend unto an ordered eternity. The land is voluptuousness itself, all curves and clefts and hollows and modest mounts. The fertile fields seem undefiled; the few buildings that there are come in the modest dimensions of a premodern age. Fencerows are low and seem to invite rather than prevent trespass, their dominions made still more appealing by their limits. A wilderness it is not, but an earthly paradise, almost. It's a country made for life, and life abundant.

Only little signs here and there reveal the constant toil behind the feint of ease. We walk along a field gouged with trenches five feet deep, dug up to drain the roots of future orchard trees. On buildings and walls the mortar between the bricks is recently repointed, expanses of stucco patched, tumbling terraces chinked, vines dressed. The grind of ongoing maintenance hides beneath the enchanting presentation.

From time to time we see the remains of bygone belfries; elsewhere, rotting chapels teeter into ruin. The land is sown with these crumbling invitations to prayer, reminders to the passing pilgrims of today that in the long term all is vanity, and even prayerful monuments dissolve into the dust—if they're not loved and constantly kept up.

Sometime in the afternoon we meet Hans, our first copilgrim since the Apennines. He's a quiet Swiss retiree, sturdily built with a head full of white hair. His tanned skin hints that he's been out hiking for a while. To inaugurate his retirement, he tells us, he wanted an adventure—something not as famous nor as crowded as the Camino de Santiago. He read about the Via Francigena in a magazine and decided it was the one for him. We walk away the afternoon together, beneath the beating sun, saying little. When we tell him that we're pilgrims, he says that he's Reformed and that he hikes more for his health than for his religion; that's about as far as we can get with him.

Walking out of Buonconvento the next morning we climb slowly out of the drainage of the Arbia, leave the Tuscan hills behind, and step into the heartland of Etruria. Here the lowlands grow still more drab and dusty, while on the skyline dark basalt intrusions rise high enough to be cool and capped with conifers. It's a landscape of volcanoes, the realm of the Etruscans.

The unencumbered view elicits an emotional release. One can comprehend all, for nothing is hidden. This is the land of confession, of unveiling, of nakedness before an all-seeing God. For miles, it seems, we march exposed for all to see, tiny vessels drifting slowly across the swells of dirt, buffeted by spiritual winds. The air bites with dust and tonic, piney odors of the steppe, carrying me back to the arid summers of my childhood in eastern Washington State. There, in the treeless expanse specked with sage, the summer heat kicked up a singular aroma—evergreens mixed with a soupçon of volcanic ash—that I smell here too. If it weren't for the walled towns in the distance, I'd almost think I was at home.

The barren dunes of this desiccated countryside are broken by San Quirico d'Orcia, where our trail funnels us into a claustrophobic canyon of a town. The village's eponymous church is a tiny jewel of the Romanesque, simple-looking at first, but then little spiritual details appear: placid lions stand guard on either jamb, writhing crocodiles devour twisting serpents across the lintel, assorted doves and carnivorous beasts spread out below the tympanum, itself inhabited by a tiny, weathered saint.

Toward the end of the day, tired and flagging from the heat, we climb a final hill up to Castiglione d'Orcia, where we meet our family in the camper. The water tank is almost empty, so we drive down just a little bit to where they had seen a farmstead. We hear the olive presses and pumps whirring away inside a modern barn. We poke around for an office, and finally a young woman wearing oil-glistened rubber boots and an apron walks out. When we ask her for some water, she guides us to a spigot with a hose, assures us that it's clean, and then apologizes for running back to work. After filling up, we go back in and ask if there are any olives or oil for sale. Again she's apologetic when she returns with a quart of oil that has no label: it's so fresh and green it smells of grass—straight from the press's tap. We park the camper that night at the edge of town in a lot looking out upon the hills to the south. The dusky batholiths fade slowly into nothingness in the warm incandescence of the twilight.

Luther must have been a friend of darkness—not only the metaphorical kind but genuine pitch-blackness too. Life in the cloister was exceptionally nocturnal, with vespers, vigils, and matins sung at night in most seasons. Candles were used—but probably more sparingly than we today would prefer. To that familiar indoor darkness was added an outer darkness of the road, as Luther must have started walking well before sunrise and finished well after dark. Unlike us, who travel in October, still in the warm light of fall, he probably walked through Italy in December. Somewhere near our spot he would have celebrated Christmas.

We continue our string of dawn starts and the next day are on the road by seven. Soon a low light streams across the dry hills in visible rays, glitteringly reflected from hundreds of tiny, otherwise invisible ponds. We make quick time downhill, flowing through aisles of live oak, corridors of *sempervivens* cedars, rows of vines and olives, finally to emerge into more vast and undulating fields, plowed along the contour lines. Looking back we can see Castiglioni d'Orcia, whence we came, glowing in the dawn above, tiny yet almost touchable in the morning air. We roll along on fields tinged with burgeoning grain, reading our Dante aloud—we've reached *Paradiso*. Now upon beige gravel, now upon abandoned swaths of hastily paved asphalt, soon we glimpse our next destination, a black mesa sticking up conspicuously to the south. It is Radicofani, a vestigial plug of basalt.

To get there we are forced to walk a ways along the Via Cassia. The originally Roman road dates from the second century BC; today's updated route is a busy two-lane highway—with wide shoulders, thankfully. Like all road walking, it's both ridiculous and terrifying as we toil along at snails' pace, while cars and trucks go screaming loudly by. We start to whine about our route again, complaining to unseen officials about their hastily drawn lines on maps, ignorant of reality on the ground. Everything above us is open fields and farmland—surely a more pleasant right of way lies up there somewhere.

Reading Dante in the open fields south of Siena

As we gripe our way along the shoulder, a car tears past us honking, its driver waving wildly. He screeches to a halt on the roadside behind us. We're certainly intrigued and not a bit alarmed as a sprightly someone jumps out and motions us toward himself vigorously, opening his trunk. When we arrive he pumps our hands forcefully, presents himself as Massimo, and announces with great enthusiasm in Italian that even we can understand, "It is your lucky day! *Fortunati, fortunati!*" Someone, somewhere, apparently, has told him we were coming, and he's been trawling around to find us.

Massimo is of middling height and age, average-sized, and dressed from head to toe in various shades of faded black. His bronzed head is completely bald, and a closely trimmed goatee surrounds a mouth that never ceases speaking. After the energetic introduction, Massimo reaches into his open trunk and pulls out two volumes, hot off the presses. Holding them into the air and gesturing toward heaven with his other hand, he assures us gravely that these books are not yet for sale. He insists again how *fortunati* we are to have met him now. These books are his very own production, guides to the Via Francigena through the region of Lazio, just to our south. All we need to know to get us safely from here to Rome is found within their pages—and painted on rocks and trees along the way in the form of his own proprietary blazes. The "official" route, he scoffs, is no good at all through Lazio. We must follow *his* blazes, he insists, from now on. All others will lead us into who knows what sort of trouble. And then, leaving us with guides in hand, Massimo is gone as fast as he arrived, tearing down the highway toward some important inauguration. We stand there stupefied for a while, holding our newly acquired books and wondering what has just hit us.

We continue along the shoulder a bit longer, hang a left at a gas station, then head up a less traveled road. As we climb, Monte Amiata comes into view in the west, skirted with its dark chestnut forest, topped with black pines, clouds growing from its summit. And before us is Radicofani, hinting just barely of Devil's Tower.

When we arrive, the town is only one long street, with pavers of black basalt below and buildings of black basalt on each side. It's old and scenic in a comforting sort of way: laundry hangs from open windows, lichen grows on tile roofs. Team Wilson awaits us in an outsized park filled with stately shade trees and with a view toward the south. There we sit upon a thoughtfully placed bench contemplating the panorama.

Our repose is broken by the screeching halt of a car. Out jumps our new pal Massimo. Again, we're *fortunati* that he found us, he says, waving a fluorescent yellow piece of cloth in our direction. Now less a magnanimous guide and more a worried mother, he scolds us for walking along the highway: "People have been killed on the very spot where I met you!" He informs us that it's illegal to walk on highways and that we could even have been fined by the police. This comes as quite a surprise to us, since we're on the government-approved Via Francigena. While our Anglo-Saxon scruples reel at the contradictions, Massimo hands over the yellow cloth, in fact a pair of reflective safety vests—his own—and exhorts us to be very careful. Then, as before, he's gone an instant. Slow tourism is fast business, apparently.

Sarah cooks up *ribollita*, a Tuscan stew of bread, beans, and greens, according to a recipe in a little cookbook my mom found. We eat inside the camper, parked beneath the pines, listening to the shooshing of the breeze through their long needles. Then Sarah and I retire to the hostel, the nicest one we've seen so far, though it is stone cold. It's so recently renovated that the air is damp and dusty with the smell of drying plaster. There's heat, but we're loath to turn it on—it must take days to warm the place up. We shiver our way to sleep beneath weighty piles of scratchy woolen blankets.

Like on so many other mornings, we begin again by swimming through the clouds, beneath the still lit streetlights. Our way through, the thick fog descends on farmers' roads, invisible pastures and their flocks indicated only by the clinking of the bellwethers. Once the fog begins to lift we spot some lanky-legged, long-haired Apennenica, their straight wool unusually free of accumulated detritus. They munch and mingle, alert and staring at us with their ears cocked sideways. Newly dropped lambs, umbilical cords still dangling blood-red from their snowy bellies, stumble about, punching their mothers' distended udders drunkenly with blunted muzzles. The ewes return our stares with curious gazes, so unlike the usual dumb and frightened look of sheep.

When finally the fog lifts, Radicofani appears behind us, its strip of stone houses circling the south side of the mesa. Far across the valley, on the slopes of Mount Amiata, vapor rises from geothermal stations. It billows gently upward, unmoved by any breeze, smoke from Vulcan's forge buried deep in the volcanic belly.

Certain signs make clear that we have moved into a new region—the former Papal States. Proceno's oversized city hall is stamped with the escutcheon of the Sforzas, with its double-eagle, double-serpent decorations. The Sforzas from Milan, who brought rice to the Po Valley, were also variously allied for and against the Holy Roman Emperor, Venice, France, and others. At the time of Luther's passage, the family had cast its lot with Pope Julius II, who with the Emperor and Spain was fighting off the French—an allegiance that would shift many times again in the decades to come.

Just below our destination, Aquapendente, we see fellow pilgrims trudging in the distance. We quickly gain on them—they are weighted down by ponderous packs—and soon we see that it's Massimo, this time accompanied by a troupe of female pilgrims. What a change from yesterday! Gone are the threadbare fashion statements and shining pate. Head to toe he's clad in hikers' garb and bent beneath a Sisyphean load. He's taking these four ladies on a two-week trek to Rome. We exchange some pleasantries but not much more than that, as they are rather out of breath. We resume our customary pace and soon leave them far behind.

The town is larger than most others on our path, and unlike so many picturesque villages abandoned by the young or transformed into open-air museums, Aquapendente is alive with real commerce. Storefronts spill over with wares: tobacco, lingerie, rainbows of plastic buckets and brooms. With this liveliness comes the unfortunate side effect of traffic. The central square with its palatial city hall is almost completely occupied by cars. Where once a thousand citizens might have assembled, chanting patriotic songs around the statue of hometown hero Girolamo Fabrizi (friend of Galileo), now sit static a couple dozen sleeping hatchbacks. In the Piazza della Constituente stands the familiar and ubiquitous memorial to the fallen of the World Wars: a helmeted soldier charges alongside a naked muscled patriot in bronze who's carrying the Roman standard with its anachronistic SPQR. "To the Fallen," the dedication reads. But how far back? To the Italian Wars of the sixteenth century? To Romans hewn down by barbarians? To Etruscans overrun by Romans? To all of them. The fickle, time-bound politics of successive dispensations dissolve into a soup of hometown piety.

That Luther walked through this town is almost certain—it's there on Etzlaub's map—but we don't know where he stayed. So it's with surprise and delight that along our Via Francigena we stumble upon a very clearly labeled Chiesa di Sant'Agostino, complete with an attached cloister dating from 1290. The edifice is another unassuming box, built of the local foamy tufa stone. Yet again, there's little left that Luther saw, for the usual reasons: fire gutted the original, and the present structure was rebuilt in Counter-Reformation Baroque. Atop its tower sprout grass and hardy saplings; nature is having her way. A sign in the entryway announces a Saint Rocco Mass and the blessing of dogs.

Saint Rocco's pilgrim hostel is next door, but we've already arranged to stay with the Sacramentine sisters on the hill outside of town. We eat another pasta dinner in the camper, then climb up to the convent. It's nearly dark as we arrive and ring the bell, which sounds distantly. As we wait among the many potted plants, cats appear and rub around our legs with bold affection. We're just about to ring again when a smiling octogenarian somewhere south of five feet tall opens the massive door and waves us in. The crickets call, the birds chirp, a fountain burbles in the center of the cloister; to this is added nothing but the shuffling footsteps of our hostess. It is a true haven of tranquility.

There are only two elderly sisters left—Suor Emilia and Suor Livia—to fill and tend this huge, meandering complex; there's probably room for eighty. But they hardly seem alone. The halls are lined with recent photos of youths and families lounging about the grounds, smiling, clowning, cutting grass, and chasing cats: a proxy family to keep the sisters in good spirits.

But from the sisters' perspective it is not *they* who need the company; instead they give company to others—especially to Jesus. For the Sacramentine order has as its vocation the perpetual adoration of the sacrament. One or another of them kneels before the tabernacle twenty-four hours a day—or as much as they can manage—the whole year through, keeping watch, adoring their Lord, proffering faithful prayers, thoughts, and confessions continually to the incarnate Christ. What drives these sisters to hold their endless vigil is not sophisticated; it is a guileless motherly concern never to let their beloved get lonely. It's a simple practice, simplistic even, but if one takes Catholic metaphysics and the practice of tabernacling seriously, it is admirable in all respects. For if Jesus remains "in, with, and under" the host (to import Luther's language), it is a pity and a shame to leave him all alone. Such gestures are often fodder for unimaginative Protestant invective, yet we see here how a gracious manner can surpass the collective virtue of whole conclaves of doctrinal skeptics. If the sacrament is to be reserved for adoration, the sisters have found the proper way to do it.

We shuffle up the stairs, their soft bricks grooved by centuries of sisters going to and from their endless vigil, and into a long corridor of dormitories. Our room is absolutely lilliputian, and to enter we must duck beneath the doorway that in other ages would not have knocked a single head.

"'The pot' is full," my father sighs with heavy exasperation as we step into the camper for our breakfast. And not the cooking pot. Now that we've left touristic Tuscany, camper services have thinned out again, leaving our captain frustrated in his scruples. It's been almost a month of life in our little mobile home, and although it's easier than the repeated separations of before, we've never quite hit our camper stride. Just one more week to go. We scarf down our cornflakes and leave the family in a mood of dour resignation, pessimistic about their chance of finding facilities.

For a couple of hours we walk through a rough-and-ready farmland: ramshackle hovels hidden in spots of forest, lean-to pigsties shut by rusting bedframes, sheep corralled by pallets wired together, sheds made out of old RVs, caves hacked into hillsides and gated with scraps of chain link fencing, half-ton rounds of hay rotting into the ground. Everything here is hoarded as if life might any day collapse into self-subsistence. The locals are poor in cash but rich in ingenuity.

We leave the fields and pad through San Lorenzo Nuovo, a one-stoplight town with a broad plaza at its heart. There stands a sizable church—much

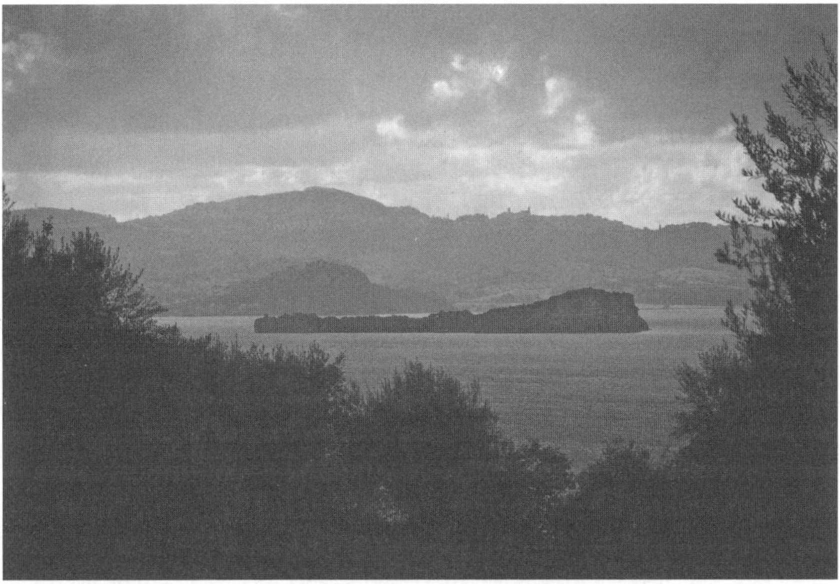

Lago di Bolsena and its volcanic islands

bigger than the city hall opposite—in imposing Baroque dimensions, dedicated to its patron, St. Laurence. Atop the main portal hangs a sculpted achievement crested by the three-tiered tiara of the papacy and mantled with the gigantic keys and lappets of St. Peter—another reminder that we are squarely within the boundaries of the former Papal States.

Out of town, just beyond the bars and service stations and miracle miles, we glimpse the shining surface of Lake Bolsena. At the very spot of this unveiling, as if made to order, we find a park lined with marble benches set at angles properly to contemplate the view. The lake's volcanic origins are obvious—it is a wide caldera filled with water, with summit cones Bisentina and Martana standing proud from the surface like freighters. Sarah and I sit and snack as we watch as the rays of sunlight race across the surface of the lake.

As we continue walking, the lake darts in and out of view, its visage always slightly altered, the islands differently arranged, the shape and shoreline wavering. It arrests us anew with each advancing angle. There's some lesson hidden in this constantly renewed attraction, some insight into the nature of human perception. I remember as a child, when we were driving around the Pacific Northwest, being always on the lookout for glimpses of the shifting volcanoes. I suppose it was the same instinct that urged the ancients to record the movements of the stars and still inspires us to contemplate the ceaseless breaking of the sea. Picture windows miss the point, it seems: the lovely landscape becomes fixed, burned into our eyes, then almost forgotten.

After we descend though more olive orchards, the silhouettes of battlements against the white reflection of the lake herald our arrival in Bolsena, the "City of the Miraculous Eucharist," as the sign tells us. According to legend, one Peter of Prague, a priest who had begun to doubt Christ's real presence, made a pilgrimage to Rome and prayed at Peter's tomb to be released of his misgivings. On his journey home, while he said mass at the church of Santa Cristina here in Bolsena, the host began to bleed. Terrified, he wrapped the tainted wafer in the altar cloth, but drops of blood still stained the floor. Pope Urban IV made the miracle a cause to extend the feast of Corpus Christi to the entire church.

Luther would probably have stopped here, seen those stains, and said a mass as well, perhaps with similar fear and trembling, perhaps not. The entrance of that church is stamped with the coat of arms of patron Giovanni de Medici—Luther's later nemesis Pope Leo X! We don't know precisely what Luther thought of such things when he was here, but later on Corpus Christi came to symbolize for him all that was wrong about the Roman mass. "This festival should be utterly abolished," he wrote in a sermon on John 6, "For it is the most shameful festival in the whole year. On no other day are God and his Christ so greatly blasphemed. This is especially evident in the procession. There you are supposed to drop everything else and to disgrace the holy sacrament in every way by its being paraded around as nothing but a spectacle, thereby committing pure idolatry."[1]

Corpus Christi seems child's play, though, compared to the festival of Santa Cristina that I saw advertised. To honor its patron saint, Bolsena recreates the adolescent virgin's martyrdom in tableaux vivants risqué enough to make Freud blush. In one tableau, the writhing nubile youth is bound to a pole and whipped by bronzed and virile men; another has her stretched out on the wheel; another shows her seething in a flame-licked cauldron of boiling oil; another depicts hot pincers removing her Christ-confessing tongue. And the pièce de résistance: Cristina standing on the millstone her father tried to drown her with—it miraculously floats—being drawn toward the lakeshore through waves of rocking papier-mâché by Grecian-bodied males. I wonder what Luther would have made of that!

Her basilica is much less plagued by double entendre than with two divergent takes on church practice. Inside we find a shrine, the floating millstone, in addition to the blood-soaked Corpus Christi host preserved in a golden reliquary. With the host, the saint, the tableaux vivants, the religion of Bolsena is so surprisingly historical, so utterly material that it is almost an offense—an anathema, a heresy against the modern quest for proof and authenticity.

A ways beyond Bolsena we see at last a long-awaited sight: a stretch of real Roman road! At every ancient pavement so far seen, all the way from Erfurt, I've been on the lookout. So single-minded have I been in my watchfulness for Roman roads that I've made many false positives; it's become a running joke between Sarah and me. But when we see this section, it's clear that all my former exclamations were premature. The road itself is rather narrow, perhaps ten or twelve feet wide at most. This one, part of the Via Cassia that Luther walked, dates from 200 BC. Its hexagonal pavers look like slices of the basalt pillars we've seen around, and they still hold out against unceasing use—much better than our short-lived asphalt! In fact, it seems to be use that keeps them from being buried by sediment.

Intact section of the 2,200-year-old Via Cassia

When we meet up with the family, they've calmed considerably from the morning's irritation and have found a nice campground for the night. We drive for a spell among the hills whose beauty is enhanced by the twilight. Parked in a grove of kiwi vines, we sleep cozily in our camper.

In the morning reminders of popes and cardinals past greet us. The gates of Montefiascone are guarded by the keys of Peter and the seal of eighteenth-century Cardinal Pompeo Aldrovandi. Atop the town, near the site of the former papal palace, we survey our momentary fiefdom—possessing the horizons with royal views. And what a pleasant reign is briefly ours: patchwork orchards, chestnut groves, hedge-bound fieldlets bright with sprouting green, and in the distance the twinkling surface of Lake Bolsena with its two volcano-islands.

On the flatland below Montefiascone rises a vaporous cloud; our muddy road heads straight toward sulfurous springs bubbling from the valley floor. Just past the last vestiges of an ancient arch we find the Parco Termale del Bagnaccio—a modern update of what in Roman times was surely a much more elaborate set of hot-spring baths. A desultory compound is parked up with campers; azure basins lined with concrete fill up with water, steaming hot into the rainy air. From a single spring streams a steady trickle, now channeled into myriad pools. Did Luther, like us, stop here to soak his tired feet?

Viterbo is another papal city, its twenty-foot-high walls topped with the squared-off merlons of the Guelph party—a sign that this town sided with the pope against Holy Roman Emperor Frederick Barbarossa. We zip through the crowded town, heads down and umbrellas up, to the summit and the Papal Palace and its companion Cathedral of Saint Lorenzo. We scurry down the hill, past ruins both ancient and modern, out beneath the layers of architectural cake, over the grassy moat, and into a labyrinth of little streets.

Outside the tight quarters of the city it's no longer buildings that press in but walls of rock on either side, ten feet wide and as much as fifty feet high. These canyons are not natural but man-made, boxed canyons hacked from the soft volcanic rock. At points it's as if we are walking through tunnels—dark, close, and overarched by oaks. We suddenly realize that "GP-Stupido" will probably instruct my parents to come this way. There's no way our whale of a camper will fit between the narrow walls. I call my dad and suggest an alternate meeting place.

After exiting this maze we meet the family and drive a bit to camp beside the walls of Tuscania. Its swallowtail-shaped battlements mark it as Ghibelline, meaning that it was for the party of Emperor Barbarosa *against* the pope. I wonder again about the insane ferocity of the papacy against Luther, then a distant, unimportant monk. It seems doubtful that, after centuries of wars, conflicts, and shifting alliances between German and papal parties, a new and critical voice—Luther's—from Germany would have been judged on theological merit rather than its dynastic implications.

Most Catholics and Protestants today are honestly confused by the temporal power accorded to the popes of Luther's day: waging wars, scuffling over rents, lending and receiving massive loans. And although those things were customarily done within the laws of the time, there was no fixed or—to us moderns, at least—any coherent distinction between these spiritual and temporal affairs. In many ways the pope was just another earthly king with added benefits. Just as confusing is the vigor with which the Holy Roman Emperor pursued papal arguments against Luther—or at least made a show of doing so—only to turn around and sack the pope's Rome in 1529. While religious matters were paramount to the unfolding of the Reformation, even the most cursory rehearsal of the facts reveals the spiritual aims of leaders such as Luther submerged in a dozen other long-term disputes: Holy Roman Emperor versus France versus Venice versus the Papal States; regular versus secular clergy; Dominicans versus Augustinians; urban versus rural magistrates; and more. Too many matters were soon involved for us to fixate honestly today on the usual set of theological disputes.

At Vetralla the next day, we pause to do some errands. While we buy some credit for our phone at the newsstand, a stranger overhears our English and accosts us as we leave. At first we only hear her voice: "You're pilgrims, surely—and Americans I think, yes?" We turn to meet a sixty-something woman with an enthusiastic mien and a sprightly gait. "So many people come through Vetralla and don't bother to stop—but there are such treasures here! It's the heart of Roman history!" commences her stream of words, and before we can object or even know what we would possibly be objecting to, she takes us literally by the elbows and marches us down the street, continuing her discourse.

"I am Mary Jane!" she announces. "I'm American, of course. I'm a writer. I'm from Boston, but I've lived in Italy for—whoof!—nearly fifty years! I came over on a one-way ticket and never looked back. Isn't it beautiful?" she gushes, herding us down the jumbled cobbles of the street toward the city hall.

After a brief and conspiratorial exchange with the guard ("an old friend—they all know me here!"), we are springing up the marble stairs to see her most recently cracked mystery. "You see," she waves her hands in well-choreographed motions, pointing to a coat of arms. "Do you know whose it is?" We see a lion, some fleurs-de-lis, and before we can stammer out a certainly incorrect response, she interrupts with an excited burst, "It's Henry the Eighth!" The one with six wives, that is, of England, who first wrote against Luther but later joined the Reformation to solve his progeny problem. "So few people realize, but this city was a protectorate of England, given to Henry by Julius II for his help in the League of Cambrai Wars, in 1512. Just look at it. Isn't it beautiful! It's been here all along, but they didn't know what it was at all. It was moved up to this stairway, and for centuries people just walked by not knowing that they were in the presence of England. That's what I'm trying to do, you see. This was such an important place. Henry the Eighth, can you imagine!" Then after the briefest of pauses her tone grows decidedly more sober as she reflects upon the fallen fortunes of her adopted Vetralla: "But it's hard, you know, the tourists come to Rome, to Florence. When really they should be coming to Etruria! It's the heart of the Roman world!"

The English theme continues as Mary Jane guides us to the council chamber, a serious room weighed down by wooden coffers and hung with gaudy chandeliers. Even now the syndics of the city hold their court beneath a friendly marble likeness of the Jacobite pretender. "King Henry, Duke of York, cardinal of the Holy Roman Church, protector of Vetralla," says the caption, "set up by the elders of the city, 1802."

Mary Jane resumes her commentary. "There's so much history here. And you know, the city council, they knew *nothing* of these ancient connections with England. *I* had to dig it up. But thanks to my work these monuments are now appreciated for the treasures that they are, and the people of Vetralla are proud of their international connections." Plummeting down the stairs she continues her ceaseless pitch: "This kind of thing doesn't happen in Rome, you know, but there are so *many* treasures hidden about the Etrurian countryside. I try as best I can to get the word out—and we're only an hour's drive from Rome!"

Back on the street, we're just about to press on our way when Mary Jane breaks off our nascent thoughts of escape. "You must come to my house for some light lunch. My partner Fulvio is there." We're already being ushered down the cobblestones as she continues, "He's written several cookbooks. We'll make *bruschette*—the real kind, you know." We murmur with sudden and genuine appreciation at her offer, as constant hunger has continued to plague us. But Mary Jane pounces on our mispronunciation: "Brus*k*ette, not brus*h*ette, with an 'e' not an 'a' on the end." She hastens on, "Fulvio picked the olives himself just this week and pressed the oil—it's from his family grove. You'll see there's absolutely nothing like it." Powerless against these epicurean seductions and not a little curious to see the sanctuary of this enthusiast, we hurry to keep up. "I never wear heels!" she proclaims, pointing to her colorful flats atop the fissured cobbles. "Can you just imagine how long they'd last on these roads?"

Fulvio greets us as at the door. He's a taciturn but vigorous retiree in a cashmere cardigan, with a cookie-duster mustache and a head of snow-white hair. He quietly retreats as we enter what Mary Jane informs us is a *palazzo*. We are dutifully stunned. It is large enough to be grand, modest enough to be owned. A spacious entryway is cluttered with ceramics, cloths, and prints and opens upon a cavernous drawing room lined with books. On one side it is a true library, with shelves two floors high and a mezzanine reached by a spiral stair. On the walls hang painted landscapes and colorful still lifes. In one corner are two large portraits of the same stolid male, one in the much decorated dress of a US Navy officer, the other in the suit and tie of a captain of industry—still adorned with his Navy Cross. This seems to be the father and patron of the good life that surrounds us.

Upon the flagstones of the floor lie acres of Persian rugs, and on them sit creaking chests woven with rattan. "The Victoria and Albert Museum wanted one of my armoires," Mary Jane comments casually as our eyes linger upon her treasures, "but as you can see, I need all the storage I can get!" All around is strewn the detritus of bibliophilia: heavy oaken furniture stacked high with leather tomes, sumptuous chairs encircled by reading lights, rolling carts ranked with hulking reference works, sheaves of paper bursting from archival boxes. It is the very essence of scholarly disorder, a warehouse for her knowledge, a staging ground for the cultivation of nostalgia. Sarah pines with ill-disguised longing.

After we loiter just long enough to absorb the magnificence (and visit the Russian-themed bathroom), Mary Jane calls us in to lunch. Fulvio welcomes us into the spacious country kitchen and seats us in stout, carved chairs. This room too is stuffed with a kind of hard-working luxury: hefty sideboards, traditionally patterned earthenware, souvenirs and treasures from throughout Europe. Mary Jane gives a brief tour: "This one's from Transylvania, I got it past the border in exchange for cigarette contraband! This one a friend just brought me from Amalfi—a former student of mine was in Rome and she took the train up to see me for lunch."

In the presence of such opulence, our lunch seems rather ascetic: toasted bread (brus*k*ette) with oil, shards of Parmigiano-Reggiano, a carafe of white wine. But the conspicuous restraint is a conceit. "Fulvio himself picked the olives this very week from his own family grove," Mary Jane says, looking possessively at her gourmand partner, "or did I tell you that already?" Seeing how we tackle the cheese with particular enthusiasm, she remarks, "I once had a visitor from Maine, and after we were done, there was no cheese left! You can't get it in Maine, you know. It's like medicine for your bones!" Fulvio tops off our glasses again and again with wine. "I buy cases of it at the museum down the road—it's in a twelfth-century tower," Mary Jane informs us. "This is our usual twelve-thirty snack," she practically giggles with delight as we continue to crunch and smack away, then pedantically corrects herself: "Well, lunch is usually at one o'clock," surely according to some unwritten and august tradition.

Our chins (and my beard) drip with oil. It's a kind of unction, our coronation, our election as children of the light. The wine flows and flows with unnoticeable effect, as does the diaphanous oil, sponged to nothingness by the airy toast. We eat and eat and drink and drink. The meal is so ethereal it seems we could continue eating without end.

When it's finally and indisputably time to go, we're all brimming with bonhomie, clicking off valedictory portraits with our companions of the light. To send us on our way, Mary Jane gives us a complimentary copy of one of her own books about Etruria. So thankful and overwhelmed—and tipsy—are we that we consent to shelling out our own euros for a second, her latest ("Oh, I would give it to you for free, but I can't, I just can't, it's just out, what would my publisher say?") as well as Fulvio's self-published cookbook.

As we stumble away, minds spinning with nobility and wine, the specter of an absent Luther rises again. Whether it was Mary Jane's incessant discourse or just plain hedonism, we'd almost completely forgotten Luther. His light footsteps are lost and silent in a landscape saturated with other histories, obscured by papal coats of arms, by English kings, by dukes, by Romans and Etruscans. How could the rough tunic and unshod feet of an Augustinian friar have anything to do with these exalted echelons swirling about, passing up and down the Via Cassia in carriage and litter?

Giddy from all these spirits and queasy from so much oil, we seem to float our way out of town, chasing away headaches and nausea with a vigorous pace. Soon we're walking through a heavy oaken forest beneath the dormant craters of the Cimini Hills. The air is damp, the trees waving in the wind, the ground moist with decay. Our forest track is parked up with the cars of mushroom hunters. Autumn is upon us, and a chilly wind swirls falling leaves before our steps.

At Capranica, our trail through the hazelnut trees gives way to concrete apartments, then passes beneath a rusticated arch—its keystone carved with the three bees and crossed keys of Pope Urban VIII—before finally narrowing to a gully of a street. Like in so many other Italian cities, the outsides of the buildings are run down and visually cluttered, their stucco streaked, discolored, and dropping away in chunks. Wires run hither and thither along with pipes and other baffling bits of infrastructure. Sarah suggests that Italians have lived with ruins for so long, they can no longer tell the difference. But when we can steal a glance through a rare uncurtained window, all is new and quite luxurious, often spartanly modern. Germany keeps its public spaces pristine, while Italy keeps its trendy elegance private and inside.

The hilltop city finally narrows to a point. Descending to the camper below, through a maze of stairs and arches and tunnels, we look back upon Capranica. It is a ship's prow, plunging through the foamy tufa sea.

In the camper we feast on piles of fresh porcini mushrooms, bought and painstakingly cleaned by my diligent dad, then cooked in butter and oil. Not even a truffle could taste so delicious, piled atop our linguine, steaming and hot, while the gale rocks the camper from without.

The next two days are mostly a blur. The same generic fields, the same hint of distant volcanic hills, the never-absent electrical wires, the invasion of our peace by constant traffic and dogs. The most striking site we find is in Sutri, where Etruscan tombs carved from the soft rock are open to explore. Elsewhere we see many similar prehistoric grottos, almost universally filled with garbage.

Now within (extreme) commuting distance to Rome, we come across whole subdivided fields filled with gated villas. Though brand new, they already manage to look like ruins in their half-completeness. Wires and satellite dishes sprout from bare-block walls; algae floats in tiny swimming pools; ambitious yet unfinished stone enclosures are inevitably patched with chain link. These architectural Frankensteins seem always to be guarded by ferocious, rabid, or absolutely terrified dogs. They tax both our nerves and our aim.

Late one day we catch up to and walk with Konrad, a tall young German doctor with floppy hair and thick leather boots. His dad was a Lutheran pastor whose best friend was the town's Catholic priest—ecumenism embodied. Our walk makes perfect sense to him—so much sense that doing something so drastic seems even a bit odd. Is it that hard to reconcile two churches already so close?

Konrad is less clear about his own reasons for walking. He has a vague sense that there is something meaningful in pilgrimage but knows not what that thing might be. He could have done some other hike, but Compostela seemed too cliché and wilderness adventures not historical enough. He started at the French border, in the Aosta valley, but had yet to have any overwhelming epiphanies from his month-long trek. He's the most earnest fellow pilgrim we've met along the way, and there's a grace to be found in his lack of expectations. In pilgrimage, as in life, the more certain we are of what we'll find, the less likely we are to find it.

Ten

Many Romes—St. Peter's—one thousand miles—St. Paul's Outside-the-Walls—celebratory supper—necropolis—Reformation Day—Scala Sancta—Luther and Rome, then and now

From our last stop in La Storta at a campground named—in English!—The Happy Camper, Sarah and I careen as quickly as possible into Rome. We accompany the morning's rush hour traffic, unhappily breathing its exhaust. When possible we scurry along the narrow sidewalk; at times it narrows to a ribbon of dirt, at others it disappears altogether.

Shrines line the blaring street. In one conspicuous roadside niche built out from a retaining wall hangs a crucified Christ. Thick bars protect the dying Jesus from car and vandal. *In hoc signo vinces*, says the inscription in Roman capitals below—"In this sign you will conquer." These are the words heard by Emperor Constantine in a dream, accompanied by a vision of the cross, just before he entered Rome victorious; they also mark the beginning of Rome's official adoption of Christianity.

Ours is certainly no triumphal entry. We soak up the stress of our fellow commuters. There they are in their cars, creeping slowly, heads in hands, fingers tapping, gazing impatiently at their watches. Above us cruise suburban trains. This city is not subject to the pope, the king, nor any other earthly power. It is subject to the automobile. Even parks, once green with grass and full of chirping birds, have become plots of hardpack dirt full of parked cars and awash in the ceaseless sonic din.

Books tell us that pilgrims approached the city from Monte Mario, which nicely blocks the view until a single dramatic reveal. The hill is now a nature park. Joggers jog, vagrants wake; cut chain link fences here and there suggest sordid rendezvous and getaways. It doesn't seem like it would be particularly

The many cupolas of Rome from Monte Mario

safe at night. All the seediness sloughs away though, as we turn a bend and there before us, shining through a blanket of light smog—or is it a heavenly aureole? an artistic chiaroscuro?—rise the spires and domes and red-tiled roofs of the Eternal City.

Luther saluted the city from this very spot, a moment he remembered well and reported decades later: "Blessed be thou, holy Rome, truly blessed because of the martyrs, dripping with their blood."[1] The phrase is not his own, but we have every reason to think that Luther uttered it sincerely. We stand there gawking, breathing the pine-tree-filtered air. I recite Luther's phrase for our camera—or rather try so many times to get it right that Sarah dissolves into hysterics.

As I stand before such a view and stutter out his sentence, it's clearer than ever that it requires a powerful filter of piety to see what Luther saw. Three disparate layers pile upon each other in our view, all working to stanch rather than contemplate the blood that seemed so important to Luther and other pilgrims.

There's Rome, the capital of antiquity, the ancient world's largest city bombinating within the capacious Aurelian walls. Of this past only a few outward signs remain.

Then there's the ecclesiastical hub, the See of Peter, celestial heir to the superseded temporal empire. Its steeples, domes, and belfries still dominate the city's silhouette—though most of these came after Luther.

But it's Rome, the throbbing modern megalopolis that meets us squarely when we descend from our hilltop park. Street sides are more packed with cars than before: double- or even triple-parked! Vehicles fill every void, even narrow medians and tiny traffic islands. The roads themselves whine with scooters and growl with buses. On boulevards the thoughtful rows of shade trees work hard to dampen the noise and clean the air. It's pleasant strolling down the cycle paths (wondrously free of cars) beside the modest apartments bristling with TV antennae.

Rome's sewers are still stamped with the imperial emblem.

Most of the outward signs of the ancient city are interred far beneath our feet and deep within our minds. The only omnipresent vestige, still stamped with the emblem of the old empire—SPQR—is the cast-iron grates and covers of the sewers, a reminder that Rome's lasting glory was its robust infrastructure, including lowly waste removal.

The Viale Angelico leads us straight toward St. Peter's Basilica, along a tram line, crowded by neo-Renaissance apartments. At one fantastically confused intersection, we glimpse, peeking from behind a gray administrative complex, through a spider-web of catenary wires, the parabolic dome of St. Peter's. And now the mingling crowds grow thicker, the entry-arches of the square appear, the statues of the pontiffs stand above with their backs toward us. Then, squeezing through the multitude, past the trinket peddlers, and finally through the towering double colonnade, Sarah and I walk into St. Peter's Square itself. We're not quite at the end of our pilgrimage, but almost.

After seventy days of walking, and just as many days before that planning, we've built the moment up to great significance. Here it is, the Eternal City, the center of Western Christendom for more than a millennium. Standing beneath the sheer magnitude of the basilica, the graceful curve of the cupola, the colossal and energetic statues all around, we are buffeted by contradictory emotions. The sheer profusion of stolid decoration, the cyclopean scale of the whole place towering above and around the milling swarms of faithful, turn our seventy days of effort into something rather small.

Such overwhelming feelings are admittedly engineered. That St. Peter's looks like an American capital building (or rather, that an American capital building looks like St. Peter's) is no mistake. The Roman church was not just sovereign over priests and bishops and their ecclesiastical affairs. It was, in its own reading of history's dispensations, the true heir of the Roman Empire. The church's faithfulness had superseded pagan idolatry and decadence, its apostles and martyrs became the charter members of God's earthly city. This inheritance endures, even if diminished. Today's Vatican is not only the capital of Catholicism but a sovereign state as well.

The Egyptian obelisk at the center of St. Peter's Square drives us even further back into the church's mixed-up ancestry and succession. On its early modern plinth, the spire stands more than one hundred and thirty feet tall, a gnomon of enigmatic origins casting shadows daily around the square—a task for which it is well made, being originally carved 3,500 years ago for the sun god Ra at Heliopolis. The granite stele was moved from Alexandria by none other than depraved Caligula himself, and it decorated the nearby circus of equally infamous Nero, where according to tradition Peter was crucified. There it stood for 1,500 years until in 1585 Pope Sixtus V shifted it ever so slightly to its present location. This Franciscan pope also replaced the gilt sphere (thought to hold the remains of Julius Caesar) on top with a cross and set it on a base decorated with the Roman eagle and four lions. Inscribed on the base are words attributed to St. Anthony: "Behold the cross of the Lord; enemies, take flight, the Lion of Judah is victorious." All the religious and political wanderings of this monument were then cleansed with a ceremony of exorcism. History piles upon history, God upon gods, power upon power, while empire after empire erects and repurposes impressive things to shock and awe.

A giant statue of Peter stands in front of his basilica. He's holding his famous key, dressed in the toga of a Roman senator. Opposite stands St. Paul, equally athletic beneath his robes, gripping a weighty broadsword. The lowly apostles now rule the earth. The story of Christ and of the church is saturated with such inversions: the Lord of the universe incarnate as a child, a scraggly band of unlearned fanatics persevering under persecution until their underdoggedness is transformed by imperial blessing. Rome inverts that humble incarnation with monuments and prestige. The incongruity of it all is quite confusing.

But Luther would have seen none of this. In 1511 the foundation of St. Peter's had only just been dug—soon to be financed by certain letters of indulgence, about which Luther would have something to say.

We'll return tomorrow to see the necropolis beneath, but for now we must continue to our true and final destination—not St. Peter's but St. Paul's outside the Walls. It is our intuition that the estrangement between Lutherans and Catholics is latent in the stories of these two apostles. Peter is the rock, the holder of the keys, the first among apostolic equals, the material bridge to Christ's incarnation, the sign of continuity. Paul's is the path of conversion, of disruption, of the startling discontinuity of Israel's election extended to the gentiles, of the rupture of old ways. Despite his persecution of early Christians, Paul became the one who carried Christ to the world at large. It is a conflict not only repeated throughout church history but evident already in the New Testament. But both Peter and Paul are pillars of the church. Neither is to be jettisoned in preference for the other. So we choose to end our ecumenical journey with both.

We walk down to and along the Tiber, here the color of bottle glass, paying close attention to our GPS. In the middle of the Ponte Sublicio, just as we cross—physically, not figuratively—the Tiber River, our trip odometer clicks over to 1,000 miles. Being modern pilgrims, we snap a selfie and tweet it.

The 1,000-mile mark, on the bridge over the Tiber River

It's only another mile or so beyond the old Aurelian walls to St. Paul's, the site, so it is said, of the apostle Paul's remains. In Luther's day it was the oldest and possibly the largest intact basilica in the city. But St. Paul's, like so many other buildings that Luther saw, has since burnt to the ground. Only bits and pieces of the ancient church remain. The golden apse dates from the thirteenth century, as do a couple of arches and a splendid medieval cloister. As with Luther's cell in Erfurt, can this really be the *same* church? Its continuity must lie not in the physical stuff but in the person—here, the person of St. Paul.

The rebuilt building is absolutely stunning in its size and luxury, its opulence and skill—and also in its coldness. It is a showcase for stone: whole quarries of Carrara marble are inlaid on the floor, ribbed in pillars and pilasters, and carved into volutes and capitals. Great rainbow panels of red and green and gold and gray hang on every wall, streaked like rain-soaked watercolors. Instead of the usual stained-glass windows, the aisles and clerestory are lit by panes of agate, arranged to highlight symmetry and order—fractal forms that luminesce. The church is a gallery of abstract natural art.

There is Paul with his sword in several iterations and vintages, and Peter jangling his keys. Christ hovers in the apse in that ambiguous judging, blessing pose. And lining the entire architrave are images of every single pope, from Peter down to Benedict XVI (Francis not being elected till 2013).

The dissonance we small pilgrims and Lutherans felt at St. Peter's Square is repeated here, even magnified. This is truly a "basilica" in the classical sense: a place for kings (*basileus*, in Greek), for holding court, for dispensing justice, and for granting favors. Yet unlike a palace for the privileged, this basilica is open to the public. With God as ruler, any and all may wander, gaze, and contemplate in person what elsewhere would stand behind lock and key and armed guard. Here the rabble could contemplate an ordered, geometrical heaven, built atop the bones of Paul.

In the middle of it all is a hole dug into the floor, a stylized archaeological excavation. We go down some marble steps to take a closer look. There's a kneeler and in front of it, covered with a thick slab of glass, is the purported tomb. Just behind, at eye level with the kneeling devotee, is a wrought grill protecting the sarcophagus. On display above are the chains in which the apostle Paul was bound—while writing many letters, we are to presume.

I try—I really try—to muster some feelings related to my proximity to holiness—or even to artistic onslaught. But I remain as resolutely cold as the church itself. Paul's words—his own testimony, his deft steering of unruly congregations through conflict toward fellowship with each other, his collection for the churches in Jerusalem, his insight into the soul's psychology, his wise teaching on sin and forgiveness, his weaving from strains of Jewish thought a theology of the world's reconciliation through the person of Jesus—live a mightier life than all these relics.

Who knows, moreover, if any of them are authentic. It's impossible to prove for sure. Besides, knowing what we do of the physical universe—of molecules and electrons, of the constant renovation of the body, of the blowing of the dust in the wind—who's to say that you and I don't have a bit of Paul physically inside us already? Our modern metaphysics trump the old, while the written word endures beyond many graves.

That night we do two things. First, we gain permission for my parents and Zeke to sleep in beds at our hostel. They're not pilgrims, technically speaking, and thus don't really have the right to stay at the *Spedale della Provvidenza*, whose rooms are reserved for religious purposes. But in the end the Franciscan sisters who run the place relent for just one night, unable to bar from use the ranks and ranks of empty bunks.

Then we head out for a celebratory supper at a fabulous pizzeria. We're joined by Will, a Lutheran pastor from the United States who's on sabbatical in Rome, and Dom Ambrose, an Augustinian Canon giddy to be studying in the beating heart of the Catholicism. Many people asked us if we were going to seek an audience with the pope—perhaps to plead for some dramatic sign of ecumenical reconciliation. But this friendly pizza party seems to fit the spirit of our pilgrimage much better. We end as we began, with a pair of fellow Christians, Lutheran and Roman Catholic, talking over dinner.

Our tiny table is packed, the restaurant crowded. As the wine in our carafes disappears, so the volume of our voices climbs. By the end, surrounded by a sea of conviviality, we're practically shouting out our conversation. And just as we wash down the last slices of our pizza, my Aunt Sally and Uncle Vince drop in—from Chicago!—adding to the festive air.

Late the next morning—far later than we've let ourselves sleep in weeks—Sarah wakes from a dream with a start. She's just crossed the finish line of a marathon. While raising her hands and shouting "Yes!" in triumph, she topples over backward and flails in front of the cheering thousands. It's some kind of deeply Lutheran commentary on the ambiguity of victory, perhaps.

This is the end of a long and stressful race for us, not just of walking but of logistics and communication, too. For weeks before we even took our first pilgrim steps, we planned and trained; booked campers and planes, cars and trains; found hotels and hostels and rooms to let. For seventy days we navigated unknown miles of unmarked paths; fought with traffic large and loud; and walked a thousand miles, too. It's with good reason that Sarah shouted in triumph—and stumbled. This is the finish of something big, something difficult.

We have an appointment at St. Peter's in the afternoon, so we take the morning to amble through the city toward it in the company of Mom, Dad, and Zeke. First we climb the Capitoline Hill. From the park on top we can see just how huge the dome of St. Peter's really is. It seems to float like a spaceship high above the rest of the city—a feat made all the more impressive, considering Rome's other mammoth monuments.

From that hill we go down and past the Circus Maximus, reciting all the lines we remember from Mel Brooks's *History of the World*. The ancient racetrack is occupied by some kind of weapons fair. Generals in fatigues and jaunty berets, military police with belts sagging with pistols, and a very few curious civilians wander about the camouflaged Quonset huts, amphibious vehicles, and the ferocious bug-like helicopters whose rotors droop like insect antennae. It seems incongruous at first, but Rome's empire was built on its army, after all, and our own peace and prosperity depend upon numerous sharpened teeth—ruffians and tyrants notwithstanding.

We then stroll by the tumbled remains of the Forum, iconic as ever, standing like the wreckage of a storm-leveled forest. It's evocative to us, but there's no evidence that Luther took any interest in Rome's classical past. He mentions the Pantheon and links other unspecific ruins to the various sackings Rome received, noting that this flattened city, sown with ashes, lay "two heights of men deep under the surface."[2]

While on the up-and-up from its medieval nadir, the Rome that Luther saw was still eerily diminished. Whereas at its apex its walls enclosed a million souls or maybe two, in 1500 it was home to merely forty or fifty thousand. Much of the classical city had been utterly erased, its only citizens the flocks of sheep grazing on its seven canonical hills. Most of the famous aqueducts and sewers had not functioned for centuries. It was as if, in the year 3500, the whole of modern-day New York City was reduced to a squatters' camp in Central Park. There were some grand administrative

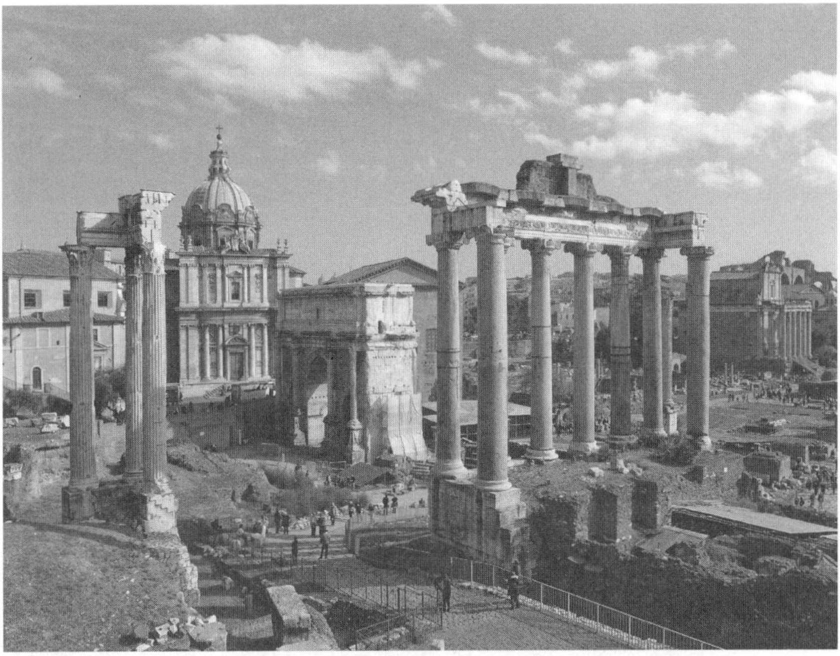

The Forum we see today was still buried when Luther was in Rome.

buildings, churches, and ecclesiastical palaces, to be sure, but it was a ghost of what it used to be.

After Rome's fall the church considered itself the empire's successor and built its houses of worship throughout the disintegrating city, repurposing much pagan masonry for a new and holier purpose. The ruins of classical Rome became archaeological lessons inscribed into the landscape, signs of the end to which all human glory comes, of the vanity of empires, indications of God's new dispensation upon earth. Many of these sentiments were shared by travelers who, starting in the seventeenth century, were out on some or another version of the Grand Tour: sketching ruins, making rubbings of inscriptions, falling into nostalgic reveries.

It wasn't really until the Enlightenment that the *philosophes* began to overturn this moral reading, looking at those huge walls, the still standing Colosseum, the truncated aqueducts, this Forum, and wondering how great this civilization must have been—and could be once again. It took Napoleon to begin the physical unearthing, a project continued with much nationalist spirit through the nineteenth and twentieth centuries. Italy, the modern nation-state, founds itself not upon the church but on its imperial predecessor.

We don't see today what Luther saw at all, either physically or allegorically. Those two storeys of dirt remained in place well into the nineteenth century, and we're more likely now to contemplate Rome's former glory than to learn from its demise.

Returning to St. Peter's Square, we find it being cleared of chairs by a large crew. Earlier in the afternoon 120,000 youth had gathered to hear an address from Pope Benedict. We linger with my parents for a while amid the clutter-cleaning hubbub, then bid them a final and heartfelt good-bye. They've been a stalwart crew, steadfast, patient helpers for all our efforts. They've bought us food, prepared our meals, found us places to sleep. They've played with Zeke, discovered wine, cheese, and olive delicacies to sate our bottomless appetites. They've tended our temperamental camper-van—fueling its thirsty engine, searching for strangely threaded propane tank adaptors, filling it with water, emptying its all too puny refuse reservoirs. All this they've managed to do where they neither speak the languages nor understand the customs and regulations. Bravo to them, and farewell. Zeke stays behind with us, and we watch my parents walk away one last time, waving to them through the crowds until they're out of sight.

Even before we left Strasbourg several months ago, we secured a spot in the restricted group that is daily admitted to see the tomb of the apostle Peter, deep beneath the basilica. It is a reminder that all the Catholic churches in Rome—indeed in the whole world—are built atop relics, material reminders that worship is not only in the present but unites in prayer with the faithful of all generations. We enter not the basilica's main portal—where a readout warns us of a two-hour wait—but through a gate off to the side. We show our reservation to the vigilant Swiss Guards, who wave us into a queue. A digital sign flashes that our wait will be seven minutes and five seconds. After our precisely calculated time in line, we descend into the dark necropolis.

We're given our tour by a young woman with long blonde hair, dark eyes, and a well-cut black suit. A doctor in archaeology, she speaks English with great command and with an accent of mystifying provenance: Italian? Or is it Slavic? Perhaps Romanian? Impossible to say. Though her script is quite rehearsed, it's delivered with gravitas and conviction—and just the subtlest suspicion of emotion.

At the time of Peter's death, this "city of the dead" on Vatican Hill was outside the city walls, and what is far beneath the church's present floor was then ground level. What we see excavated looks remarkably like the mausolea we've seen all over Italy. Our guide leads us through a bricked corridor where we peer into what seem like rooms, stacked with evocations of great patrons and their petty clients—such a space was probably owned by an entire family. Smaller niches were meant for bones of lesser members; greater niches were more ornately carved, some with statues of the deceased or their patron gods; other dead had their own ornate sarcophagi. It's unlikely that fisherman Peter would have had the means, social or financial, for a spot in such a cemetery, but tradition tells us that certain Roman Christians guarded his remains and eventually interred them in their family's memorial room.

When the recently converted Emperor Constantine wanted to build a church on the spot of Peter's bones, he planned to knock the entire cemetery down. But instead, to appease the vociferous and still pagan local notables whose ancestors were interred within, the aisles and rooms of the necropolis were simply filled in to make the foundation. And so from the fourth century on, building after building, century after century of stones and storeys piled atop the tomb.

No one seems to have thought much about whether Peter's bones were really there or not (though shameless peddling of bogus relics by spiritual entrepreneurs made the cautious investor suspicious). According to tradition, Peter's skull was at rest with that of St. Paul down the road in the church of St. John Lateran. But the living piety of the people made these kinds of questions quite absurd. Martyrs and their tombs were the very first places of Christian celebration. The festival traditions were passed on from generation to generation. Skepticism was not a virtue, if it existed at all. Even as scathing as Luther was against the relic trade—and the costly pilgrimages that drove it—it was not because he doubted that Rome's churches were built on top of myriads of martyrs.

The necropolis was briefly rediscovered in the sixteenth century during the earthworks for the current building, but it took until 1939 for the hunt for Peter's bones to begin in earnest. After Pope Pius XI expressed his wish to be laid to rest beside his famous predecessor, academics and archaeologists took up the task, emptying portions of the necropolis, which they dated to the second and third centuries. It was painstaking work that continued all through World War II—done in secret to avert the prying eyes of Italy's Nazi allies, always strangely eager for sacred artifacts. The forty thousand cubic yards of excavated dirt were spread clandestinely throughout the Vatican's gardens to hide the dig.

Finally, they found inside a box some peculiar remains, largely intact, of a sturdy working man judged to be in his sixties or seventies, who had died in the first century. The bones were of the same body, and no others were mixed with it, so it seems to have been well cared for. Certain stresses on the bones seem even to suggest an inverted crucifixion. Conclusion: St. Peter had been found! And there we see him, through a tiny slot, behind some bars and Plexiglas, lit by spotlight. Here is the material link to the ascended Christ, preserved through the ages by faithful remembrance, the executed witness who in death preached even louder than in life.

The tour was nicely done: the dark cellar, the context of the place, the pious papal desire, the careful excavation, the secrecy, the Nazi villains, the carbon dating, all leading up to the dramatic discovery and the church's solemn confirmation. As for me, I find it educational, agreeable, but unconvincing; too many slim odds, multiplied. Sarah is more inclined to give the bones the benefit of the doubt. But such responses—yea or nay, belief or unbelief—serve only to confuse two real and important points that have little to do with science or superstition, Lutheranism or Catholicism.

Christianity is a historical religion based on people and events that occurred not in some airy ether up above but in time, in space, in bodies, and in spoken words between human beings. That somewhere, somehow, the bones of an apostle—perhaps all of them—exist (or at one point did) is not really a matter of belief or disbelief but simply an expression of the nature of the Christian faith. And if that is the case, it's not unreasonable at all to offer such remains a kind of honor above others, to pay respects to our ancestors in the faith just as we do the ancestors in our family.

I struggle to identify what irks me. Is it my Protestantism? My modernity? My scientific mind? That Peter's bones are here is a matter of tradition, not dogma. But the presentation was all science, pure and simple, urging us to trust not just in the church but in its intellectual due-diligence—and implying ever so slightly that only the irrational would object. When Luther labeled many relics shams, his objections were all mixed up too: part denial of phony patent medicine, part vitriol at broken trust. But his challenge was not really scientific. He did not reject the existence of apostles' bones (though possibly their abundance) but rather their effect in certain sorts of Christian practice.

He aimed to point believers' trust toward its only worthy object: Christ and his promises.

The rhetoric of Luther's opponents at the time, however, served to flatten diversity of Catholic teaching, turning Luther's scruples about indulgences—and pilgrimages and relics and other modes of penance—into rejection of the entire Western tradition. This caught Luther off guard, as he felt his criticisms to be part and parcel to his calling as a "doctor of the church." His own responses, many of them less than temperate, fueled the fire, thereby complicating any prospect of reconciliation.

This much is now recognized by Catholics and Protestants alike. The 2013 joint statement of the international Lutheran-Catholic dialogue, "From Conflict to Communion," admits as much:

> Luther believed that his protests were in conformity with the teaching of the church and, indeed, even defended that teaching. Any thought of dividing the church was far from his mind and was strongly rejected by him. But there was no understanding for his concerns among the ecclesiastical and theological authorities either in Germany or in Rome. The years following the famous "95 Theses" of 1517 were marked by increasing polemics. As the disputes intensified, Luther's primarily religious concerns were increasingly intertwined with questions of church authority and were also submerged by questions of political power. It was not Luther's understanding of the gospel considered by itself which brought about conflict and schism in the church, but rather the ecclesial and political concomitants of the Reformation movement. (§13)

Luther's later judgments were hardened by the fires of persecution and attack. His sense of betrayal was heightened by his former piety. In his mind he was furthering a broad and fully faithful movement, with roots in the mendicant orders, to take Christian discipline more seriously, to separate sordid earthly affairs from the task of preaching, and to practice and spread what we now call discipleship.

I struggle with this all, contemplating Peter's purported bones. Are they really his? It seems unlikely. Does it truly matter? If bodies matter, bones must matter, too—and whose they were. But even if the bones here on display aren't precisely those of Jesus's apostle, even I can appreciate—standing beneath the millions of tons of marble, bronze, and statuary, after those thousands of years and lives spent building, cleaning, updating this gargantuan shrine in honor of a fisherman—that it does matter where things happen, and that such bones, wherever they may be, exist—or did. And I appreciate in a way I didn't before—and struggle still to do, Lutheran that I am, and a shallow-rooted American, too—that an earthly place can carry heavenly significance.

Many are the Protestants who call Jerusalem and Galilee "the Holy Land" and do so because it is the land of Jesus, of David, of Joshua, of Abraham, and of Isaac. It is the Bible's stage. Precisely the same spirit is at work in Rome, but it extends that same concept to the life of the apostles, giving those who took Christ's news an honor fitting their courage and inspiration. For if they—if Peter and if Paul—had not preached Christ, had not persevered under violent opposition, the message had been lost.

St. Peter's above stands on its own artistic merit, but visiting it is a very different pilgrimage—for art, for awe, for bucket lists. But you'll find the beating heart of the basilica's religion not in the marble or the Michelangelo but in the necropolis below, bathed in martyrs' blood, bones awaiting the resurrection's call.

In the end the Western church, despite its many monuments, determined that the center of its life was not in shrines or in basilicas, fixed to one single place, but in the supper of the Lord, which is intrinsically portable. The body and blood of Christ can travel anywhere on earth with equal merit and effect. The work of Christ does not depend upon ready access to holy sites. Jesus is present where the people gather, where God's promises are evoked, where Christ in teaching and in body is truly present. These are things upon which both Lutherans and Catholics can and do agree.

The next morning Zeke, Sarah, and I do what we could not in the past weeks: attend a Lutheran church. And what a stunning space it is, the *Christuskirche*, appropriately Italianate without, all dim and Byzantine within, coruscating softly with gold leaf. It's built from materials brought expressly from various cities of Lutheran Germany, an attempt to reconcile in stone the differences of the past, to construct a harmony from formerly irreconcilable geographies.

This is where Pope John Paul II made the first-ever visit by any pope to a Lutheran church. He did so in 1983, during Luther's five hundredth birth year; a stone plaque in the back of the nave commemorates the occasion. It was the site of further ecumenical occasions as well. In 1998, Cardinal

Ratzinger (the future Pope Benedict XVI) came here to talk about the future Lutheran-Catholic "Joint Declaration on the Doctrine of Justification," which both churches signed the following year. Most recently, Pope Francis visited in November 2015, provocatively hinting that he would be willing to ease the restrictions on receiving the Supper for Catholic-Protestant couples, a small gesture that could open wide the doors for the sharing of holy communion.

It's not until the organ begins to thump and the congregation to belt out the earthy strains of "Ein Feste Burg Ist Unser Gott" that we realize—with feelings somewhere between shock and uncanniness—that today is Reformation Day! But the hymn, instead of reverberating with Protestant triumphalism, heralds an ecumenical occasion. The aisles and porch are filled with extra chairs for visitors; up in front is Catholic prelate Max Eugen Kemper, who gives the sermon—about grace, *selbsverständlich!* of course! The confession of faith, instead of the usual Apostles' Creed, is an antiphonal recitation of selections from the "Joint Declaration," the one and only binding doctrinal statement that the Catholic Church has ever promulgated in concert with a Protestant church.

The anthem is Luther's *Nun Freut Euch*, "Dear Christians, Let Us Now Rejoice," begun by the choir hidden in the loft. Luther's heartfelt verses recount the whole history of salvation. In exchange for taking on our sin and despair, Christ gives us his very own heavenly glory. "I give myself all up for thee / And I will fight the battle," pronounces Luther's Christ. "For I am thine, and thou art mine / And my place also shall be thine." The words float down from on high, resounding from the golden vault, ecstatic strains descending straight from the heavenly host. And then the congregation joins the choir's strains, becoming one, both Catholic and Protestant, both angels and humans, belting out good news that's neither limited in scope nor punitive in judgment but uniting in its purpose: "So that God's Kingdom may be spread / All to his glory reaching."

At the end of the service the pastor invites Sarah forward, who hopes her German is not too compromised by five weeks of pretend-Italian. Before the confessionally mixed crowd, she introduces our thousand-mile pilgrimage, says we've just arrived, and lauds the day's festivities. It is a fitting punctuation for our trip. We return to Luther, not the Luther as he once was, in unremitting struggle with the pope, but Luther as he now can be, freed from confessional barricades, a teacher for the entire church. Today's celebration is a joyful contradiction of many centuries of slander.

There's one last stop on our abbreviated itinerary: the Archbasilica of St. John Lateran and the Scala Sancta beside it. It's not called "arch" for nothing. Despite the renown and size of today's St. Peter's and its status as crown of Vatican hill, it is not the capital of Catholicism. If any church deserves that title it is this, the pope's cathedral, dedicated to the Johns—both the apostle and baptizer. Destroyed by fire and crumbling, its grandeur lagged in Luther's day—but not its significance. He longed, but failed for lack of time, to say a mass in its erstwhile nave to win a plenary indulgence for his mother.

Today the edifice is almost comically imposing, all pillars and pediments of Brobdingnagian portions, lorded over by hulking, vigorous statues of Jesus and Mary, evangelists and popes. It's the very picture of the church triumphant, exactly as it's meant to be. Like so many churches we've seen on this trip already, it is Baroque in style, imbued with the dynamism of a world-expanding, Europe-dominating church. This kind of cyclopean display, according to art historian Alessandro Castrini, owes itself in part to Luther—who by his part in kicking off the Counter-Reformation pushed Catholic buildings toward this colossal scale: "Paradoxically, we see the architectural outcome of the Reformation nowhere in the world more clearly than here" in Rome.[3]

It seems so out of place, so out of pace with our own times. The church has lost its struggle for universal jurisdiction, conspiracy theories aside. So many other spirits wrangle for our attention and allegiance, not least of which are nation-states and cities and their own competing architecture and social consciousness. And as for spectacles, the processions, the drama of the mass, the pomp and ritual of ordinations and prelate visits are ousted in our minds by more compelling constructions and spectacular events. What is a church service to the Super Bowl?

As for us, our eyes and minds are exhausted by Rome's magnificence, and our time is too short to wait out the dress-up affair that's blocking the portal of the church. So we head across the square to our last stop of all, the Scala Sancta, the Holy Stairs, dismantled and transported from Jerusalem at the behest of Emperor Constantine's mother Helena. They are, according to tradition, the steps of Pilate's palace that Jesus climbed during his passion. Here we have not just the occasion for reverence or contemplation but a piece of interactive drama. The pilgrim ascends the steps, painfully and slowly, and in so doing enters into a simple, unequivocal *imitatio Christi*. That's what the pilgrims did and do here still, crawling on their knees, reciting a *Paternoster* on each step.

The Scala Sancta, which Luther climbed to earn an indulgence for his grandfather

For such an act the pilgrim still gets an indulgence. The panel at the bottom still reads (rather bureaucratically): "PLENARY INDULGENCE: on all Fridays of Lent, and once more each year on an occasion of one's choice; PARTIAL INDULGENCE: on all other days of the year, as long as one is sincerely repentant of one's sins." This is what Luther sought here five hundred years ago, not for himself but for his deceased grandfather.

It's perhaps the most iconic scene of Luther's stay in Rome. Elsewhere in the city he was hurried through his masses by less-than-patient priests, unsettled by the openly debauched lives of cardinals and prelates, disgusted by the jarring cohabitation of utter squalor and ostentatious opulence. But none of these reveal the slightest chink in Luther's pious armor. Despite the glaring managerial deficiencies, the church itself and its meritorious deposit, the accumulated good of all the saints, remained pure and essentially intact. Its rituals and teaching, despite the consummately flawed delivery, were both adequate and upright.

But here, at least according to his later reports, we glimpse a hairline crack in Luther's fervent youthful monkdom. He ascended these very steps as prescribed, imitating Christ, full of his most sincere intent, duly winning all the merit ascribed to such an act. Then at the top, where satisfaction and triumph ought to have awaited, a tiny drop of doubt leaked out: "Who knows if it is true?"[4]

The simple phrase swells into a flood of questions. What exactly is this *it* that may or not be true? Is *it* the quantified merit attached to a certified religious work? Is *it* the release of a suffering soul from purgatory? Is *it* the assurance of the church at large that such an indulgence was trustworthy?

Is *it* the certainty that these steps are really those that Jesus climbed? Or, more profoundly still, is *it* the conviction that God could be more closely approached, piously prayed to, and fervently believed when one is physically closer to the relics of the past?

This statement is at odds with other—arguably hyperbolic—claims Luther makes about his former zeal. But above all, in the shadow of the muscled manifestations of church power sprouting all about us here in Rome, we should take due note that it was not the splendor or depravity that put him off. It was the promise of a thing that could not be promised.

When Luther later railed against such religious good works—and this he did with great volume and exquisite vituperation—his opponents ingested his peptic tone but didn't really get his meaning. And perhaps this is understandable, for the atmosphere was so politically charged and the stakes so apocalyptically high that no one was really in the mood to listen. Many of Luther's heirs and partisans have misread him, too, not to mention generations of Catholics who libeled Luther as arch-heretic and hater of God's law. Any honest reading of Luther will reveal that he is, in fact, fixated on works—what he calls true good works, not the pilgrimages, indulgences, and masses promoted by his antagonists. Being upright, honest, faithful, humble, and in all ways a good neighbor is the fruit—not the essence—of Christian faith for Luther. Christians are to plunge their spades into the earth, not struggle up the stairs to heaven.

Luther mentions Rome countless times throughout his many works: in Scripture commentaries and treatises, in pamphlets and letters, in his *Table Talk*. Most of these refer not to the city as a place at all but as a stand-in for the Roman church, the new Babylon, capital of apostasy, chief enemy of the gospel. But these were later interpretations, born of Luther's excommunication, the failure of his church to hear him out, political machinations and convoluted interests working to discipline loud critics such as him.

The younger Luther seems less interested in all that. He went to Rome with great sincerity and did his pilgrim duties with an energy and thoroughness befitting his great fervor. "As I was a true saint," he recounts, "I ran through all the churches and cloisters, believing everything"[5]—which is why it hurt him so to hear other priests cynically hurrying through the mass, saying, "Bread you are, and bread you shall remain." Rome's hypocrisy could not have been a secret to any traveler of the day, yet it's clear that Luther went to Rome expecting greater holiness than he found—not just the former holiness of the martyrs but also the present holiness of his church's leadership. What ought to have been a shining beacon of confessors was a cesspool of unbelief and vice, as full of prostitutes as priests.

Luther's disillusionment with his fellow clergy, however, mutes the central sensibility that underlay his trip: that places mattered, that artifacts of saintly people had a wondrous, numinous effect, that martyrs' blood was cleansing in its copious flow. The last point in particular was important—Rome was "truly blessed," as we recall from his entry salutation—not because of the pope, not because of rich ecclesiastical architecture, and certainly not because of classical splendor, but "because of the martyrs, dripping with their blood." And what quantities of blood were believed to have flowed—great gushing rivers of it! Of his visits to the catacombs, which were then advertised to pilgrims as martyrs' graves (something we know now to be false), Luther calculates the number of martyrs at "two hundred thousand." Yes, Luther came to say his masses and to win a giant pot of merit, but it all was based on the notion of proximity to this holy suffering.

If Luther had been heard, his criticisms worked into a program for internal reform of the Western church, he might not have had such bad memories of Rome. Good Augustinian that he was, anyway, Luther felt that the truly faithful were few—even in his own Wittenberg—and that trust in God and in the gospel were under constant attack everywhere. Luther later said enigmatically of his trip, "I carried onions with me to Rome, and brought back garlic." Had history turned out differently, he might instead have said he'd brought back honey.

In his own day it was not clear that Luther or the movement he spearheaded would survive at all. The compromise between his prince and the Holy Roman Emperor was fragile and at times broke down. Luther could easily have become another Hus, another Wycliffe, or Waldo: executed, disciplined, sidelined, absorbed, or mostly ignored. We can make our own retrospective judgments on why the Reformation survived. Luther believed God firmly on his side; he certainly had a powerful message that won support from powerful princes and fellow intellects. But it also seems quite possible that it was precisely the harassment from his opponents, their disproportionate persecution of him that forged a lasting movement out of Luther's Reformation. One thing is quite certain, though: it was *not* his trip to Rome that made a Lutheran out of Luther.

After five hundred years, Germans and Rome seem to have made a kind of peace. Northern tourists are rather starry-eyed when it comes to Italy, coveting its cuisine and art. One cannot claim the same enthusiastic rapprochement between all Lutherans and Roman Catholics, who after centuries of ill will continue to regard the other with suspicion. Representatives of the two estranged parties are able now to voice a common appreciation of Martin Luther, though, and can acknowledge that he taught correctly on justification even if he was excessive in his polemics. That he was a teacher for the whole church, on this many Lutherans and Catholics can and do agree.

The world has moved on since Luther's day, of course—not necessarily in one way or another, just moved on. As the Rome that Luther saw is buried under storeys of dirt, so interred is Luther's Europe. We've seen traces of this lost world all along our hike. Almost all the man-made things he saw are gone. The crops are different, as are the trees, even rivers' courses. Our roads and rails, planes and wires—and all their implications—are far beyond what Luther could have dreamed.

The close entanglement of church and state is gone as well, and with it many of the reasons for Luther's excommunication, and for subsequent wars and conflicts. We can certainly continue to rehearse our bygone grudges, but if we do we risk ignoring present problems. A century ago—or even half—it was a scandal for a Catholic to marry a Lutheran. Today both churches would be content if their members married at all. Churches Protestant and Catholic still have a certain sway in the world at large, but that it's different and vastly altered from Luther's time is clear to all, as much as some may pine for former glories.

As for Rome? The city seems to have made its peace with Martin Luther. In 2015, at the impetus of some local Protestants, and with the blessing of Pope Francis, the city of Rome inaugurated Piazza Martin Lutero. You can visit it today, on top of the Oppian Hill. It's the most conspicuous sign of all that Luther came and saw Rome and, after five hundred years, in a small way, he conquered.

Epilogue

Wittenberg

We walk down the steps into the metro and out of the world of saints and relics. The next morning we fly away. One moment we're taxiing down the tarmac in Rome, the next we're splashing through the puddles of cold and rainy Wittenberg, traveling in just a few hours what took Luther (and us) months to walk. Though it seems an appropriate coda to our journey, this side trip is not a planned part of our pilgrimage at all, but work for Sarah. She's teaching a course on Luther's theology to a group of students from around the world.

But our brief visit to Luther's city is even more germane than we imagined. For we were wrong to think that Luther left for Rome from Erfurt—as we were wrong to think he left in 1510. The five hundredth anniversary observance of Luther's pilgrimage itself inspired a reevaluation of the evidence; new facts were unearthed, old ones thrown away as speculation. It turns out that Luther left from Wittenberg in the fall of 1511; and it was to there that he returned from Rome sometime in the spring of 1512—facts we ourselves could not possibly have known before our trip. So much for our historical reenactment. Instead of commemorating the poetic five hundredth, we've observed the four hundred and ninety-ninth anniversary instead.[1]

The contrast with Rome could not be more acute, almost as much for us as for Luther. Gone is the noise, the traffic, the cosmopolitan ambience, the vestiges of classical greatness, the saturation of sumptuous ecclesiastical architecture. Wittenberg is a two-street, two-church town.

In the middle is St. Mary's, the "City Church." The internal decorations were destroyed by the iconoclasm of 1522, and it still feels austere. Its masterwork is a later altarpiece by local Lucas Cranach. In it layman Philip Melanchthon baptizes while Luther preaches and holds the keys of the confessional—that emblem usually found in apostle Peter's hands. The center panel assembles Jesus and his disciples around the Last Supper—a rare theme in medieval art, one given new life by the Reformation. The most striking scene of all, though, is painted across the bottom: a congregation of sixteenth-century burghers on the left listens to Luther preaching on the right. It is an allegory of a sermon, for though Luther is necessarily silent, he directs the gaze of his congregation toward the floating figure of Christ crucified, hanging in the air between them.

And at the far end of town is All Saints', called the "Castle Church," as it is attached to the elector's castle. Its tower is capped by a conspicuously regal crown inscribed: "A Mighty Fortress Is Our God." Luther's tomb is here inside, beneath the pulpit, opposite that of his friend, Melanchthon. It was on this church's wooden door, in the path of student traffic, that Luther purportedly posted his Ninety-Five Theses. The present door pays tribute to the event, its tarnished bronze heft inscribed with all the Theses, looking rather like Moses's two tablets of the law. One legend says the new door was needed because the old one kept getting chipped away by the faithful. In truth the whole church burnt down in the eighteenth century, but I rather like the idea of Protestant pilgrims taking home their "piece of the true door."

In a way this legend isn't too far from the truth, for it's obvious that Wittenberg has become a city-sized shrine to Luther—and to his colleagues Melanchthon, Bugenhagen, and a few others. But mostly to Luther. It wasn't always this way, though, something travelers of the nineteenth century lamented. Back then Luther's house was a dump, the university had moved to neighboring Halle, and the whole town was rather miserable. That's clearly not what the likes of Harriet Beecher Stowe expected to find when in the 1850s she visited what she and others deemed the "Protestant Mecca."[2]

For a long time Wittenberg lay forgotten, pieces of the true door notwithstanding. It never had been a great city like Rome or even nearby Leipzig or Erfurt. The only real fame it ever had came from Luther, from the fact that for a little while in the sixteenth century it was the center of the Reformation.

In the past few decades the city, now renamed Lutherstadt Wittenberg after its patron, has been completely cleaned up, renovated, and readied for the throngs of visitors streaming in to honor Germany's most famous figure. The erstwhile dust-filled *Lutherhaus* (originally Luther's own Augustinian cloister) is now a very nice museum. Besides delivering a thorough introduction to the Reformation, it offers spine-tingling proximity to Luther artifacts: his handwritten notes, his black academic gown, the pulpit from which he preached, and even officially stamped and sealed letters of indulgence.

But as we've learned from our pilgrimage, we don't see the Wittenberg Luther saw. Even his house has been completely reconstructed. Five hundred years is long enough that archaeologists were needed to identify Luther's former study. The foundation of the building is on display, under glass, the old cellars dug up and looking less like an early modern house than the ruins of Pompeii.

It's a stroke of luck that there was a Wittenberg left to excavate at all. Despite its nearness to arms-producing factories, Wittenberg was largely spared the bombing that destroyed so many other German cities during the Second World War. Ordinary American Lutheran soldiers, it turns out, pleaded with their generals to go easy on the geographical source of their religion. Even for Protestants, supposedly free of saints and relics, places still mattered.

The physical world is surprisingly ephemeral, though. We began our trek imagining we'd learn a great deal about Luther by seeing what he saw, but we soon discovered that his world, in so many of its facets, is gone for good. Roofs leak, fires destroy, stones crack, frost heaves, mountains crumble, rivers meander, languages and cultures disappear, artistic styles come and go. Wittenberg's recent renovations too will fade, for nothing survives long without constant maintenance. Five hundred years in the future, as today, pilgrims will see only what human love has determined worthy to preserve.

There's wisdom in Isaiah's prophecy—and the Reformation's later motto—"The Word of the Lord endures forever." Nothing else does. There's a power in words and their remembrance—even words that aren't the Lord's—that defies nature's tendency toward disorder and decay, an endurance that outlasts geography, even geology. While Wittenberg has crumbled and been rebuilt, Luther's thoughts remain as fresh today as when he wrote them.

Luther certainly didn't put much stake in the importance of his location, anyway, but rather reveled in its insignificance. The Reformation happened, he said, "while I slept, or drank Wittenberg beer with my friends. . . . I did nothing; the Word did everything."[3]

From the Other Pair of Feet

Sarah Hinlicky Wilson

Andrew is the kind of person who has to run seven miles every day to be happy. Seven miles barefoot and uphill both ways, if possible. Sometimes instead of running, he swims a mile and a half. Scaling walls or leaping along the top level of jungle gyms is what he does just to relax.

I am not like this. Until I met Andrew, due to a combination of bookishness, bad experiences in gym class, and a poor grasp of human physiology, I had acquired the conviction that the human body is a very fragile and delicate piece of sculpture, liable to snap and collapse at the slightest exertion. I accordingly considered the ability to sit very still for hours on end the highest physical achievement. I did not sweat. I did not walk. I certainly did not walk for seventy days on end.

So when we were approaching La Storta—the last stop before Rome—and I suddenly realized we'd done it, *I'd* done it, a whole thousand miles, I burst into tears of joy and victory. Andrew couldn't figure out what the big deal was. He seemed to regard the walk thus far as the light stretching that precedes *real* exercise, like an Ironman competition or an ultramarathon in Death Valley.

I gather most people are more like me than like him. In these pages Andrew has offered to you the spiritual, theological, historical, and ecumenical significance of Luther en route to Rome, the ensuing split, and the recent efforts at repair. But the first reactions we got along the way and ever since have centered on the sheer *impossibility* of walking as far as we did. So now, at the far end of both the journey and the book, I'll offer some words about the proven *possibility* of walking so far.

It's pretty simple. You just put one foot in front of the other.

This may sound absurd, but that's really all there is to it. Pilgrimage does not require physical feats of Olympic prowess, which explains why children, cloistered nuns, and fat burghers have all managed to do it over the centuries. All you have to do is take another step. If you can walk at all, you can walk to Rome.

That is not to say it is effortless. We trained in advance of departure, starting with two-hour walks, building up to four hours, and a couple of times we devoted most of a day to walking. That probably helped, but nothing really prepares you for walking all day, every day. The first week was by far the worst for me, not least of all because for some curious reason I completely lost my appetite—as far as I can recall the only time in my life that has ever happened, apart from stomach flus. By the third week, I realized that my only job was to walk and to sleep, and even the sleeping part was only to facilitate the walking part. By our last stop in Germany, my hunger had gone from nonexistent to huge. I choked down my first banana in twenty-four years. In Italy we consumed countless ham-and-pecorino sandwiches, lightly perfumed with hand sanitizer. By then we hardly even stopped to sit while we ate. We nicknamed our daily dose of chocolate "Vitamin CH." By weeks eight and nine, we had learned the necessity of eating every single hour to prevent emotional and physical "crashing." Beforehand I would have thought a valid excuse to eat every hour was heaven. In reality it was revolting, and during the last week I willingly started scaling back in preparation for normal life.

There were other deprivations that made the walk hard beyond the physical challenge. First and foremost and like a constant nag was the separation from our Zeke. The weekly visits during the first half of the walk—through Germany and the Alps—were never long enough, and the good-byes were always wrenching. In Italy it was much easier with the knowledge that we'd see each other again every evening, but it was still no picnic putting ourselves through a good-bye every morning.

Then on quite another level, for this bookish pilgrim the absence of written material in my life bordered on torture. I was far too tired in the evenings to read, and what little time we had—less and less as our treks stretched farther and the daylight got shorter—was spent communicating with the outside world via social media. I remember vividly one particular day in Switzerland when the astounding scenery could not interrupt the circuit of about a dozen thoughts that raced through my brain, over and over again, till in desperation I started bellowing out to the peaks and valleys how bored I was. It didn't help much.

And add to that a particular malaise of mine: an extreme susceptibility to "earbugs." Once in my early twenties I flew to France to join the Orthodox community in Paris for Holy Week and Easter. The last music I heard on the radio before I left home was the Rolling Stones. It never left me, not once, to the point that during the great vigil, in a crypt in the middle of the night, the priest's solemn intoning of "Wisdom, let us attend" alternated with my mental scourge of "It's the honnnnnnnky-tonk women!" Not quite as jarring but nevertheless torturous was an entire week of pilgrimage to the tune of Bruce Springsteen's "Dancing in the Dark," which I had overheard in a café. It was not a particularly amenable accompaniment to prayer.

And yet. Here's the funny thing. I do vaguely remember the hunger and the earbugs, but it wasn't until I reread my journals that I discovered again how often my feet ached (in the intervening years I'd convinced myself that my feet didn't hurt *even once* the whole entire time), how often I got despondent at the number of miles that lay ahead, or how much trouble it cost us to manage our sleeping arrangements or find our next meal or coordinate with the camper. What I do remember and have remembered is the beauty. The elation. The startling insights. The serendipitous meetings. The gift of time outside of time. And none of these would have happened or been possible without the sore feet and the pressing on just a little farther to the day's goal. You can't get it hopping from city to city on a plane or roaring through the countryside in a car. You have to take each step and see what it will bring you.

This is the ancient wisdom in ascetic practice. It is not done as an end in itself or to accrue merit or to become a superior religious person—as Luther so devastatingly critiqued—but to strip away the clutter and distractions and to simplify life to something as plain as walking and sleeping. And praying. You will assuredly pray on pilgrimage, because all the conventional supports of life have been stolen from you. I know now why Luther prayed for help when caught in a thunderstorm! And I know now what Hebrews 13:2 means by "Do not neglect to show hospitality to strangers, for thereby some have entertained angels unawares," though I think it was the angels who were showing the hospitality to us rather than the other way around. We still have the honey jar that Horst and Rosemarie gave us, though the honey itself is long gone. We still have Mary Jane's Etrurian histories and Fulvio's unread-because-in-Italian cookbook.

Luther's ethic was neighbor-oriented, and in going on pilgrimage we discovered all kinds of neighbors we never knew we had, from the fearless-in-the-face-of-death Hans and Regine in Oettingen to the exuberantly-Catholic-and-yet-Luther-friendly Emanuela and Stefano in Chiavenna to the motley other pilgrims on the trail. And that happened by walking. Nowadays we know our neighbors less and less because we just don't get out and walk around in places where we might bump into them. We live sealed inside our houses, offices, and automobiles; and should we get stuck at a bus stop, airport, or any other public space, we have earphones to declare our unavailability for conversation and screens to connect to anyone except the one who's right in front of us.

Walking is an act of deliberate vulnerability and exposure: to strangers and the elements, to traffic and discomfort, to divine interruptions and neighbors unawares.

And it's just putting one foot in front of the other.

Gear

- Backpack
- Waterproof pack liner (a garbage bag works fine)
- Foam pad to sit on
- Button-up shirt
- Pants
- Long underwear top + bottom
- Fleece
- Windbreaker
- Two T-shirts
- Two pairs of underwear
- Two pairs of socks
- (all clothing light and synthetic, for fast drying)
- Comfortable, lightweight walking shoes
- Sun hat
- Sunglasses
- Umbrella
- Water bottle
- Pot + stove
- Small folding knife
- Plastic cup + plate
- Wooden spoon
- Spices, salt, pepper
- Smartphone
- Laptop
- Camera
- Something to read (like Dante)
- Journal + pen
- Toothbrush
- Soap
- First Aid kit
- Passport, wallet, other documents
- Nothing else

A Recipe from the Road

Pilgrims' Vegetable Stew

When we still had the time to stop and cook during our daily walk or in the evenings, we made this a lot. We never got tired of it.

Ingredients

- 1 tablespoon extra-virgin olive oil
- 1 onion, diced
- 1 large eggplant, diced into small cubes
- 2 tomatoes, diced
- 1 yellow bell pepper, diced into small cubes
- salt and black pepper, to taste
- 6 ounces of feta cheese, cubed
- fresh basil, shredded
- 1/2-pound of small pasta, like penne or macaroni, cooked by the time the stew is done

Directions

Heat oil in pot over medium heat. Add onion and eggplant and cook till they begin to sizzle. Sprinkle with 1/4 teaspoon salt, cover the pot, and cook until the eggplant softens, about 10 minutes. Add tomato and bell pepper, cover the pot again, and cook another 10 minutes. When all the vegetables are very soft, taste for salt and add more if needed, along with black pepper. Serve over the pasta and top with feta and basil.

Variations

Top with other fresh herbs, like parsley or chives; season with cayenne pepper to taste; pour additional olive oil on the finished dish; scatter black olives on top.

Notes

Preamble

1. Lucien Febvre, *Martin Luther: Un destin* (Paris: Presses Universitaires de France, 1928), translation mine.

2. Heinrich Boehmer sums up this new consensus in *Luthers Romfahrt* (Leipzig: U. Deichert'sche Verlagsbuchhandlung Werner Scholl, 1914).

3. Ibid., 77–79.

One

1. Boehmer, *Luthers Romfahrt*, 82–87.

2. Scott Hendrix, *Martin Luther: Visionary Reformer* (New Haven: Yale University Press, 2015), 38–39.

3. Martin Luther, in *Luther's Works*, American Edition, 55 vols., ed. J. Pelikan and H. Lehmann (St. Louis / Philadelphia: Concordia / Fortress, 1955–), 31:129 (hereafter cited as *LW*).

Two

1. Translated by F. Bente and W. H. T. Dau, in *Triglot Concordia: The Symbolical Books of the Ev. Lutheran Church* (St. Louis: Concordia, 1921), http://bookofconcord.org/lc-3-ten commandments.php#para11.

2. My translation; the original German reads:

St. Leonard, in deine Hand
  empfehlen wir den Bauernstand.
Breit' über jedes Tier im Haus
  beschützend deinen Mantel aus.

3. Altered for American English. *Story of a Soul: The Autobiography of Thérèse of Lisieux*, ed. T. N. Taylor (London: Burns, Oates & Washbourne, 1912; 8th ed., 1922), http://www.ccel.org/ccel/therese/autobio.xvii.html.

4. *LW* 60:73.

5. Boehmer, *Luthers Romfahrt*, 82.

6. See Erwin Weber, "Luther in Rome," *Lutheran Journal* 52, no. 3 (1985). Weber gets this from Luther's hamartiographer Johannes Cochlaeus. See Boehmer, *Luthers Romfahrt*, 8.

7. Jürgen Krüger and Martin Wallraff, *Luthers Rom: Die Ewige Stadt in der Renaissance* (Darmstadt: Primus Verlag, 2010), 69.

Three

1. Slightly altered for the modern reader. Translated by Albert T. W. Steinhaeuser, edited by Robert E. Smith, from *Works of Martin Luther with Introductions and Notes* (Philadelphia: A. J. Holman Company, 1915), http://www.projectwittenberg.org/etext/luther/babylonian/babylonian.htm#3.42.
2. I later looked it up and discovered that this piece was BWV 914.
3. *LW* 42:101.
4. "Temporal Authority: To What Extent It Should Be Obeyed" (1523), *LW* 45:91.

Four

1. Boehmer, *Luthers Romfahrt*, 88.
2. "Temporal Authority," *LW* 45:113.
3. Manuel Eisner, "Modernization, Self-Control and Lethal Violence: The Long-Term Dynamics of European Homicide Rates in Theoretical Perspective," *British Journal of Criminology* 41, no. 4 (2001): 618–38.
4. Sarah Hinlicky Wilson, "A Thousand Miles in the Footsteps of Martin Luther," *Wall Street Journal*, August 20, 2010, http://www.wsj.com/articles/SB10001424052748704868604575433283501270518.

Five

1. "Descriptive Sketches," *Poetical Works of William Wordsworth* (London: Longman, Rees, Orme, Brown, Green & Longman, 1832), 1:72.
2. Andrew Beattie, *The Alps: A Cultural History* (New York: Oxford University Press, 2006), 116.
3. Richard Bangs, "Here Be Dragons: The 'Sacred Terror' of the Alps of Switzerland," *Huffington Post*, December 25, 2015, http://www.huffingtonpost.com/richard-bangs/here-be-dragons-the-sacre_b_8874978.html.
4. Boehmer, *Luthers Romfahrt*, 83.
5. "On Translation" (1530), *LW* 35:190.
6. Heiko Oberman, *Luther: Man between God and the Devil*, trans. Eileen Walliser-Schwarzbart (New Haven: Yale University Press, 1989), 330.
7. Elda Simonett-Giovanoli, *Bivio und das Bergell: Märschen, Geschichten, Legenden*, 3rd ed. (Chur: Bischofberger AG, 1995); quotes below from 11 and 12.

Six

1. Conrad Bonorand, *Riforma e società nei Grigioni: Valtellina e Valchiavenna tra '500 e '600* (Roma: F. Angeli 1991).

Seven

1. David Steinmetz, "Luther and the Late Medieval Augustinians: Another Look," *Currents in Theology and Mission* 44, no. 4 (1973): 246.
2. Hendrix, *Martin Luther*, 30.
3. Scott Hendrix, *Recultivating the Vineyard: The Reformation Agendas of Christianization* (Louisville: Westminster John Knox, 2004), 14.
4. *LW* 34:337.

Eight

1. Boehmer, *Luthers Romfahrt*, 84.

2. Charles Beard and John Frederick Smith, *Martin Luther and the Reformation in Germany until the Close of the Diet of Worms* (London: K. Paul, Trench, & Co, 1889), 179.

3. *Inf.* 19:115–17. Trans. Dorothy L. Sayers (New York: Penguin Classics, 1950), 191.

4. Martin Luther, *The Letters of Martin Luther*, trans. Margaret A. Currie (London: Macmillan, 1908), 5; cf. *LW* 48:12–13.

Nine

1. Martin Luther, "Sermon on John 6," in *Festival Sermons of Martin Luther*, trans. Joel Baseley (Dearborn, MI: Mark V, 2005), 43.

Ten

1. Quoted in Martin Brecht, *Martin Luther: His Road to Reformation* (Minneapolis: Fortress, 1985), 100.

2. Peter Maier, "Aussagen Luthers über die Stadt Rom seiner Zeit," in *Lutherania: Zum 500 Geburtstag Martin Luthers von der Mitarbeitern der Weimarer Ausgabe*, ed. Gerhard Hammer and Karl-Heinz zur Mühlen, Archiv zur Weimarer Ausgabe der Werke Martin Luthers 5 (Cologne: Böhlau Verlag, 1984), 284.

3. "'Wer weiß, ob es wahr ist?' Vor 500 Jahren reiste Martin Luther nach Rom—Nur wenig gesicherte Erkenntnisse," *Sontaggsblatt*, January 16, 2011, http://www.sonntagsblatt.de/news/aktuell/2011_03_13_01.htm.

4. Maier, "Aussagen Luthers," 283.

5. Maier, "Aussagen Luthers," 282. The quotes from Luther in the following paragraphs are from this source (283, 286, 288).

Epilogue

1. Hans Schneider, "Martin Luthers Reise nach Rom: Neu datiert und neu gedeutet," *Studien zur Wissenschafts- und Religionsgeschichte* 10 (New York: De Gruyter, 2011), 1–157.

2. Hartmut Lehmann, "Nineteenth Century American Tourists in Wittenberg, the 'Protestant Mecca,'" *Lutheran Quarterly* 29 (2015): 428.

3. "Invocavit Sermon #2" (1522), *LW* 51:77.